The Biography
of a Building

The Biography
of a Building

How Robert Sainsbury and
Norman Foster Built a Great Museum

Witold Rybczynski

50 ILLUSTRATIONS, 34 IN COLOR

 **Thames & Hudson**

In memory of Anna Zofia Rybczyńska (1915–2010)

Note to the Reader

The story of the Sainsbury Centre for Visual Arts is partly told through
the words of those who took part in the events described. Where quotations
are unsourced, they are taken from conversations between the author and the
speakers. Sources for other quoted material are supplied in reference notes
at the end of the book. Information that enhances the narrative, but would
interrupt its flow if it were included in the main text, is provided in footnotes.
Some additional details may be found in the endnotes.

The titles and dates of works in the Sainsbury collection follow the catalogue,
prepared under Sir Robert Sainsbury's direction: Steven Hooper, ed., *Robert and
Lisa Sainsbury Collection*, 3 volumes (New Haven: Yale University Press, 1997).

Dimensions and other units of measure are given in metric values except
where it would be anachronistic or otherwise inappropriate to do so. Where
necessary, metric equivalents of imperial values are provided in footnotes.

Frontispiece: Interior view of the Living Area. Nigel Young/Foster + Partners

First published in 2011 in hardcover in the United States of America by
Thames & Hudson Inc., 500 Fifth Avenue, New York, New York 10110

thamesandhudsonusa.com

Library of Congress Catalog Card Number 2011922557

ISBN 978-0-500-34276-3

Printed in China by Toppan Leefung

CONTENTS

A Tribute to Sir Robert and Lady Sainsbury
BY NORMAN FOSTER   6

Prologue   14

A Tribute to Sir Robert and Lady Sainsbury

BY NORMAN FOSTER

It was the first day of 1974, and I had been summoned to a meeting at the London residence of Sir Robert and Lady Sainsbury in Smith Square, close to Westminster and the Houses of Parliament. The Sainsburys, their home and its extraordinary display of modern paintings and sculpture made a deep and lasting impression on me that day. The eventual outcome of the visit was the Sainsbury Centre for Visual Arts, which would house their extraordinary collection, as well as a major university faculty and research centre.

It is well known that Sir Robert and Lady Sainsbury amassed a great collection of art and donated it, in their lifetime, to the University of East Anglia in Norwich. Equally well known is that the Sainsburys and their son David (later Lord Sainsbury) provided generous funds for a building that would evolve and grow over time.

However, what is not known is how much more the Sainsburys put into their project – beyond the materiality of their works of art, their funding and their endowments. As I saw it, they put their very hearts and souls into the venture – with manifest end results. This unusual form of patronage was inquisitive, industrious and creative, so much so that it is an important and inseparable part of the story of the building itself.

The Sainsburys' approach to architecture late in their lives was as radical as their approach to contemporary painting and sculpture in their earlier years. It was open-minded and remarkably free from preconceptions, other than an appetite for the avant-garde. Many of the artists that they supported were, at the time, virtually unknown outside their immediate artistic circles. Only later would they be recognized as masters of their age – Bacon, Giacometti and Moore, for example. I know from conversations with the Sainsburys that they engaged very personally with many of these artists, and the friendships that they developed were often inseparable from their acquiring what would eventually be acknowledged as great works of art. At the time that I met the Sainsburys, several of these significant paintings and sculptures graced the more accessible spaces of their London home. This was to be the primary venue for the most important discussions on the project and where all of the final decisions were made.

I was fortunate to spend much time with the Sainsburys, and my personal insights will, I hope, complement Witold Rybczynski's full and remarkable account of their project. I would like to pay tribute to them by revealing how they, and their Smith Square home, would significantly influence the design of the Centre.

Sir Robert — or Bob, in our friendship — had a very particular way of operating. His style was not to delegate or over-formalize relationships but instead to focus on the two people he had decided were the key individuals on the project. The liaison would then be one-to-one and face-to-face. From the outset he pinned responsibility for the interior on Kho Liang Ie and for the architecture on me. As the book explains, through tragic circumstances, I would eventually become responsible for both the architecture and the interiors. I have no doubt that behind the scenes he and Lady Sainsbury — whom I would know affectionately as Lisa — were in total accord on this strategy. They were always together for any meetings that involved design. Only occasionally would Bob separately discuss certain contractual issues, such as cost.

I realize now that Bob probably knew more about the contractual background than he gave away. For example, he took for granted that my wife and architect partner, Wendy, and I would be working together on the design, and that I would be directing a talented team of architects and designers in our studio. He was also aware that our practice was responsible for the environmental engineering, which was overseen by our partner Loren Butt. Beyond our own colleagues there were other, separate consultancies for structural engineering, estimating and cost control. Bob would have understood all the legal niceties in which these responsibilities were separately defined. Nonetheless, as far as he and Lisa were concerned, the architect was responsible for everything and the architect was Norman.

It followed logically, therefore, that I would engage directly with Bob and Lisa at every client meeting. Most of the time it was just the three of us in Smith Square, although sometimes we might be joined by another consultant or individual. On one research trip it was just the Sainsburys, Wendy and myself, who travelled together. A meeting to look at mock-ups on site or in our studio would provide a rare opportunity to bring more members of the team into the picture.

My personal responsibilities increased as the project developed because over time the relationship between the Sainsburys and the university became somewhat strained. So, for example, I might leave a typical Smith Square meeting knowing that I would then have to go to East Anglia to negotiate again the decisions that had emerged, this time with the university. Looking back, I now realize more fully the extent to which I became central not just to the design process but also to the politics of its implementation.

On this project Bob and Lisa scorned the trappings of bureaucracy, preferred not to delegate responsibilities and were, in today's parlance, totally 'hands-on'. They tolerated, with some impatience, the charade of the few formal meetings that, in the early days, passed for committees.

Initially strategic decisions on the links between the university component of the project and the Sainsburys' private initiative were handled directly between Bob and Frank Thistlethwaite. There was a warmth early in this relationship, which I can particularly remember from a small but very convivial dinner party that the Sainsburys hosted at Smith Square, with the vice-chancellor and his wife, Wendy and I.

Not surprisingly, the thinking at the beginning of the project assumed at least two buildings, one publicly funded for the university and the other privately sponsored by and for the Sainsburys. The direction that emerged later, which brought together all the spaces under one roof, offered several benefits. For example, the single building created greater cross-fertilization between the public world of art and the academic community devoted to its study. It also provided greater flexibility for changes of use over time – a potential that has since been validated in practice. In addition, the more compact building had a better ratio of wall to floor surface and was therefore more sustainable than a collection of separate structures – an important consideration in the quest for a green build-ing, at a time before such ambitions had become widespread and, in one sense, fashionable. I recall saying at the time that an energy-conscious architecture was not about fashion, but about survival.

To implement these design strategies meant that all the parties had not only to embrace them but literally to buy into them. The simple idea that the same finishes and standards would flow throughout the academic spaces, which were funded by the central authority of the University Grants Committee (known as the UGC), and the major areas paid for by the Sainsburys created a bureaucratic night-mare. It defied what passed as conventional wisdom. As a small example: how, it was argued, could the School of Fine Arts possibly afford a carpet like the gallery spaces that flowed into it? University standards had been forged over time and had become sanctified. Such issues contained the seeds of an explosion between 'the haves' and 'the have nots'. The worst prospect was an exterior of calm simplicity with a riot of conflicting standards within.

To create the seamless experience inside meant bending some rules and breaking others. As someone in the middle of this conflict, I could see and understand the frustrations of both sides. The Sainsburys, for their part, felt that the complications of resolving such issues was a result of the university being over-bureaucratic. This situation was not helped by the friction that developed between Bob and Lisa and the Chief Estates Officer, Gordon Marshall. It reached a point where they could not be in the same room together. The situation was only resolved by my having separate meetings, first with the Sainsburys and afterwards with Marshall. Gordon was a powerful voice and could make or break the project. I recall him telling me the story of his battle with the original architect for the university – Sir Denys Lasdun – and how, in his words, they both 'lost out'. He described how he had succeeded in having Lasdun dismissed, but said that he then suffered a heart attack as a result of the stress involved.

If the Sainsburys thought they were hard done by in terms of the university's procedures, then Thistlethwaite and Marshall, each in different ways, felt underappreciated for their efforts to subvert the bureaucracy in the cause of a single architecture for all. I could sympathize with the irritations felt by both sides. It was in essence a classic demonstration of the different protocols that govern the ways of private business and public bodies.

My first allegiance was always to Bob and Lisa, but I was fortunate to be able to establish genuine working relationships with Frank Thistlethwaite and Gordon Marshall. It could be suggested that it was in my interests as an architect to do so, as well as in the interests of the Sainsburys to help achieve their objectives. But I also had responsibilities to the university as their architect for a significant part of the totality. Inevitably the meetings it created were of different kinds from those that took place in Smith Square, but they were also significant in their own right and central to the realization of the project. I remember that they were marked by a feeling of goodwill and hard work – as well as a shared sense of humour.

I sometimes refer to a building as being like the tip of an iceberg: the process that generated it, with all the many intrigues, lies hidden below the surface. As in so many projects the heroic struggles between differing cultures and personalities are largely untold. The Sainsbury Centre is no exception, and the deceptive simplicity of the outcome belies those many conflicts that can never be detected in the official transcripts – not even by reading between the lines.

It would be unfortunate and misleading if my description suggested a cavalier approach on the part of the Sainsburys. Of course, like anyone bestowing resources on such a grand scale, they could be firm, even impatient, and would not mince their words, but they were always reasonable. Bob was nothing if not precise in the few contractual meetings that were convened.

I recall how, from time to time, as we sat together, his hand would slip into the inside breast pocket of his immaculate dark suit to produce a small pack of white cards in a black leather holder. He would jot a note in passing, transfer the card to the back of the pack and replace the clip in his inside pocket. Only some months later, when the real consequences of that conversation came to fruition, would Bob pull out a card from the past and advise us of the mismatch between our predictions and what eventually emerged. These occasions were thankfully very few. I remember one meeting when he used this system to point out to the quantity surveyor, John Walker, the discrepancy between an early first estimate and the final cost of the basement. After making his disapproval clear he graciously moved on to other issues.

I was privileged to have an insight into Bob's philosophy when the project overlapped with his involvement in reworking the pension scheme for the employees of the Sainsbury supermarket. He confided that everyone expected him to research other organizations to find out their pension plans before making any proposals. 'Nonsense,' exclaimed Bob. 'First of all I am going to explore what I think we should be doing and only then will I compare that with what the others have done.'

Research for the Sainsbury Centre took a somewhat different tack. I had identified three museums for Bob and Lisa to look at in Denmark and Germany. There was never any expectation of our seeing something that might sway the direction of the evolving design. It was more in the nature of intelligence gathering, particularly to find out how public museums worked behind the scenes. In Copenhagen we spent an evening together in the then elegant interior of the SAS Hotel designed by Arne Jacobsen. This was to prove pivotal. After dinner and long into the night we debated the siting and design of a single unifying structure, and they effectively signed off the design strategy there and then. On that occasion I think we all slept well afterwards. However, I know that some critical points in the unfolding of the design caused them to suffer sleepless nights.

Many lessons were learnt from that study trip about some of the more controversial aspects of the design. Alvar Aalto's sublime use of roof lights in his North Jutland Art Museum was helpful in reaffirming the decision we had already taken on using natural top light, although the system proposed for the Sainsbury Centre was unusual in offering a range of control, down to a total black-out. But it was the Louisiana Museum of Modern Art that underscored the differences between a museum created as an institution and one that had been generated by art-loving individuals, starting with their own home. This is a vitally important point and I will return to it later.

After the trip, Wendy and I were amazed by the stamina and endurance of the Sainsburys and confided to our friends that Bob and Lisa were so energetic that we had difficulty keeping up with their pace, despite the disparity in our ages. London, like many cities, is nothing more than a village when it comes to dinner-table gossip, so we soon discovered that in talking to their friends about the tour they were saying how difficult it was for them to keep up with us!

Design is not a linear process, in which one decision leads smoothly to the next; it is often a zigzag pattern with setbacks and frustrations along the way. It is only later that the images produced over time can be shuffled to reveal the big sequential picture of a design's evolution. Sometimes there are 'eureka' moments when not only is a seemingly intractable problem that has long been wrestled with solved by a sudden shift in the design, but, as a consequence, the total outcome is dramatically enhanced. It is like turning a camera lens to the point when everything snaps into sharp focus.

There were two such 'eureka' moments in the evolution of the Sainsbury Centre and they both taxed the patience of Bob and Lisa. The first was the late realization that the change from a shallow, solid structural arch to a deep, triangulated one would produce a significantly better building. This structural change solved a host of other problems that had been compromising the purity of the interior spaces.

The second moment of breakthrough was the birth of the basement. I had left the studio in mental despair one evening. Overnight I nagged further at how to solve the problem of servicing a single-storey building, and the next morning came back with the idea of adding a basement spine. It immediately resolved a range of other issues that were starting to erode the integrity of the design. On reflection, and for the first time as I write this, I realize that this development was probably a delayed consequence of that earlier research trip. What I was not to know was how far-reaching that decision would prove to be, as a basis for the longer-term expansion of the building some thirty years later.

All such situations of change test the confidence and strength of the client–architect relationship. Why, when an accord on one version of a concept has been reached over months of painstaking preparation, would one risk undoing it in striving for something even better? It is to the credit of the Sainsburys that they were always open to debate and exploration. On these two significant issues they were finally enthusiastic and totally endorsed the critical changes. In this and other ways they were always supportive.

But not all such meetings with the Sainsburys would result in agreement. I can recall one occasion when I was showing some variations on the internal planning and presented an arrangement in which the main entrance led directly into the restaurant. Before I could even start to explain it Lisa dismissed it out of hand, enumerating the problems of smells and housekeeping sufficient to banish the idea forever. Of course she was absolutely right – it was (in retrospect) not a good idea at all! However, the final concept of a café conservatory as an entrance space grew out of that idea, and the restaurant itself was, as a consequence, more sensibly located at the western end, where it commanded fine views of open countryside beyond.

My presentations tended to trace the various options that had been explored to show how they resulted in a final recommendation. For most of the time this method served the project well and did justice to the considerable amount of work that was taking place back in the studio in Fitzroy Street. However, I will never forget one occasion when this approach was totally by-passed. Typically the scene was the main dining room, on the corner of the house overlooking Smith

Square. On the mantelpiece, staring out at the meeting, was the powerful and commanding portrait of Lisa by Francis Bacon. I ritualistically laid out the presentation on mounted boards at the far end of the room, so that I could reveal them one at a time as part of a carefully planned sequence. This time, however, Lisa took charge and said 'Norman, why don't you get straight to the point and tell us what you'd like us to agree?!' I cannot remember too much about the rest of that meeting except that, like all such exchanges, it reached a good conclusion. I suspect that afterwards Bob ended up seeing all the work, but in reverse order. In that sense he was by nature more analytical. On reflection, perhaps one of the reasons why Bob and Lisa were so wonderfully effective together was the combination of his methodical approach and her intuition and spontaneity.

Over the years of the project and then way beyond it, I realized that on all issues of art and architecture they did everything with a single accord. But additionally they had their individual passions, though they also shared them. Lisa, for example, had a discerning eye for pottery and greatly appreciated the works of Hans Coper and Lucie Rie. In a similar spirit Bob had a personal treasure trove of tiny objects – for example, delicate ivory figurines crafted by Eskimos, the indigenous people of Alaska and Greenland. The smallest of those were barely the size of a thumb, and I was told that he kept them in glass cabinet by his bedside, which his children humorously described as 'the toy department'. Their universal appeal is such that, so many decades later, they still have a particular attraction for the younger visitors to the Centre. These, and the more conventionally sized ethnic carvings, arguably some of the purest forms of abstract art, would normally be found in museums of ethnography rather than galleries devoted to the fine arts. It is a measure of the vision of the Sainsburys that they could appreciate the aesthetic dimensions of such works and chose to acquire them well before other collectors. A part of Bob's collection of so-called primitive art was housed in his study, which was the most intimate space in Smith Square. It was designed by Kho Liang Ie, with cases beautifully crafted in slabs of acrylic, lit by tiny spotlights, each connected by a visible tracery of fine wires.

But Bob's study was only a small part of Smith Square and not typical of the main spaces of the Sainsburys' relatively modest central London home. Building on its Georgian origins, they combined tasteful furniture and elegant decoration to create a gracefully quiet background for radical art. Against this backdrop, their own outward appearance was conceptually a part of the place – always stylish but never ostentatious in dress or lifestyle.

I hope that I have been able to give a flavour of the way in which the Sainsburys went beyond the role of patrons and played an unusual part in helping to shape the building that bears their name. I can recall the conversations between them to determine the official name, which is a reflection of Bob's precision in his use of language. Not 'Art Centre', because that might have encompassed the performing arts, which would not be accurate. 'Visual Arts' neatly embraced not just their paintings and sculptures but also the historical study of those forms of art. Like their philosophy and the building that embodies it, the title is inclusive.

Less easy to pin down, but nonetheless tangible, is the role that their home, Smith Square, played as an influence on the design of the Centre. The magic of Smith Square was its homeliness – the casual ease with which great works of art were treated. The Sainsburys and their many visitors were immersed in paintings and sculptures, which were an integral part of the very fabric of the spaces of the house. Unlike so many collectors, they never engaged with fashionable decorators, who might use gallery-style lighting to draw added attention to a painting or sculpture. It was the informality of their home setting – its low-key qualities – that inspired the nature and name of the main gallery of the Sainsbury Centre, the Living Space. The domestic-style furniture and soft, easy seating in informal groups was also an extension of the Smith Square experience. The accessibility and flow between spaces, with soft carpet underfoot, was the opposite of most institutionalized spaces and welcoming by comparison. A building with family roots is always going to be more personal and less anonymous.

I talked about the special qualities of a museum like the Louisiana, which literally grew out a family home to eventually engulf it. Although Smith Square was not close to Norwich, a fairly remote corner of Great Britain, it is the birthplace of the Centre and its very presence is still felt there so long afterwards. Even the Special Reserve storage of the Crescent Wing extension echoes a small room in the Sainsburys' home, with its sliding rack of works too numerous to be displayed at the same time.

One special quality of Smith Square was its deceptively casual juxtaposition of modern masters and indigenous art. This eclectic mix, unified by a discerning eye, is continued on a magnified scale in the Centre. So the Sainsburys' very personal stamp is carried forward as a tradition, and perhaps outshines even their munificence as founders.

These recollections bring me full circle to that vivid memory of standing, apprehensively, on the doorstep of Smith Square on that chilly New Year's morning. Later, just before being introduced to Lisa before lunch, I overheard Bob say that I, like David, was young enough to be his son. Nearly forty years later, it is a great pleasure to pay tribute to David Sainsbury and his vital role of seamlessly continuing the initiative of his parents. I am grateful for his invitation to contribute to this 'biography of a building' and sincerely hope that I have done justice to the memory of his parents and their generosity of spirit. They were a truly exceptional couple. I have many reasons to be grateful to them – far beyond that of being privileged to act as their architect.

Prologue

It begins, this very English story, in Miami. I was there in December 2006 on a book tour to lecture about Vizcaya, an early twentieth-century estate in Coconut Grove. The first talk had gone well but I'd come down with a virus and, instead of enjoying the balmy weather before my next appearance, I was stuck in my hotel room, drinking bottled water, popping Tylenols, and generally feeling miserable. My cell phone rang. It was Andrew Wylie, my agent. He was calling from London, and despite his usual calm and deliberate manner he sounded excited. He said that he was calling about the Sainsbury family and a museum they had built.

I assumed that Andrew was referring to the Sainsbury Wing, Robert Venturi's controversial addition to London's National Gallery, but he said no, this was a different museum. He wasn't sure of the name, but the building was somewhere outside London, and he believed the architect was Norman Foster. Lady Sainsbury, a friend, had asked him whether he could recommend someone who might write what he characterized as the biography of a building. Would I be interested? I said that I admired Foster's work, but explained that I was in no condition at the moment to give the subject serious thought. I promised that I would look into it when I got home.

The first Foster building I'd ever seen was the Hongkong and Shanghai Bank. The high-rise office building was a dramatic celebration of technology, similar to the Pompidou Centre in Paris, but unlike the famous 'oil refinery', whose exposed pipes and ducts seemed largely intended to *épater le bourgeois*, the bank tower was low-key, almost sombre. Since then I had seen the Sackler Galleries at the Royal Academy and the British Museum, both buildings to which Foster had made significant additions, and I'd been impressed by his combination of technical dexterity and elegance. My friend Martin Pawley had written a monograph on Foster's work. Once I had shaken the virus (which took all of a week), I leafed through his book and found the building that Andrew had mentioned. It was called the Sainsbury Centre for Visual Arts and it was on the campus of the University of East Anglia in Norwich. The Sainsbury Centre looked like a well-designed aircraft hangar, and its cavernous interior contained a curious mixture of antiquities, African masks, Henry Moore sculptures and Giacomettis. What surprised me was that the building had been built a decade *before* the Hongkong Bank – it was now more than thirty years old. Had Andrew's friend been the client? And why did she think it deserved to be written about after all this time?

Books have come to me from different places. Occasionally through inspiration – when I first saw a Palladio villa I knew I wanted to write about the architect one day – but often by accident. A friend's idle question during an after-dinner conversation, 'Why aren't our cities like Paris?' led to an exploration of American urbanism; a magazine editor's request to write about the best tool of the millennium grew into a history of the screwdriver; the suggestion of an acquaintance, who said 'You should write about this,' when I told him the story of how I built my own house, resulted in an architectural memoir. So I was not averse to Andrew's suggestion, at least not in principle. The hangar-like art gallery intrigued me, since it was so different from most contemporary museums. 'The biography of a building' was appealing, too, since I'd always been interested in how architecture was created. Architects tend to be close-mouthed about this process, preferring to preserve an impression of creative autonomy. Asked where his designs came from, Frank Lloyd Wright once said: 'I just shake them out of my sleeve.'[1] Maybe he did, but most architects engage in an extended dialogue with engineers, builders, fabricators and colleagues, and especially with clients; indeed, great buildings are often said to be the result of great, or at least special, clients. A book about the Sainsbury Centre would be an opportunity to explore this subject in detail.

I told Andrew all this, or rather emailed him, and in his economical fashion he forwarded my message to Lady Sainsbury. In due course, she replied that perhaps we should all meet. We fixed a time the following January when she would be visiting New York, and met in Andrew's office on West 57th Street. Lady Sainsbury was accompanied by Dame Elizabeth Estève-Coll, who was introduced as a former vice-chancellor of the University of East Anglia, and was evidently a family friend, and Chris Foy – no title – who was a trustee of several Sainsbury charitable foundations and worked for Lady Sainsbury's husband.

Lady Sainsbury, an animated woman, spoke at length about the art collection and the museum. It took me several minutes to realize that the builders were not herself and her husband, but rather her husband's parents. (I also learned that the Sainsbury Wing of the National Gallery had been built by a different branch of the supermarket-chain-owning family.) She described Robert and Lisa Sainsbury as private people, and was at pains to point out that, while the pair had established a museum, their intention had not been to build a monument to themselves. Their chief goal, according to her, had been to create the same sort of intimate surroundings as in the London townhouse where their collection had previously been displayed. Having seen photographs of the Sainsbury Centre, which seemed anything but domestic – or diffident – I found her characterization a little far-fetched, but I bit my tongue. We spoke for an hour or more. I was, at this point, non-committal, and we decided I should take some time to consider the subject, and if I thought there might be a book here, I could come to London to meet Lord Sainsbury, visit Foster's office, and, of course, go to Norwich.

Lady Sainsbury lent me a privately published book of conversations with Sir Robert Sainsbury, recorded some years before his death. I read parts of it on the train back to Philadelphia. The oral history described his long collecting career, which started when he bought two drawings and a small sculpture in 1931. I found his voice engaging, a combination of a businessman's clear-headedness, an art collector's wilful self-absorption and a rather endearing simplicity. 'I always say that I am an old-fashioned aesthete and ours is not an ethnographical collection, or an archaeological one, not a Collection at all. It goes back to what we have said – not a collector but a passionate acquirer of what one likes for better or for worse.' He also said of his museum that he wanted students to be able to experience art as part of their everyday lives. So, perhaps Lady Sainsbury was right about him not wanting to create a monument.

My favourite museums are those built by individual collectors: Isabella Stewart Gardner in Boston, Pierpont Morgan and Henry Clay Frick in New York, Albert Barnes in Philadelphia, Charles Freer and Duncan Phillips in Washington, DC. It's not just that private museums tend to be small and domestic in scale – in the case of Frick and Phillips they are actually converted houses – it's also the pleasure of sharing someone's private passion. Visiting a personal collection is like paging through a scrapbook; not 'Everything that's Important' but rather 'The Things I Like.' Quite different from visiting a conventional museum, which is like opening an encyclopaedia where the entries are categorized, labelled, certified, A to Z – one of these and one of those.

The private museum frequently embodies idiosyncratic ideas about art and how it should be displayed. When Charles Freer left his collection of Asian art to the Smithsonian, he reserved personal curatorial control, and insisted that his dining room, designed by his friend James Abbott McNeill Whistler, be installed in the museum. Duncan Phillips mixed periods to create unusual juxtapositions, and scattered comfortable seating among his paintings. Isabella Gardner produced theatrical settings, in one case displaying Titian's *Rape of Europa* next to a sixteenth-century Persian carpet because her friend John Singer Sargent told her that the colours would be an interesting match. Albert Barnes hung pieces of Pennsylvania Dutch hardware among his Impressionists. As a collector, Sir Robert Sainsbury seemed to fall somewhere in between: as eclectic as Freer, more knowledgable than Gardner, less conventional than Frick, not as eccentric as Barnes.

Although the idea of writing about private collectors and personal museums was appealing, I had serious misgivings about the project. It appeared from our conversation in New York that what the Sainsbury family wanted was a sort of literary memorial. My books often end up in unpredictable places; indeed, for me, writing is an excuse to explore a subject, wherever it leads. How would the Sainsburys feel about that? Moreover, did it really make sense to have a North American write about a British topic? I still remember an irritating London review that treated one of my early books as the work of a talented colonial bumpkin. As for American readers, would they be interested in a thirty-year-old museum in a distant part of England, built by a British supermarket magnate? I emailed Andrew summarizing my views. 'In general, my conclusion is that I'm probably not the right person to write this book.'

The next day I changed my mind; it seemed impolite to just say no. I jotted down some general thoughts about a book, which I imagined as a far-ranging exploration of personal collecting. 'This is not an outline, since I still don't know enough, but it does describe the sort of book I would actually enjoy writing,' I wrote to Andrew. 'This gives Lady S. at least a general sense of where I would be heading, and a chance to stop now, rather than waste all our times with UK trips, etc. You should tell her that I completely understand that this may not be what they are looking for.'

The Sainsburys were not dissuaded, and two months later, during my university's spring break, I spent a week in London. I visited the Foster office, a vast and airy workroom overlooking the Thames, met Foster's partner Spencer de Grey (who has been with Foster for more than thirty years), and examined the drawing archive. I spoke to Steven Hooper, who had recorded the conversations with Sir Robert that I had read. We had tea in the courtyard of the British Museum, beneath Foster's vast glass roof. Hooper, an anthropologist whose field is Oceanic art, told me that Robert and Lisa Sainsbury's treatment of non-Western artefacts as art was very unusual for its time, and is still uncommon. I saw Lady Sainsbury, whom everybody calls Susie, and over dinner at the Royal Academy she introduced me to Ian Ritchie, an architect who had worked for Foster in the 1970s when the Sainsbury Centre was being designed. Ritchie had recently designed the temporary Courtyard Theatre in Stratford for the Royal Shakespeare Company, on whose board Susie sits, and on another evening she invited me to a cast dinner, following Patrick Stewart's spirited performance in *The Tempest*.

The idea of a book about the Sainsbury Centre had originated with Susie's husband, David Sainsbury, whom I met in his Westminster office. He had recently retired from the government, where he had served for eight years as Minister of Science and Innovation, and was currently occupied running his charitable foundation. I had never met a lord before, especially not a billionaire lord, and I found him unassuming, serious and disarmingly direct. We spoke about his parents. I asked him if he was a collector. No, he said; after having a father with the record of discovering artists such as Henry Moore and Francis Bacon, how could he be? He told me a story about receiving a postcard from his parents, who were in Paris on an art-collecting trip. The postcard was written in a café, where they had met some friends and were discussing whether fifteen-year-old David should be allowed to read *Lolita*, which had just been published. They had agreed that he should. The postcard was signed by his parents, as well as Henry, Alberto and Sandy; that is, Henry Moore, Alberto Giacometti and Alexander Calder, probably the three greatest sculptors of the mid-twentieth century. Later, Sainsbury and I walked around the corner from his office to see his parent's townhouse in Smith Square. He pointed to the window of his bedroom on the top floor, which had had a sculpture by Moore under the sink, since this was one of few places in the house that could structurally support the weight. A number of his boyhood presents had been paintings and drawings by Moore, who had been his godfather. 'This was just how we lived,' he explained. 'I thought everyone grew up with Bacons on their walls.'

We agreed to meet the next day at Liverpool Street Station, to catch a train to Norwich and visit the Sainsbury Centre. All buildings look good in photographs – that is, after all, the architectural photographer's job – but the experience of the real thing is sometimes a disappointment. Not this time. Foster's design had a powerful presence, and the intense sense of conviction that is the mark of all good architecture. The space inside was vast – 120 metres long with a ceiling 7.5 metres high – but it was neither overwhelming nor inhuman. At first glance it reminded me of Mies van der Rohe's open exhibition space in the New National Gallery in Berlin, but there were subtle differences: the daylight filtered down from above, and the side walls were solid, not glazed. The materials and details were industrial, but the effect was austere rather than machine-like. The paintings, sculptural objects and many very small artefacts looked at home. We walked up to Henry Moore's *Mother and Child*, which Robert Sainsbury had acquired in 1933. The metre-tall sculpture, which had originally stood in the hall of the Smith Square house, was in the open so that people could touch it. 'Moore used to tell me to stroke the back,' David Sainsbury recalled. He stopped to examine a painting that was among his father's last acquisitions. It was by Zoran Music, an Italian artist who was ninety when he painted it, the same age as Sir Robert Sainsbury when he bought it.

After lunch, David Sainsbury went back to London, and I stayed to wander about the building. By now I had decided to write about this place: the story was simply too compelling. But I had many questions. What made Robert Sainsbury, by training an accountant, and by his own admission someone who had no youthful exposure to or interest in the arts, amass what many consider one of the great private collections of its type in Europe? Why did he pick Norman Foster, who was not well known at the time, and had never designed a museum, or indeed any public building? Whence came the impulse for the unusual design – from the collector or from the architect? Or did they do it together? And what role did the university play? After all, this wasn't a private museum.

The rapport between the architect and his clients was evidently close; I read that Foster once described Robert and Lisa Sainsbury as 'a vital part of the design team'. He also said that they were 'the toughest clients that I had ever worked for'. David Sainsbury told me that a decade after the Centre opened, Foster had been invited back to design a major extension, and that he had recently finished making further modifications to the building. This work represented an ongoing relationship between Foster and the Sainsbury family of more than thirty years.

There are broader questions as well. Where does this austere art hangar fit in the flamboyant history of museum design in the late twentieth century? The Sainsbury Centre is a very early example of an architectural movement known as 'high tech'; the Pompidou Centre, which opened at about the same time, is another. Both museums were designed by British architects. Why did this approach take root in Britain? And how did this building style come to dominate airports, office buildings and institutional buildings – as well as museums – around the world? When I visited the Sainsbury Centre I was surprised how little it showed its age. This is in part a testament to David Sainsbury's careful stewardship and in part a reflection of Foster's resistance to fashion, but the building also looks new because so many of the architectural concerns that it embodies have remained current. That is unusual, too.

I have, for over forty years, been a passionate acquirer – a passionate acquirer of works of art that have appealed to me, irrespective of period or style, subject only to the limitation of size, in relation to the space available, and, naturally, cash.

Architecturally Norman Foster was given only two guidelines, we did not want a monument to ourselves nor to him, and we did want a positive statement.

ROBERT SAINSBURY

I once described the design process as being like an iceberg – if the visible tip was a building, then out of sight and out of mind, below the surface was the process – those many thousands of man-hours spent in discussion, research, exploration, negotiation, drawing, modelling, and finally the making of the building itself.

In the leap from drawing board to reality the human factor is paramount, regardless of the shift of technology, and loving care remains a vital ingredient throughout the process of manufacture and assembly.

NORMAN FOSTER

ONE HAS TO CHOOSE

Robert and Lisa Sainsbury create an art collection. Exhibitions in America and the Netherlands. Meeting Kho.

ROBERT SAINSBURY ACQUIRED HIS FIRST WORKS OF ART IN 1931 when he was twenty-four – a pair of drawings by Jacob Epstein, bought from the Redfern Gallery in London's Old Bond Street, and, shortly after, a small Epstein bronze of a sleeping infant's head, from Zwemmer, a gallery in Lichfield Street. Robert had just started working in the family business, and he was still living with his parents in their flat in Portland Place in central London. The sculpture sat on the mantelpiece in his room. Epstein was an adventurous choice for a budding businessman who had just passed his accountancy exam. 'You have to understand that this is a period in which Epstein was vilified,' Robert later recalled.

> His name stood for everything that was terrible in modern art and I can remember an occasion when there was a family dinner party and as always, it was eight people (two tables of bridge) I was the ninth. I was at home, so I was having dinner and the subject got on to this terrible creature Epstein and I looked at my mother and said 'Excuse me a moment, do you mind if I go to my room and get something' and I disap-peared – I came back, plonked the baby's head on the dining room table and said 'Now what do you think of this as art?' All the women swooned and I said 'As a matter of fact *that* is by the monster, Epstein.' I now blush to think how extremely rude I was to my parents, but I was so furious.[1]

The story succinctly describes a conventional upper-class family – dinner parties, bridge, gossip. It was not a household in which aesthetics were prized. 'In the house in which I spent all my childhood in Hampstead there was no art whatsoever … I had no encouragement in matters of art and was never taken to any museum.' The story also reveals something about his character: a young man who excuses himself to his mother, and an older man who ruefully acknowledges his youthful impetuousness – both unfailingly polite. On the other hand, 'I was so furious' suggests deeply concealed emotions. A split personality? Not so unusual in the world of art collectors, which has included men of the cloth, flighty heiresses, hard-boiled business tycoons and haughty socialites. Why shouldn't a grocer's grandson have an artistic soul?

John James Sainsbury, Robert's grandfather, opened his first shop in 1869, a small establishment in Drury Lane, selling butter, eggs and milk. The son of a picture-frame maker, he had married a dairyman's daughter, who encouraged him to go into retailing. Victorian Britain prospered and the Sainsbury family – there were six sons, who all worked in the business – prospered with it. A sturdy fire-plug of a man, John James was a determined entrepreneur, who expanded into groceries, bought directly from producers, and eventually owned his own farms. By the time he died in 1928, 'J. Sainsbury' was a household name in southern England: there were 182 shops and annual turnover was an astonishing £9 million.[2] Much of this extraordinary growth was engineered by his eldest son and sole partner, John Benjamin, who in turn groomed his two sons, Alan and the younger Robert (1906–2000), to take over the business.[*]

Robert Sainsbury's mother, Mabel, was Dutch, the daughter of Jacob Van den Bergh, scion of a prominent Jewish family that had made its fortune in margarine.[3] So while Robert had an unremarkable boyhood – boarding school, holidays at the seaside, Cambridge (he read history) – his family background was slightly exotic.[4] Perhaps it was this, as well as his temperament, that led him to art. When he was eighteen, his mother,

---

[*]   John Benjamin Sainsbury also had two daughters, Nora, who died in childhood, and Vera.

who loved horse racing, placed a five-shilling bet on his behalf, and Robert won five pounds. He used the money to buy a book that he saw by chance in the window of an antiquarian bookseller in Charing Cross Road. This impulsive purchase started him collecting books from private presses and special editions. It was an almost secret hobby. He once came home with a leather-bound book, and his father observed that it looked expensive. 'Yes,' the young man replied. 'You gave me an allowance. As far as I know I have no debts and if I choose to buy books instead of silk pyjamas [which were much in favour in Cambridge at the time], is that all right?'[5] He became friends with a talented young engraver and printer, Blair Hughes-Stanton, and sponsored his Gemini Press. 'As time wore on, I got more and more interested in the plain printed page without any embellishments,' Robert Sainsbury remembered. 'I didn't at the time query this except I realised that this was what meant most to me – the perfect placing of the type on the page and the capital letters – typography, not too much decoration on the page … it is not a far step from the plain printed page of beautiful proportions on lovely paper to a drawing.'[6]

Two years after buying the Epstein drawings, Robert Sainsbury moved into his own flat, not far from his parent's home. When a young man strikes out on his own, he often acts up. In Robert's case, the acting up took an unusual form: he bought art, lots of it. He began with an India ink drawing by another sculptor, Henri Gaudier-Brzeska, and followed that with several little Tang-dynasty earthenware tomb figures. The ancient Chinese pottery was bought on the advice of the great collector and Orientalist George Eumorfopoulos, whose brother was a friend of Robert's parents. By his own admission, Robert was a 'young man who knew absolutely nothing', and people such as Eumorfopoulos, and later the dealers John Hewett in London and Pierre Loeb in Paris, were a great help to him, although he always made his own final decisions. He bought several more Tang figures – two horses and a camel – as well as a painting, *Peonies* (*c.* 1930), an expensive oil by Matthew Smith, which hung in his dining room for years; he later sold the painting. 'I guess it was to make way for other things,' he said of the sale, 'the realisation that, not being able to have everything, you have to choose what you want – and I realised early on that what meant most to me – paintings as well as drawings – was the human figure, not either flower pieces or above all, landscapes. It doesn't mean to say I wouldn't love to have great landscapes and great still lifes but one has to choose.'[7] The view of a sensible man.

Robert ended that first year on his own with a major acquisition. He was introduced to the artist at a party. Henry Moore, thirty-five and still teaching part-time in an art school, invited him to the opening of his second exhibition, at the Leicester Galleries in London in November 1933. 'I toured the exhibition, so to speak, with Henry – bought *Mother and Child* and then we went and had lunch together in Leicester Square at a café on the north side of the square,' Robert laconically recalled.[8] It was the way he would always buy, not impulsively but, once he knew what he wanted, without hesitation. '*That* is *my* drawing, *my* object – the one that I like,' he once said.[9] *Mother and Child* (1932) is now generally recognized as one of Moore's great early works. Robert paid £158, a significant sum (the equivalent of about £8,000 or $12,000 today), and he placed the metre-tall green Hornton stone figure in the corner of his living room. Two men with very different backgrounds, Sainsbury and Moore would become lifelong friends, drawn together by a shared love of sculpture.

Collectors collect for different reasons. Some to advance themselves socially, some to fill their spare time, some to broaden their horizons. Robert Sainsbury seems closest to the last; art was a release for a part of him that the business world left unfulfilled. He spent his working days at the family firm, becoming a director and company secretary in 1934, but on Saturday afternoons he browsed the London galleries. Art was his chief pastime – his entry in *Who's Who* did not list any clubs, hobbies or sports. And he continued to buy. During the second year on his own he acquired a small reclining figure by Moore, drawings by Picasso, Degas and Charles Despiau, a painting by Rouault, Modigliani's exquisite *Head of a Woman (Anna Zborowska)* (*c.* 1918), and two bronze sculptures, Ossip Zadkine's

Accordion Player (1918) and Despiau's beautiful *Eve* (1925). The following year, the Tate asked to borrow *Eve* for a sculpture show. Robert agreed, but only if they would include a work by Moore. 'Over my dead body will Henry Moore enter the Tate,' the director told him.[10] *Eve* stayed on her pedestal in the dining room.

Robert Sainsbury had begun to visit Paris. In 1934, in the gallery of Paul Guillaume, he saw his first examples of African art: a reliquary head from Gabon and a dance mask from the Ivory Coast. He was intrigued, but declined to buy on grounds of cost. Back in England and ill with mumps, he regretted his caution, and was further pained when he read of Guillaume's death. The following year he bought the two pieces from the dealer's widow. Later, he said of his initial reaction: 'I knew nothing about African art. I had never seen it consciously before. I didn't *appreciate* it, I didn't *understand* it, or know anything about it. I straightforward liked it in sensual terms … it really was the purest form of reaction because I didn't even know what I was looking at.'[11] He was obviously not a conventional collector; he had no interest in rarity or completeness, not even exclusively in modern art, as the Tang figurines and the African objects attest. He *was* drawn to depictions of the human figure, and to sculptures, especially very small sculptures.

In 1937, Robert married Lisa Ingeborg Van den Bergh (b. 1912), his second cousin. 'Butter weds margarine again', the newspapers quipped, referring to the two families' business interests. Although she was born in the Netherlands, Lisa's background was cosmopolitan. Her father, Simon, the first Van den Bergh to snub the family business, had gone to Germany to study philosophy and married a Russian refugee, Sonia Pokrojska, whom Lisa described as 'more like a Chekhov character than you can possibly imagine'.[12] Lisa grew up in Geneva, where her father worked for the League of Nations, and later in Paris, where he taught Islamic philosophy at the École des hautes études. She was sent to a private school in Paris, studied in Oxford for three years and, influenced by the pioneering almoner Cherry Morris, undertook hospital social work at St Thomas's

THE SAINSBURYS

John James Sainsbury opened
a small dairy shop in 1869 in
London's Drury Lane, and with his
six sons created a successful chain
of grocery stores across the south
of England. Part of the appeal of
J. Sainsbury was the combination
of luxury and cleanliness, clearly
represented by the branch at 143
Guildford High Street (*below*) on
opening day, 6 November 1906.
In the post-war years, Sainsbury's
grandsons, Alan and Robert,
expanded the business into a
nationwide network of self-service
supermarkets.

Robert Sainsbury acquired his first sculpture, Jacob Epstein's *Baby Asleep* (1902–4) in 1931 when he was twenty-five. The human figure was the central theme of his eclectic collection, which included Charles Despiau's *Eve* (1925), a Khmer torso (11th century; *opposite, top*) – in his view, the greatest sculpture in his collection – and a reliquary head from Gabon (19th–20th century).

Bob and Lisa Sainsbury's collecting produced close friendships
with several artists, including Jacob Epstein, Henry Moore, Alberto
Giacometti and Francis Bacon. In 1939, Epstein created a bronze bust
of Lisa (*opposite, top right*), and a few years later made a companion
piece of Bob (1942). Bacon, who did not accept commissions, painted
a portrait of Bob in 1955, and over the next two and a half years
painted eight portraits of Lisa; this (from 1956) is one of three
that he did not destroy.

The Sainsburys' home at 5 Smith Square, London, was full of art. Henry Moore's *Mother and Child* (1932, *right*) stood in the entrance hall, and Degas's *Little Dancer aged Fourteen* (1880–1), shown here with Bob and Lisa, occupied the first-floor landing. Bob's study contained cases with small sculptural figures, and larger works stood on every available surface. He particularly loved small objects, such as these Tang-dynasty earthenware tomb figures, which were acquired in 1933.

In 1957, Bob and Lisa visited the Barnes Foundation in Philadelphia, where Impressionists hang among Pennsylvania Dutch hardware and African art (*above*). When the Sainsbury collection was exhibited in 1966, in the Rijksmuseum Kröller-Müller in the Netherlands (*right*), visitors could experience a similarly unconventional juxtaposition of modern and tribal art.

Hospital in London. She met her cousin Robert Sainsbury at a London charity ball, and they married four years later. Although the BBC News would characterize the wedding as 'secret', David Sainsbury disagrees.[13] 'My parents both came from large families, and they could either have had a huge wedding or a private one. They decided on the latter, and since neither was religious, they married in a register office.' All the same, Lisa's father did not approve of his daughter marrying a businessman, and his opinion of his son-in-law did not improve when he saw his taste in art.[14] Simon Van den Bergh was an academic and an intellectual and, in his daughter's words, 'had no visual sense whatsoever', which was part of what attracted her to Robert – as well as his directness and lack of intellectual pretension.[15]

Bob and Lisa, as they came to be known, were, in some odd way, a perfect match, though in temperament they were almost opposites. He was of medium height, mild-mannered, self-sufficient, and somewhat withdrawn; she was small – 5'2" – forceful, and more sociable. She spoke French and English fluently, as well as Dutch; he spoke no foreign languages at all. Of the pair, she was the practical one; he was entirely unmechanical – never learned to drive a car, for example. A family story has it that he had to stop smoking because the butler who changed the flints in his lighter left and Bob didn't know how to do it for himself. As the episode of the Epstein head demonstrates, whatever views Bob held – and he held strong ones, especially about art – he was always scrupulously polite, and is invariably remembered by people as 'absolutely charming'. Lisa, blunt and unsentimental, could be abrasive; her manner has been described as 'aristocratic' in the sense that she could be very direct, almost peremptory, in her demands. A family friend of long standing remembers once having an argument with her, 'which reduced Bob to a condition of admiration mixed with fear – not many people took her on.' According to another close friend, 'Lisa has a strong personality, which made some people find her "difficult" – but you simply needed to have confidence to deal with her.'

The following year, after suffering a mild heart attack, John Sainsbury abruptly retired from the firm, leaving his two sons to take over as joint general managers. A *New Statesman* profile paints a contrasting picture of the brothers: Alan, who had worked at the firm since he was seventeen, was the dynamic retailer, 'a fiery personality and an energetic shopkeeper'; Robert was 'a gentler soul', who oversaw administration, property management and personnel matters.[16] It proved to be an extremely successful and long-lived partnership. They guided the company through the food shortages and rationing of the Second World War, and the difficult post-war years, and navigated Sainsbury's enormously profitable transition from a regional collection of grocery shops to a national chain of self-service supermarkets.*

As a marriage gift, Bob and Lisa had bought themselves an exceptional Modigliani, *Portrait of Baranowski* (1918). This makes it sound as if art had brought them together, but that was not the case. 'I came from a completely different background,' Lisa later recalled, 'and it took me some time to recover from having been trailed around most of the world's great museums and told what I should like and what I should despise. However, we lived in Montparnasse in Paris and that gave me an opportunity of seeing quite a lot of modern art.'[17] Bob and Lisa had slightly different tastes, he being attracted to line, she to colour, but collecting became a shared pursuit and they never bought anything unless they both wanted it. 'I was with Bob and Lisa once in a gallery when they were buying,' recalls Elizabeth Estève-Coll. 'They circled the artworks – separately – not saying anything, then made a decision extremely quickly, on the spot. I couldn't really see why they liked the particular piece, but later came to understand that they had, for them, made exactly the right choice.'[18] Buying art often meant travelling. 'We are those monsters who didn't take our holidays with our children,' Bob recalled. They eventually bought a country house, a handsome Georgian vicarage in Bucklebury, a village in Berkshire, about

---

* Robert Sainsbury ran the firm single-handedly during the war, since his brother and cousins were seconded to the Ministry of Food.

50 miles from London, where Lisa and the children spent the summer, Bob visiting them at weekends. 'Then we went on our travels when they went back to school in September. I always took two holidays a year.'[19]

Bob and Lisa's collecting was constrained by the so-called Art Account, a self-imposed annual £1,000 limit on what they could spend, instituted immediately after the war. Although the sum was not inconsiderable (about £40,000 or $60,000 today), Lisa chafed at Bob's rectitude, thinking it needlessly puritanical. But he was cautious. 'People have a little bit tended to think, because my name is Sainsbury, that even when I was young I had unlimited means at my disposal,' he explained. 'I did not, because all those years Sainsbury's was a private company. I may have owned a large number of shares, but those shares were not marketable and paid virtually no dividends.'[20] When one of their uncles quit the business, Alan and Robert were obliged to buy him out, which consumed most of their liquid capital. The Art Account, which was in place for thirteen years (although the spending limit was gradually increased), had an important effect. If Bob and Lisa wanted a more expensive piece, they would either sell something, or forgo the pleasure. The Art Account was also a reflection of Bob's sense of propriety. 'I have been fortunate in having a job which I enjoyed, which enabled me to, if you like, indulge a passion for art, but having that passion for art, what would have happened if I hadn't had self-discipline and limited my expenditures? I know the answer would have been financial problems for me and trouble for Sainsbury's.'[21]

The other limit on the quantity and size of the works they bought was simply space. Shortly after they married, Bob and Lisa bought a house on the corner of an eighteenth-century Georgian terrace in Lord North Street, facing Smith Square in Westminster. Here they raised their four children: Elizabeth, the eldest; David, who was born at the outbreak of the Second World War in Montreal (where Elizabeth and the pregnant Lisa had been sent to family friends for safety); Celia; and Annabel. The narrow, four-storey house, one room deep, was elegant but hardly palatial: an entrance hall, dining room and kitchen on the ground floor; a sitting room and a nursery on the first; Bob and Lisa's bedroom and a study on the second; and on the third floor, under the roof, bedrooms for the older children. The basement contained a flat for the live-in couple who kept house for the Sainsburys, and a cellar. Before they moved in, Bob and Lisa engaged a young London architect and furniture designer, Roderick Eustace Enthoven, to decorate the interior. Enthoven had just completed an art deco restaurant for the Regent Street store of the Belfast linen merchants Robinson & Cleaver, and the Smith Square décor was similarly spare, mostly white and very modern, rather daring for 1937.

In time, there would be art all over the house. Moore's *Mother and Child* stood within the curve of the staircase in the hall, and a Picasso hung above a simple antique side-table. Degas's *Little Dancer aged Fourteen* (1880–1) occupied the first-floor landing, opposite Modigliani's *Portrait of Baranowski*; an Arp sat on the window-sill. A visitor recalls seeing a work of art on top of the toilet tank in the powder room.[22] In the wood-panelled dining room, a Francis Bacon triptych hung behind Bob's chair; at the opposite end, Soutine's *Lady in Blue* (*c.* 1931) overlooked two fifteenth-century Flemish alabaster sculptures on a table. A small Parisian street scene by Pierre Bonnard, a wedding present from Alan Sainsbury, occupied the third wall, while a tall polished hardwood club from the Marquesas Islands stood in the corner. In the sitting room, in the place of honour above the mantelpiece, was another Modigliani; nearby stood a Giacometti bronze figure, and two paintings by the same artist hung on the opposite wall. Behind Bob's chair was an eleventh-century Khmer torso purchased from the Eumorfopoulos collection, and behind Lisa's the Gabon head. The walls of the study were lined with vitrines (glass-panelled display cases), suspended from the ceiling by metal rods, and built-in bookshelves filled the space beneath the windows. There were many more paintings than there was wall space, and extra canvases were stored in a contraption that the children christened the Bicycle Rack. A long, slim, wall-hung cabinet that Bob filled with tiny sculptures was known as the Toy Department.

A French journalist admiringly described the atmosphere at Smith Square: 'There is no concern with decoration. It is like the idea of Chinese collectors: a few art works on display, and in a small room, accessible only to art lovers, cases full of objects that you examine one by one. Paintings and drawings by masters are stacked against the walls, and are shown individually, but only if you ask and are really interested. There is no hint here of the ostentatious collector who demands admiration, and smothers you by the quantity of his paintings. The Sainsburys know that even the most beautiful works of art eventually get "worn out".'[23]

Bob and Lisa frequently entertained dealers and artists at Smith Square, which became an institution in the London art world. They had many artist friends: Moore, of course, but also Alberto Giacometti and Francis Bacon. It was not just a question of buying their work – although that was important, for none was well known when the Sainsburys started collecting them – but of personal relationships. Lisa, always practical, bought Giacometti a raincoat to replace his tattered garment. She lectured an ageing and rheumatic Henry Moore on central heating. 'He said, well my mother didn't have it,' she recalled. 'I said your mother couldn't afford it but you can, and you will feel much better for it.'[24] Bob personally guaranteed Bacon's bank account for £500, since 'Francis was, just as usual, in a financial muddle.'[25] The artists reciprocated and Smith Square contained bronze busts of Bob and Lisa by Epstein, drawings of the children by Giacometti, a portrait of Bob and three of Lisa by Bacon (who never painted portraits). It was hardly a Bohemian household, but it was definitely unconventional.

By 1958, with the Sainsbury firm growing by leaps and bounds, the Art Account had been discontinued. Bob and Lisa bought their first bronze by Giacometti (their previous purchases of his work had all been paintings and drawings), as well as a large reclining female figure by Henry Moore, which was installed at the foot of the garden at Bucklebury. As the prices for contemporary artists rose – in the case of Bacon and Moore, thanks in no small part to Bob and Lisa's early patronage – the Sainsburys turned increasingly to non-Western art. They frequented dealers, auctions and galleries, not only in London and Paris, but also in New York City, which they visited annually. In 1962, Bob and Lisa were approached by Robert Goldwater, then director of the Museum of Primitive Art on West 54th Street.[26] He wanted to know if they would agree to show part of their collection at the museum. 'I wasn't aware I had a collection – what are you talking about?' was Bob's first response.[27] But Goldwater, an art historian and a respected scholar of African art, was persuasive, and the following year 123 objects from Smith Square went on display in the museum; Africa, New Guinea, Polynesia and the Americas were represented, as well as antiquities from Europe and the Middle East. The exhibition, which ran from May to September 1963, was billed as 'The Robert and Lisa Sainsbury Collection'. In an introductory essay in the exhibition catalogue, Bob wrote, 'The objects in this exhibition should not be regarded as a consciously formed collection of primitive sculpture … they are part of a seemingly more heterogeneous whole, containing not only modern sculpture, drawings and paintings, but Ancient, Medieval and Oriental objects which by no argument could be called *primitive*.' He went on: 'in my art acquisitions I am essentially eclectic, intuition largely taking the place of intellect. The result, after 30 odd years, is a collection only in the literal sense, unless it be found that a strong predilection has of itself produced the cohesion usually regarded as the essence of a *collection*.'[28]

Bob was touchy about being labelled a collector, perhaps because he did not want to be mistaken for simply another wealthy businessmen buying up art. 'As I say I am sensitive – it may be sort of inverted snobbism, but it is very largely, I think, the result of all these Americans out to form what I call "instant collections" whether it be African or Impressionist … They may not be the greatest masterpieces, but you could still buy, a few months ago, one of the great Degas's – you can still buy this, that or the other if you have enough money. You don't even have to have the taste to do it – there are plenty of people who will tell you how good it is!'[29] However, despite Bob's remonstrations, the New York show had an effect. The Museum of Primitive Art was in a large townhouse, so the scale of the rooms was not entirely different from Smith Square, but seeing their possessions in a public gallery *was* different. 'It wasn't until then really that I thought in terms of a collection,' Bob said later.[30]

In 1965, Bob and Lisa were contacted by Rudi Oxenaar, the recently appointed director of the Rijksmuseum Kröller-Müller in the Netherlands, a respected museum with the world's second largest collection of Van Goghs. Oxenaar proposed to mount a major exhibition that would display the full scope of their collection – modern as well as primitive – and to arrange the works according to purely aesthetic criteria. This was particularly attractive, as was the venue – not only its being in the Netherlands, with which Bob and Lisa had so many ties, but also the museum itself, which had been founded thirty years earlier by a famous private collector, Hélène Kröller-Müller.[*] 'I can only say that I am sure that Mrs Kröller-Müller, always our example in such matters, would have loved to see your collection in her museum,' wrote Oxenaar.[31]

The exhibition, which opened in July 1966, occupied seven rooms – all the temporary galleries of the museum – and included 180 pieces, or about two-thirds of the entire collection. The work was roughly balanced between modern, ancient and tribal art. The exhibition began with Zadkine's *Accordion Player* on one side, and a twelfth-century *Virgin and Child* on the other, which signalled the theme of the collection: a far-ranging celebration of the age-old impulse to represent the human figure.[32] Francis Bacon's portraits of Lisa and Bob, flanked by Moore's *Mother and Child* and a prehistoric Celtic head, occupied a prominent position. Picasso's *Woman combing her Hair* (1906), which Bob had bought in 1935 from the British impressionist painter Fred Mayor, was there, so was the wooden reliquary head from Gabon that had caught his eye in Paris. The

---

[*]   Hélène Kröller-Müller's story is recounted in detail in Chapter 2.

display was characterized by a close mixing of objects and periods: sculptures by Giacometti, paintings and drawings by Modigliani and César, as well as younger artists such as Antonio Saura and John Wragg, among Benin masks, Maori figures, Melanesian heads, Haida rattles, Cycladic figurines, Chinese pottery and the Khmer torso, which Bob considered the greatest piece of sculpture in the entire collection.

'As I now understand more than ever, it is extremely difficult, in the normal course of events, to be objective about one's own possessions in one's own house, when one knows them so well and is used to them being about,' Bob wrote to Oxenaar. 'In the Kröller-Müller we were able, mentally, to stand back and survey them.'[33] The exhibition changed the way that Bob and Lisa thought about their art. In his introduction to the catalogue, Bob admitted that 'apparently I must now take my "collection" a little more seriously than hitherto', and he included what is perhaps the clearest statement of his philosophy of collecting.[34] He asked that each object, painting and sculpture in the exhibition 'be looked at and judged as a work of art in its own right, irrespective of provenance and date, or its creator's purpose.' He added: 'I naturally have in mind particularly the so-called "primitive" objects, which I am proud to show alongside modern sculptures and sculptures of other cultures and periods long recognized as works of art.'[35] The reviews in the Dutch newspapers, which were forwarded to Bob, were complimentary. At the end of September, the Sainsburys stopped on the way back from a holiday in Venice, to see the exhibition a second time.

In a warm speech at the opening of the Kröller-Müller exhibition, Bob conveyed his and Lisa's excitement. 'You will understand that as we do not live in a large mansion, but an ordinary-sized house, there is, shall I say, a certain amount of congestion at home. It is, therefore, a very real joy for us to see so many of our favourite possessions with space around them and displayed in a manner which does them more than justice.'[36] The exhibition layout was the work of a thirty-nine-year-old Dutch designer.[37] Kho Liang Ie was of Chinese parentage, born in 1927 on the island of Java, then part of the Dutch East Indies. In 1949, in the aftermath of Indonesian independence, like many ethnic Chinese his parents left Indonesia for the Netherlands, where Kho enrolled in the Institute for Applied Arts (today the Gerrit Rietveld Academy) in Amsterdam. His Bauhaus-influenced training included interior architecture and furniture design. After graduation, he made a name for himself as a design consultant to the furniture company Artifort. In 1959, Kho established his own design studio, quickly building an international reputation in furniture, graphics, exhibitions and office interiors. At the time of the Sainsbury exhibition, he had just completed the main waiting lounge of Amsterdam's Schiphol airport, to great acclaim, and was working on the interior of the Lagos airport terminal.*

The Sainsburys were very impressed with the sensitive way that Kho designed the Kröller-Müller exhibition. He displayed the sculptures so that they could be seen from all sides, the larger ones on plinths and the smaller pieces grouped in glass cases. The overall design was extremely simple and unaffected, allowing the art to speak for itself. (The identification labels were tiny, according to Bob's instructions.) The temporary galleries at the Kröller-Müller are somewhat rustic, with rough brick floors and white painted walls, and Kho mounted some of the drawings and paintings on canvas panels. The muted aesthetic, so similar to their home in Smith Square, pleased the Sainsburys. 'One of the great revelations to me was your use of colour in the display. I know that this will have a permanent effect on my pleasure in the collection,' Bob wrote in an appreciative letter to Kho.[38] In 1966, when the British Arts Council raised the possibility of an even larger exhibition of the Collection (as Bob now referred to it) in the new South Bank Gallery, Bob and Lisa's first choice to design it was Kho. They had already discussed with him the design of another possible exhibition of the collection in Jerusalem.[39]

---

* Kho was a significant figure in post-war Dutch design. His 1960s sitting furniture for Artifort is still in production, and the leading Dutch industrial design award is name the Kho Liang Ie Prize. The firm Kho founded is still in existence.

Neither of these exhibitions came to pass, but, as they did with many young artists, the Sainsburys forged a friendship with the Dutch designer. In 1967, with the children grown, Bob and Lisa decided to make some alterations to their house in Smith Square in anticipation of their retirement. They had a lift installed, and they asked Kho to turn the nursery into a study and to transform the old study on the second floor into a separate bed-sitting room for Bob.*[40] Working with British architect Martin Caroe, Kho installed display shelving and vitrines, and wall-mounted stands. For the new study, he designed a massive walnut desk that also served as a stand for sculptures. The furniture he chose included Le Corbusier's chaise longue, his sling chair and Grand Confort club chair, and Mies van der Rohe's Brno armchair, all designed between 1927 and 1930, and already considered classics. According to a contemporary description, 'the walls were lined with panels covered in mushroom coloured silk, the floors carpeted in a slightly darker shade of the same colour, and the windows curtained in silk of a darker shade still.'[41] The combined effect of the severe décor and the delicate cases and stands gave the impression – even more than before – of a personal museum. 'My mother's room had one or two favourite pieces of art – I remember a Morandi,' says David Sainsbury. 'But it was more like a normal room than my father's room.' Bob's specially designed bed was in the centre of the room, surrounded on two sides by built-in shelves so that he could be close to the figurines and small objects he so loved. The counter-height shelves were covered by a white marble slab and immediately became known as the Milk Bar. On it stood an Arp terracotta and African figures. Opposite the bed was the Toy Department cabinet, with an up-swinging Perspex lid to allow Bob to adjust the positions of the tiny sculptures when it pleased him, which was often. The room had a Bacon portrait of Lisa, and vitrines and wall-mounted stands similar to those Kho had used in the Kröller-Müller exhibition. Steven Hooper recalls being stunned on his first visit

---

*   Kho refused payment for the work. Bob and Lisa later gave him a sculpture by John Wragg, a recent young protégé, although Bob felt this was 'hardly adequate recompense for all the time and trouble involved.'

by seeing three great Polynesian sculptures ranged along one wall. After dinner, instead of convening a game of bridge, Bob would announce to his guests: 'Now let's go up to my bedroom', where he would conduct a tour of the latest acquisitions.

LIFE EVER AFTER

The gift. How three private collectors founded notable museums.

ALAN AND ROBERT SAINSBURY, 'MR ALAN' AND 'MR RJ' as they were known in the firm, built Sainsbury's into the largest food retailer in Britain, with more than two hundred branches, 28,000 employees, and an annual turnover exceeding £100 million.[1] In 1967, Alan retired and Bob succeeded him as chairman. He served long enough to see the firm through its centenary celebration two years later, before stepping down. Following a family tradition, Bob handed the management of the company to the next generation, in this case Alan's son John. His own son, David, having completed a degree in history and psychology at Cambridge, as well as an MBA at Columbia University, had also joined the firm. One senses that, at sixty-three, Bob was not entirely unhappy to leave. 'God didn't particularly intend me to be a businessman,' he once said. 'I have no regrets and I enjoyed it very much, but it wasn't a question of the only thing in the world I wanted to do was to be occupied by Sainsbury's.'[2]

After their retirements, Alan and Robert Sainsbury were named joint life presidents, and had adjacent offices on the seventh floor of Sainsbury's headquarters in Stamford House in the Blackfriars area of London. While Alan, who had once stood as a Liberal parliamentary candidate, pursued his interest in politics, Bob was occupied with art. He was a member of the board of trustees of the Tate Gallery, service for which he was knighted in 1967, and two years later was elected chairman of the Tate board, a powerful position on the London art scene. He and Lisa now had more time for travel, regularly visiting galleries and dealers in Paris, Milan, Rome and New York. But they faced a vexing question:

What was to become of their collection? None of their children was sufficiently interested in art to take it over. David Sainsbury remembers a conversation with his father. 'He asked me if I wanted to inherit the collection. By then there were four hundred objects, and it had gone beyond something you could keep at home. I didn't see myself living in a house full of art, with young children and a family it simply wasn't practical. I suggested that he should consider leaving it to a museum. It followed that it would happen in their lifetimes.'

A strong philanthropic streak runs in the Sainsbury family.* In 1938, shortly before the outbreak of the Second World War, the British government decreed that unaccompanied Jewish children victimized by Nazi persecution would be allowed into the country if they had British sponsors. Bob and Alan Sainsbury founded a hostel in Putney for twenty refugee children, part of the so-called *Kindertransport* that brought about ten thousand children to Britain The brothers and their wives paid regular visits to the children, took them sightseeing, supplied pocket money, and even provided a seaside house for summer holidays. Bob and Lisa's philanthropic roots went back to their common ancestor, Simon van den Bergh, the early twentieth-century 'Margarine King', who was known for helping European Jewish refugees seeking passage to America. In the late 1950s, Bob and Lisa established a programme to assist two or three young sculptors a year. 'The Sainsbury Awards were for during the first year after leaving art school to enable them to exist without spending their entire time earning their living as warehousemen and so on,' Bob said. 'We didn't give them enough to avoid other work but sufficient to enable them to have two or three days a week in which to be sculptors.'[3]

Thinking of the collection, Bob and Lisa briefly considered creating their own gallery. 'I mean if, for example, we bought the house next door and set up our own museum – great fun, I would have loved it,' said Bob. 'But what the hell happens when we die? You couldn't expect

---

* At the time of writing there are seventeen Sainsbury charitable trusts.

Westminster to do anything about it. Perhaps two people a week might visit it.'[4] They decided not to go it alone but to leave the collection to an institution – not a museum but a university. They were not interested in creating an academic centre for scholars and researchers, however. Bob explained: 'It is because we want to give some men and women – and who better than undergraduates in a School of Fine Arts – the opportunity of looking at works of art in the natural context of their work and daily life, not just because they have been prompted to visit a Museum or Art Gallery – to give them the opportunity, when young, of learning the pleasures of visual experience – of looking at works of art from a sensual, not only an intellectual point of view – above all, of realising that certain artefacts are works of art as well as evidence of history.'[5] This highly original and personal goal influenced and shaped their decisions throughout the long process that would follow.

Bob had preliminary discussions with his alma mater, Cambridge, but the university wanted to divide the works between the Fitzwilliam Museum and the Museum of Archaeology and Anthropology, and proposed to put most of them in storage, which did not suit him. Having always nurtured young talent, Bob and Lisa decided that, rather than leave their collection to an established, well-endowed university, they would consider a fledgling institution. In the late 1960s, that meant one of the seven so-called 'new universities' – Sussex, East Anglia, York, Lancaster, Essex, Kent, and Warwick – which had been founded in the immediate post-war period. They were also known as the 'plate glass universities', thanks to their modernistic buildings, which contrasted with the Victorian red-brick universities, and the older stone quadrangles of the medieval and Renaissance colleges. 'We looked at the architecture of various universities, none of which appealed to me,' Bob later recalled. 'The thought of my collection going to Sussex was anathema.'*[6] Bob and Lisa often made decisions on the basis of personal experience, which is what drew them to

---

* Sussex had a picturesque brick-and-concrete campus designed by Sir Basil Spence, but Bob may have been referring to its radical student politics.

the University of East Anglia, whose vice-chancellor, Frank Thistlethwaite, had become a good friend.

They had met Thistlethwaite in July 1964. He was then forty-nine, a Cambridge history don, who had come to Norwich only four years earlier to create and lead the new university. He had a cosmopolitan background, having studied and lived in the United States, married an American, and written a bestseller on American history. A small, lively man, he was a talented pianist and interested in the arts. He had an entrepreneur's flair: when the university considered establishing a music school, Thistlethwaite sought the advice of Benjamin Britten, whom he had never met; when it needed academic regalia he approached the acclaimed photographer, Cecil Beaton, who had designed prize-winning theatre and film costumes. Thistlethwaite came to know the Sainsburys through their friend Andrew Ritchie, an expatriate Scottish art historian, who was director of the Yale University Art Gallery. Ritchie's and Thistlethwaite's wives, both Americans, knew each other. Ritchie convinced Thistlethwaite that a new university should have an art collection, and to that end he introduced him to the London art scene, which included Bob and Lisa Sainsbury. The three must have hit it off, for the week after they met, Thistlethwaite wrote to Bob, 'we are much concerned to see that the undergraduates should have the opportunity of enjoying the arts ... I have been encouraged by Andrew Ritchie to overcome a natural reluctance to go begging and to ask you whether you could possibly consider the loan to us of a few pictures or prints from your own collection.'[7] In due course, the loan was made, and over the next four years a warm friendship developed. The Sainsburys were impressed by Thistlethwaite's commitment to the visual arts: he had recruited Peter Lasko, a talented young Berliner, graduate of the Courtauld Institute and expert in medieval art, to start a school of fine arts, and the university had established a small art gallery. Bob and Lisa lent more pictures and sculptures, and also made substantial anonymous contributions (totalling £3,500) for the purchase of art books. A further personal connection developed when their youngest daughter,

Annabel, enrolled at East Anglia as an undergraduate in mathematics and physics.

Thistlethwaite and his wife, Jane, were occasional guests at Smith Square, and, after a dinner on 30 May 1968, Bob made a surprising announcement: he and Lisa had decided to leave their entire art collection to the University of East Anglia. 'I was too stunned the other evening to be able to convey the depth of my appreciation for your very generous remarkable intentions,' Thistlethwaite wrote in a follow-up note.[8] It was decided that for the moment there would be no public announcement, since it was unclear exactly where the collection would be housed, the university having no museum and no funds to build one. It was obvious that the large collection, which was now estimated to be worth £5 million, required a proper home. Bob hoped that the university would provide a new building, but 'he did not rule out the possibility that his estate might be in a position to contribute handsomely.'[9]

Thistlethwaite's attempts to find external support for a new university arts centre proved unsuccessful. Five years passed. 'I began to wonder whether we should ever be able to take advantage of the Sainsburys' good will,' he recalled.[10] In the spring of 1973, while Thistlethwaite and his wife were on sabbatical in California, they received a message that Sir Robert had invited them to spend the night at Smith Square on their return, since there was an important matter to discuss. 'Over dinner Bob and Lisa outlined their proposition to us,' Thistlethwaite recalled. 'Recognizing the intractability of our problems – our inability to fund, either from our own exiguous resources or from Government grant, the capital and recurrent income for such a project – they proposed to give their collection to the University of East Anglia outright together with the sum of £3 million, half to cover the cost of a building and half for an endowment, the income of the latter to be used to buy art objects to expand the collection.' The Thistlethwaites were staggered by the offer. 'We knew the Sainsburys were wealthy but, in our somewhat academic naivety, we had never dreamed of such munificence, that Bob's unassuming modesty masked such a veritable Maecenas.'[11]

In fact, the Sainsbury family was about to become very affluent indeed. Later that year, the Sainsbury firm went public, with the largest new stock offering in the history of the London Stock Exchange. The 10 million ordinary shares, which represented only a small fraction of the company's worth, sold out in minutes. The public stock offering represented a significant windfall for the family, which retained ownership of eighty-five per cent of the company. According to David Sainsbury, 'it was only when the company went public that the family became very wealthy'. And he adds, 'My father had given me all his Sainsbury shares when he retired. At the time, this was largely a matter of exercising control within the company, but it also meant that when the company went public he did not get a huge financial boost. It was understood between us that I would cover the cost of the East Anglia endowment and the building.'[12]

It took six months to finalize the details of the gift. Since Bob and Lisa wanted to retain ownership of the collection until their deaths, rotating works between the university and their home, the Inland Revenue had to agree that the gift would be exempt from death duties.[*] The University Grants Committee, the government body that allocated funds to universities, had to agree to include the operating cost of the new building in their annual block grant to the university. There were other details to iron out: Bob claimed for himself and Lisa the right to enlarge the collection during their lifetimes, which the university accepted; on the other hand, he also wanted to retain the right to approve the investment policy of the endowment, which the university felt was unreasonable. To preserve confidentiality, Thistlethwaite waited until the day of the public announcement – 26 November 1973 – to inform the University Council of the Sainsbury gift. 'The scale of the proposition stunned members of Council, as I expected it would,' he informed Bob. 'It was like an exploding bomb.'[13]

------

[*] Under British tax law at the time, the gift of the collection and the endowment to the university provided no direct tax relief to the Sainsburys.

Bob and Lisa Sainsbury had joined a long line of British collectors who founded museums at institutions of higher learning. In 1677, Elias Ashmole, a politician, solicitor and antiquary, gave his extensive collection of botanical and mineral specimens, antiquities, coins and rare manuscripts to the University of Oxford, on the understanding that the university would erect a new building to house it. Designed by Thomas Wood, a local master mason, the elegant two-storey structure on Broad Street is widely considered to be the world's first purpose-designed museum. In 1816, Richard Fitzwilliam, an Irish viscount and a successful Dublin property developer, left his library and art collection to the University of Cambridge, which engaged George Basevi, a pupil of John Soane, to design a new museum. In 1932, Samuel Courtauld, an industrialist, left his collection of French impressionist and post-impressionist paintings to the University of London, and included an endowment to create the Courtauld Institute of Art, whose first home was in a townhouse in Portman Square, designed by Robert Adam.

Ashmole's eclectic museum was known locally as 'The Closet of Rarities', and it resembled a *Wunderkammer*, or cabinet of curiosities, a type of display room fashionable among sixteenth- and seventeenth-century collectors. These studies were crammed from floor to ceiling with a variety of objects: geological specimens, precious stones, antiquities, rare books, stuffed animals, maps and engravings. Intimacy and self-expression were the hallmarks of these private museums, as indeed they are of all personal collections – one visitor to the Sainsbury home in Smith Square described it to me as a *cabinet de merveilles*.[14]

When Bob and Lisa Sainsbury filled their home with art, they were following a cultural practice of long standing. 'Art collecting starts with the Italian Renaissance,' wrote art historian Nikolaus Pevsner, 'for the Renaissance developed a sense of history, enthusiasm for the products of Classical Antiquity and whole genres of contemporary art suited to, and indeed made for, the private house: paintings with mythological subjects, paintings by Flemish artists, small bronzes and, in the North, graphic art.'[15] Paintings and sculptures were exhibited around the house, or rather around the palace, for the first collectors were nobles or potentates of the Church.

According to Pevsner, the first architectural space specially designed for the display of art was built for Pope Innocent VIII in 1508. Designed by the great Donato Bramante, it was part of an extensive conversion of the Vatican's Belvedere into a summer retreat. Bramante created a square courtyard intended to recall the atrium of a Roman villa, and surrounded it with an open-air colonnaded portico. Within the portico were a series of niches containing the pope's personal collection of ancient statuary, including the famous *Apollo Belvedere* and the Laocoön group.

The covered porticos surrounding Bramante's courtyard were called *gallerie*. As displaying works of art in the home became popular, such long narrow spaces, whether open or enclosed, proved convenient for displaying not only sculptures but also paintings. Indoor galleries typically had windows along one long wall, and space for hanging paintings on the other. By the end of the sixteenth century, architectural plans for palaces and grand residences regularly included a 'gallery', and throughout Europe the term signified a special room for displaying art. 'Long time thy shadow hath been thrall to me, / For in my gallery thy picture hangs,' the Countess of Auvergne tells Talbot in Shakespeare's *Henry VI*.[16] It is the first recorded use (1591) in English of the word in this sense.*

The first collector who built an entire building devoted solely to the display of art works was Cardinal Alessandro Albani, a nephew of Pope Clement XI. In 1755, Albani commissioned his long-time friend, architect Carlo Marchionni, to design a *casino*, or garden house, for his extensive collection of antiquities. The lower floor of the long, two-storey building, which stood at the foot of the garden of Albani's Roman estate, was an open loggia for the display of sculpture, while the upper floor contained

---

* The origin of the word is medieval French – *galerie*. The word was adopted by all European languages: German and Czech (*Galerie, galerie*), Italian (*galleria*), Spanish (*galería*), Dutch (*galerij*), Russian (*galeryeya*), even those perennial outliers Hungarian (*galérián*) and Finnish (*galleriassa*).

an enclosed gallery that occupied the entire length of the building. Johann Joachim Winckelmann, the cardinal's secretary and the man generally recognized as the world's first professional art historian, called it 'the most beautiful building of our time.'[17]

The wish to create special surroundings in which to enjoy, and to display for the enjoyment of others, one's art collection is at the root of all personal galleries. But the impulse that guided Ashmole, Fitzwilliam and Courtauld – as it would guide the Sainsburys – has a greater ambition: to preserve the collection intact long after its creator has departed the scene. It seeks a kind of life ever after.

Dulwich Picture Gallery

Noel Joseph Desenfans (1744–1807) was a French émigré living in London. A native of Flanders, he had come to the city as young man to work as a tutor, and eventually married Margaret Morris, thirteen years his senior, the sister of a wealthy Welsh industrialist. Desenfans, ambitious, well educated, and with close connections to Parisian art collectors, set himself up as an art dealer. He was a prominent if somewhat louche figure on the London art scene; 'well known, if not well liked' one art historian has put it, 'distrusted and admired in not quite equal measure' according to another.[18] It is hard to know if this reputation was the result of British snobbery or envy, or if it was due to the Frenchman's irritating habit of denigrating English art and promoting his own connoisseurship.

Desenfans's position as an outsider was underlined by his unusual domestic situation. He and his wife had no children, but their household included a young man who was the dealer's protégé and sometime business associate. Peter Francis Bourgeois (1756–1811) had lost his mother at an early age and had been abandoned by his father, a Swiss watchmaker. Desenfans arranged for the young man to take painting classes and sent him on the Grand Tour of the Continent. Bourgeois was never more than a middling landscape painter, but his lack of talent did not discourage Desenfans, who advanced Bourgeois's career, even engineering his election as an associate of the Royal Academy. Paul Sandby's watercolour of the two men at home shows the younger man, conventionally handsome and a bit of a dandy, dozing on the sofa next to an animated Desenfans, who is puckishly attired in a turban and is clearly a 'character'.

In 1790, Desenfans was approached by an unusual emissary, Prince Michael Poniatowski, the brother of Stanisław Augustus, the king of Poland. The king, a cosmopolite who had lived in Paris and spoke six languages, was an enthusiastic patron of the arts. Although the royal collection numbered more than two thousand paintings, few were first-rate, and the king had engaged agents in Paris, Genoa, Venice, Florence, Rome and Naples to buy art on his behalf. Now he wanted someone in London.[19]

Whatever Desenfans's reputation among his London colleagues, he was an accomplished dealer, and his wide continental connections made him a good choice for the job; he agreed to devote himself full-time to the task. To cement the arrangement, he had himself appointed consul-general of Poland to Great Britain, and wangled a Polish knighthood and an appointment as a royal painter for Bourgeois, which facilitated Bourgeois's election a few years later to full membership in the Royal Academy.

Over the next five years, Desenfans assembled a remarkable collection, representative of all the great European schools of art, especially Dutch, Flemish and French old masters, who were Stanisław's favourites. Trolling the dealers of Europe and taking advantage of the availability of artworks belonging to aristocrats fleeing the French Revolution, Desenfans was able to put his hands on such masterpieces as Poussin's *The Triumph of David*, Vernet's *Italian Landscape*, Veronese's *Saint Jerome and a Donor* (a fragment of an altarpiece), and three Rembrandts, including the wonderful *A Girl at a Window*. He bought several Murillos and two large paintings by Guido Reni, a Baroque painter much admired at the time. Desenfans's most expensive acquisition was Reni's *Saint John the Baptist in the Wilderness*, for which he paid a Scottish dealer 1,000 guineas.[20] The enterprising Desenfans even found three Leonardo da Vincis, although *A Young Man* is now considered to be by Piero de Cosimo, and the two others are unattributed. On the other hand, a charming portrait of a young woman that caught his eye, long thought to be by a lesser painter, turned out to be a Fragonard.

While Desenfans was buying paintings, things were not going well for his Polish client. The king had supported – and participated in drafting – the first written constitution in Europe. Hailed as a democrat in France and America, he was seen as a threat by the rulers of neighbouring Prussia and Russia and, after Catherine the Great successfully invaded Poland in 1792, large parts of that country were ceded to Russia and Prussia. In 1795, following a failed insurrection and another foreign intervention, the Polish kingdom was entirely dissolved.

Desenfans was left holding 180 paintings, for which he had, personally, paid £9,000. Stanisław, forced to abdicate and now penniless, was in no position to settle the account. Desenfans made repeated offers to Tsar Paul I, hoping that he might buy the pictures, but the Russian ruler was not interested. The dealer then unsuccessfully tried to sell the collection to the British government, as the basis for a 'national gallery'.* In 1803, increasingly desperate, he organized a well-publicized auction in London. With a French war on the horizon it was hardly a good time for selling art, nor did Desenfans help himself by his behaviour. As art historian Dennis Farr writes, the auction's two-volume catalogue 'extolled French connoisseurship and damned the mediocrity and jealousy of British dealers – a foolish exercise which earned him lasting animosity. Many of the attributions were very optimistic and the sale was a failure.'[21]

Following this public debacle, Desenfans's health deteriorated, and he left his business largely in Bourgeois's hands. Desenfans, his wife and Bourgeois (who never married), lived together in a large house in Portland Place, which also served as their showroom. In 1807, Desenfans

---

* Desenfans was ahead of his time. The National Gallery was founded in 1824, although with far fewer – and less important – paintings than he originally offered.

died, bequeathing his property equally to his wife and Bourgeois, but willing all his paintings – numbering 350 in all – to Bourgeois.

Even before Desenfans's death, Bourgeois had started thinking of his friend's pictures as a collection that should be preserved intact to honour his friend's memory. In 1810, Bourgeois and Desenfans's widow, who was of like mind in this endeavour, tried unsuccessfully to buy their leased house in Portland Place, intending to open the collection to public viewing. Realizing the impracticality of founding their own museum, they looked elsewhere. Dulwich College, a boys' school south of London, was a likely candidate, if for an odd reason. The college had been founded in the seventeenth century by Edward Alleyn, a famous Elizabethan actor and wealthy theatrical entrepreneur; Desenfans, who had been involved in theatre during his youth in France, was a long-time friend of the great Shakespearean actor John Philip Kemble, who introduced Bourgeois to the college. Bourgeois liked the suburban location, outside the city but easily accessible; moreover the college already had a picture gallery, albeit in somewhat decrepit condition. No doubt, thumbing his nose at the London art establishment was also part of the attraction.

Matters came to a head in December 1810, when Bourgeois, who was fifty-seven, suffered a serious fall from his horse. He dictated a will on his deathbed, leaving the collection to Margaret Desenfans, on the under-standing that at her death the paintings would go to Dulwich College. Bourgeois included a princely endowment of £10,000, and a further £2,000 (to be matched by the college) for the refurbishment of the old gallery. Mrs Desenfans announced that she did not want to wait – she was seventy-nine – and that if the renovation work started immediately, she was prepared to donate the collection to the college as soon as the gallery was ready.

Bourgeois had stipulated that his friend John Soane should be the architect of the renovation. The college authorities protested, for the style of their buildings was Jacobean, and Soane was known to be a committed classicist. But Bourgeois insisted, adding that, since Soane was wealthy, 'you may depend upon his treating you as a friend and that he will not make it an expensive business.'[22] Under the circumstances, the college could hardly deny the dying man's wish.

John Soane (1753–1837) was one of the most successful architects of the day. Although his social origins were unremarkable – his father had been a bricklayer – by dint of talent and hard work he had risen fast. He was apprenticed at fifteen to a distinguished architect, George Dance the Younger, and thanks to Dance's tutelage was accepted into the Royal Academy as a student. At twenty-three, Soane won the academy's gold medal and a three-year travelling scholarship to Rome, and by the age of thirty he had completed the first of many country-house commissions. Soane's combination of practicality (severe and almost plain exteriors) with romantic fancy (extraordinary interior spaces) proved immensely popular. His architectural prowess gained him the lucrative position of architect to the Bank of England, and the death of his wife's guardian made him independently wealthy. Soane had met Peter Francis Bourgeois at the Royal Academy, where the two men were frequent allies in academician intrigues and became close friends. Soane owned several of Bourgeois's paintings and was a frequent guest at Portland Place; his wife, Eliza, was a friend of Margaret Desenfans, and attended Bourgeois on his deathbed.

The day after Bourgeois's death, Soane walked to Dulwich to examine the site. Four months later he presented the college with several alternative designs (his usual practice). Soane had determined that Bourgeois's idea of renovating the old gallery was impractical (the room was too small, and in such poor condition that he recommended its demolition). Instead, he proposed building a new quadrangle, consisting of an existing chapel, and a new library and gallery.* The alternatives, which showed different configurations of the quadrangle, all had an uncommon feature: a mausoleum. Years earlier, when Desenfans died, Bourgeois had asked Soane to design a small mausoleum in the stable yard behind the

---

* The library was to house Soane's own collection of books and antiquities, which he considered leaving to Dulwich College. When the library plan fell through, the collection remained in Soane's house.

Portland Place house. The domed room with top-lit alcoves had space for three sarcophagi for the three friends. Bourgeois's will stipulated that Soane should provide a similar structure as part of the Dulwich gallery.

The college authorities rejected all five of Soane's alternatives, and asked the architect to confine himself to the gallery, but to add six almshouses for indigent women – known as the 'Poor Sisters' – who were currently housed in a wing of the old building. It was a queer mix, but Soane dutifully prepared three more designs, one of which met with the college's approval. Before construction could begin, however, a problem familiar to all building projects arose: excessive cost. Soane and the builder had prepared an estimate of £11,270. The college building fund, the bequest, and an additional £1,000 that Bourgeois's estate had set aside for the mausoleum, left a shortfall of £2,500. The college was reluctant to start; Soane offered to pay the difference himself but was politely refused. Finally, it was Margaret Desenfans who saved the day with a gift of £4,000 to the college.[23] The foundations of the new building were laid on 19 October 1811, nine months after Bourgeois's demise.

Soane's design is extremely simple. A long, narrow, single-storey building divided into five rooms – three cubes and two double cubes, following Palladian proportions – contained the gallery; the six almshouses were ranged down one side; and the mausoleum, jutting out slightly, occupied the centre. The exterior of the gallery was austere, no ornament, no classical orders, basic details, very little stonework; the predominant material was a yellowish London stock brick. Such simplifications allowed Soane to reduce the final construction cost to less than £10,000.*

What makes the design of Dulwich such a pivotal chapter in the design of art museums is that the galleries are lit entirely from above – there are no windows. London art dealers sometimes had top-lit showrooms, and the Desenfans house in Portland Place had a so-called Skylight Room on the top floor. But at Dulwich Soane convincingly demonstrated

---

* Presumably at his friend Bourgeois's request, Soane did not charge the college for his own work.

how top lighting could become the main organizing feature of an entire building. He was familiar with skylights. At the Bank of England, which covered a whole block, he regularly used skylights to introduce daylight into inner rooms. Soane was particularly interested in how art objects were displayed for, at the time he was designing Dulwich, he was turning part of his own house in Lincoln's Inn Fields into a museum (which is still open today). The extraordinary series of rooms (many with skylights) house his vast collection of books, drawings, prints, models, architectural fragments and antiquities. For Dulwich, Soane designed hexagonal roof lanterns, supported by vaulted ceilings (to further diffuse the light). The lighting wasn't perfect – there were complaints about insufficient light on dull days, and the design of the lanterns was later modified to allow more daylight to enter – but the advantages of top-lighting galleries were obvious: even illumination, no glare from windows, more wall space.

Dulwich Picture Gallery, which opened to the public in 1817, was the most accessible of the important London art collections, and 'the first independent building erected to be a picture gallery', according to Pevsner.[24] More important, it was the first *modern* art gallery. Dulwich celebrated natural light, as almost all galleries would henceforth do, and the open plan, a series of standardized spaces linked by broad arched openings, made the entire gallery a single unified experience. Soane restricted architectural detailing to the vaults and lanterns, keeping the lower portion of the design – red-ochre walls – unadorned, their plain expanse allowing the arrangement and rearrangement of paintings over time.

Soane paid careful attention to how the collection was displayed, always giving precedence to the art. Nevertheless, he also honoured the memory of his friends and, thanks to his artistry, this is an intensely personal museum. Although in his first studies Soane placed the mausoleum in a secondary position at one end of the building, he soon realized that this made it seem like an afterthought, and moved it to the centre, opposite the entrance. The tiny mausoleum was the one place where the architect allowed himself a measure of theatricality. 'We have only to fancy the Gallery brilliantly lighted for the exhibition of this unrivalled assemblage of pictorial art,' he wrote, 'whilst a dull, religious light shews the Mausoleum in the full pride of funereal grandeur, displaying its sarcophagi, enriched with the mortal remains of departed worth, and calling back so powerfully the recollections of past times, that we almost believe we are conversing with our departed friends who now sleep in their silent tombs'.[25] The visitor enters the mausoleum through a circular vestibule, whose domed ceiling is supported by black Greek Doric columns. The burial chamber beyond is lit from above by a tall lantern, similar to those in the galleries but glazed with translucent yellow glass. Bourgeois's sarcophagus stands in the centre, flanked by those of Desenfans and his wife. Depictions of serpents, symbols of eternity, adorn the space above the arches. Soane repeated ancient signs on the exterior: three sarcophagi, three funerary urns, and three never-to-be-opened doors, lacking handles or even hinges. The overall effect, as John Summerson observed, is 'toy-like but sinister.'[26] Life ever after, indeed.

The Barnes Foundation

To be a collector is to live surrounded by art. The Desenfans home in Portland Place had paintings all over the house: fourteen Poussins in the dining room, twelve Cuyps in the library, a Rubens in the parlour. The Skylight Room at the top of the house was more than 6 metres tall, and the large paintings hung in tiers, two and three high (as they later were displayed in the Dulwich gallery) – a Veronese, two Murillos, and Reynolds's *Mrs Siddons as the Tragic Muse*, a full-length portrait of John Philip Kemble's sister, Sarah. Like all private collections, Desenfans's mirrored his own taste: turgid historical scenes by his friend Bourgeois next to old masters, Nicolas Poussin beside portraits of friends and family, including a charming copy of a lost portrait of a young Margaret Morris. Gustav Friedrich Waagen, a noted German art historian, who visited Dulwich in the mid-nineteenth century, observed drily that the collection consisted of 'much that is excellent mixed with much that is indifferent and quite worthless'.[27] That was a professional's view; but collectors saw things differently. 'It is pleasant to be nonsensical in due place,' said Soane, quoting Horace and describing the unusual juxtaposition of objects in his own house–museum.[28]

Intimacy, more than merely possession, is what the collector seeks. That is the quality that Soane captured in his design for the Dulwich gallery – an atmosphere and scale that were domestic rather than institutional. The impression was of entering someone's home. There was no sign over the door (except in the mausoleum), and no explanatory texts; identifying labels were affixed to the picture frames, as was the custom at the time, and the paintings were only loosely arranged according to schools, and were densely hung in large-scale symmetrical wall compositions. The overall aim was aesthetic rather than academic or pedagogical, and to interfere as little as possible with the viewer's ability to enjoy the art.

While the collector's appreciation of art involves connoisseurship, and sometimes scholarship, it is above all the product of direct experience. As one noted collector put it:

> The enjoyment of art is one of the experiences which are desirable for their own sake. It is, of course, capable of acquiring other values also. It may enable us to make a living; it may improve our morals or quicken our religious faith; but if we attempt to judge a work of art directly by its contribution to these ends, we have abandoned the track. A work of art presents to the spectator an opportunity to live through the experience which by its own quality vouches for its right to existence, and whatever other value it has depends upon this value. If it lacks this, it is a counterfeit.[29]

Few collectors have had the opportunity to live in as intimate contact with their collections as the author, Albert C. Barnes. According to a 1928 *New Yorker* profile: 'When he can't sleep he puts on his dressing gown and walks through a passageway that connects the house and the museum, and in the gallery he studies his pictures and sometime spends hours arranging them to suit his taste.'[30] The 'pictures' included 150 Renoirs, 100 Cézannes, 40 Picassos and Matisses, and dozens of Soutines and Utrillos. In all, the *New Yorker* estimated, a thousand paintings.*

Albert Coombs Barnes (1872–1951) was born in Philadelphia; his father, who had lost an arm in the Civil War, was a letter carrier. Young Albert was bright enough to get into the city's premier public high school, and from there he was accepted into the University of Pennsylvania's medical school. Although he completed his internship, he never practised medicine. He was ambitious to get ahead – and to get rich. He determined to become a chemist, took courses, and eventually got a job with a leading Philadelphia pharmaceutical manufacturer, where his fierce drive led to an appointment as manager of advertising and sales. Nevertheless, dissatisfied with his prospects at the company, Barnes began experimenting at home with a chemist colleague, Hermann Hille, whom he had been instrumental in bringing from Germany. In 1902, Barnes and Hille announced that they had invented a silver nitrate solution to treat infections. Encouraged by successful tests, the two men left their jobs, formed a company and began manufacturing what they named Argyrol. With Hille overseeing production and Barnes handling sales and promotion, Argyrol, which was used to prevent gonorrhoeal blindness in newborn infants, proved a national and ultimately an international success. A few years later, Barnes bought out his partner and in time became extremely wealthy.

The business ran itself and, at thirty-eight, Barnes was effectively retired – and bored. Now happily married, he had built a house in Merion, on Philadelphia's Main Line, and acquired a country estate in

---

* That was an exaggeration: when Barnes died his collection numbered 800 paintings.

rural Chester County, west of the city. Although he took up riding and fox-hunting, the social scene did not appeal to him. Nor he to it: a skilled boxer, he never lost his pugnacious south Philadelphia manner. The *New Yorker* profile called attention to 'a solid beefiness that would suggest an Irish police captain', and described him as 'ostentatiously aggressive'.[31] As a pastime, Barnes began to collect paintings, and in his methodical way he set about teaching himself art appreciation. In the process, he contacted a former high-school classmate, William J. Glackens, a successful New York City painter. As often happens, the boyhood friendship rekindled. Glackens didn't think much of his friend's collection, and said so. He introduced Barnes to contemporary artists, took him to galleries, and opened the doctor's eyes to impressionism and post-impressionism. In 1912, when Glackens announced that he was going to Paris for two weeks, Barnes entrusted him with the not inconsiderable sum of $20,000 (more than $400,000 at today's values) to purchase paintings. Glackens returned with a dozen canvases, including Renoir's *Girl Reading*, Van Gogh's *Postman*, Cézanne's *Mont Sainte-Victoire and Valley*, and works by Monet, Gauguin, Degas and Picasso.'[32] Although Barnes loved the Renoir, some of the others puzzled him. But in time, with Glackens's encouragement, he was hooked.

After that, Barnes continued to buy on his own – voraciously and astutely. He regularly travelled to Europe, where he met artists, collectors and dealers. Some of them found the blunt American millionaire vulgar, pushy, even boorish, but those who could see beneath the rough-hewn exterior, such as the art collector and critic Leo Stein and the important Parisian dealers Paul Guillaume and Pierre Loeb (who would also influence Robert Sainsbury), recognized an acute artistic intelligence. Barnes bought not only impressionists, who formed the bulk of his collection, but also contemporary artists such as Picasso, Matisse and Douanier Rousseau, as well as younger lesser-known painters such as Modigliani, de

---

* This was early for an American to collect painters such as Picasso and Cézanne; the famous Armory Show, which introduced modernism to New York, did not occur until the following year.

Chirico, and Soutine, whom he effectively discovered. Under Guillaume's direction, Barnes also bought African art.

In January 1923, the *New York Times*, reporting on the arrival of the S.S. *France*, noted the presence of 'Albert C. Barnes, Philadelphia art collector, who brought with him 100 pictures painted by modern French artists'.[33] During what one biographer has described as 'one of the most extravagant buying sprees in the history of art collecting', Barnes also made another purchase: 900 tons of tawny-coloured limestone from the Burgundian village of Coutarnoux.[34] With his home overflowing with paintings, the doctor was building an art gallery.

The previous year, Barnes had bought 12 acres across the street from his house in suburban Merion. This would be the home of the Barnes Foundation, to which he donated his entire collection as well as $6 million in company stock. The objective of the foundation, stated in its charter, was 'To promote the advancement of education and the appreciation of the fine arts; and for this purpose to erect, found and maintain … an art gallery and other necessary buildings for the exhibition of works of ancient and modern art.'[35] In other words, a museum that was also a school.

'The key to Barnes's personality was that he believed in human perfectibility and was messianic about it,' wrote his friend, Henry Hart, a journalist and editor.[36] The means to perfection, in Barnes's view, was education. In his own factory, for example, he established an eight-hour shift, six hours for work and two hours for daily discussion groups, led by himself and occasional visitors. He also hung paintings on the shop floor, and established a lending library for his employees. His ideas about learning were formed by reading William James, George Santayana, and especially John Dewey. Barnes enrolled in Dewey's weekly seminar at Columbia University, and the eminent philosopher and the millionaire doctor became lifelong friends.[37]

Although Barnes collected modern art, and held progressive views on many subjects, when it came to choosing an architect for the new foundation he did not hire a modernist. He was aware of Parisian firebrands such as Le Corbusier, who would soon thereafter design a large villa for Leo Stein's brother, Michael, as well as a studio for the sculptor Jacques Lipchitz, whom Barnes knew well. (Le Corbusier was certainly aware of Barnes – he published an article on the doctor's collection in his art magazine, *L'Esprit Nouveau*.) The most prominent American modernist was Frank Lloyd Wright, who was then living in Los Angeles, but there is no evidence that Barnes considered him. Perhaps, as John Lukacs has written, 'Barnes's common sense kept him from falling in with those avant-garde or highbrow temptations which were intellectually endemic to rich American humanists of that period.'[38] In any case, the doctor had not previously shown much interest in architecture; it was his wife, Laura, who had overseen the construction of their Merion home, an unremarkable Tudor-style mansion.

Barnes had deep family roots in Philadelphia, and in his own way he was devoted to the city. Philadelphia's leading architectural practitioner in the early 1920s was Horace Trumbauer, who had a national reputation, having built several mansions in Newport, Rhode Island, and Harvard's Widener Library. However, he was currently designing the Philadelphia Museum of Art, which probably disqualified him in Barnes's eyes, since the doctor did not want to be seen to be following the city's art establishment. George Howe and Paul Cret were two younger Philadelphia architects. Howe had designed exceptional country estates in the Philadelphia area, but the work of his firm, Mellor, Meigs and Howe, was almost exclusively residential. Cret, on the other hand, had designed an important art museum, for the Detroit Institute of Arts, then in the final stages of completion. He was a French émigré, which would have appealed to the Francophile doctor; moreover, the architect was also a professor at the University of Pennsylvania, with which Barnes hoped to establish closer relations in the future. In the late summer of 1922, he invited Cret to be his architect.

Paul Philippe Cret (1876–1945) was born in Lyon, in circumstances not dissimilar to Barnes's own; his father (who died when Cret was a boy) was a labourer, and his mother supported the family by working as a dressmaker. Thanks to an architect uncle, Cret was able to study architecture in Lyon and won a prize that gave him the opportunity to attend the École des beaux-arts in Paris. There he distinguished himself further, winning more prizes and earning a coveted *diplôme*. In 1902, he accepted an offer to teach at the University of Pennsylvania, whose architecture department was looking for a leading École graduate to head its senior design studio.

Cret was a gifted teacher and, thanks to him, the University of Pennsylvania's architecture programme became the foremost in the country. His university contract left him free to do his own architectural work; in 1905, he was placed first in a competition for the prestigious Pan American Union Building, in Washington, DC, and, eight years later, won a competition to design a central public library for Indianapolis. Shortly after the end of the First World War, Cret received the commission to design a new art museum for Detroit. He had definite ideas about how museums should be planned. 'The idea of making of museum rooms a mere shelter, as inconspicuous as possible, is wrong,' he wrote in a report to his client. 'Nothing is more dreary than passing from a cream-coloured room with a coved ceiling and inconspicuous door to another cream-coloured room with the same ceiling and the same door.'[39] He pointed out that some of the most respected museums in Europe were housed in old palaces, which had a variety of rooms, offering different settings for art works, and different qualities of light. Cret believed that a museum should be a sequence of custom-designed rooms, whose architectural character reflected their contents, depending on whether these were paintings, sculptures, or decorative objects. In a paper that he wrote for the *Journal of the American Institute of Architects*, he criticized 'scientific' theories of museum design, and derided the notion of the neutral museum, calling it a 'cemetery for works of art'.[40]

The brief that Barnes gave Cret included, in addition to the art gallery, a residence for himself and his wife, staff quarters, a four-car garage, and stalls for stabling horses and milking cows. Cret organized the programme into three buildings: the gallery in the centre, flanked by a service building on one side, and the residence (on the architectural drawings it is referred to as an 'Administrative Building', which is what it became after the Barneses' deaths) on the other.[41] The residence is linked to the gallery by a bridge that forms a porte cochère. The main entrance to the gallery is through a central portico, flanked by Tuscan columns. Although the style of the Barnes museum is often described as 'French Renaissance', it is really an early example of what Cret called 'new classicism'.[42] A dedicated classicist, he believed in simplifying classical elements to bring them into line with contemporary tastes.

Cret laid out twenty-three exhibition rooms of varying sizes and proportions on the two floors of the gallery. The main gallery, which occupies a central position, rises the full height of the building, 10 metres, to a vaulted ceiling. This impressive space was to serve as an occasional music room and classroom. Only two of the galleries had skylights. 'The gallery with top light is open to several criticisms,' Cret explained to Barnes. 'A museum made up of such rooms is gloomy. The visitor, jailed between walls, longs very soon for a glimpse of outdoors. The paintings themselves, under the cold light filtered through various diffusing sashes, seem to be drowned in an aquarium. Painted in a studio, or outdoors, they ought to receive the same quality of light to be fully appreciated.'[43] In four of the galleries, Cret made subtle adjustments, slightly angling the two walls perpendicular to the windows to improve the lighting. 'Throughout, no decoration,' the architect emphasized, 'the paintings composing the collection being of the modern school, which strives for simplicity of expression.'[44]

The walls of the galleries were built out of wooden boards covered with burlap, an unusual arrangement, suggested by Barnes, which allowed paintings to be easily rearranged. The paintings were hung in tiers, all the way up to the ceiling; no identifying labels distracted from the experience of the art. Barnes did not organize the art chronologically or according to individual artists, but thematically, according to his aesthetic theories. An El Greco might be above a Picasso, an old master next to a Matisse, a Glackens facing a pair of paintings by Horace Pippin, a Pennsylvania-born African-American artist, whom Barnes discovered and promoted. Barnes called these compositions 'wall pictures'. In addition, the crowded rooms contained his large collection of African sculpture, ancient Chinese art and antique furniture. After 1940, when Barnes started collecting old Pennsylvania Dutch hardware, wrought iron hinges, keys and locks appeared among the canvases. This wilful display is eccentric, but it accomplishes what Barnes wanted – it makes us look at art afresh.

During the first year of construction, relations between the collector and the architect were cordial. Barnes lent Cret four watercolours to hang in his office. The pair exchanged many letters (some in French, in which Barnes was fluent). The doctor had heard his building referred to as a museum, and he jokingly suggested that Cret should find a way to discourage casual visitors. 'I thought of a mitrailleuse [machine gun], an electric chair, a loose stone leading to an underground dungeon,' Barnes wrote, 'but all these devices are too subtle and inadequately expressive of my contempt for the prominentists [sic] that one meets in the art circles of Philadelphia.'[45] But when the pace of construction lagged – Cret had promised a building in eighteen months – the doctor exploded. 'In my opinion, your inspection, as I understand that function, has been and is a farce,' he scolded the architect in early September 1923.[46] Two days later: 'We have never in all our experience seen greater negligence and stupidity than thus far has characterized both your superintendence and your inspection.'*[47]

It is possible that Cret, who had associated with larger firms in his previous projects, was unused to handling American building contractors. Moreover, since Barnes lived across the street, the client spent more

---

* The 'experience' Barnes referred to included building seven houses on land he owned in Merion.

time on the building site than did the architect or his representatives. Cret attempted to placate Barnes: 'I shall entertain the hope to construct in a dignified and orderly manner a series of buildings, in spite of the difficulties that you seem to enjoy putting in my way,' he wrote.[48] Then, after receiving a particularly scathing letter, in February 1924 he offered to resign. Barnes turned conciliatory, yet eight months later, fuming about a badly executed linen closet, he again lambasted the architect: 'It is most annoying to be put in the position where one has either to waste so much time in straightening out your errors or to be put under the disagreeable necessity of reminding you of them.'[49] At one point, Cret sought legal advice, sure that his client was about to sue him. Somehow they got through it, although construction took twenty-eight months, not eighteen. Shortly before the building was formally opened in 1925, Barnes generously offered Cret an opportunity to arrange a private visit for his friends. The two men parted on good terms, although years later, when Theo White, who was writing a monograph on Cret's work, asked the architect if he would help him gain admittance to the gallery by interceding with Barnes, Cret responded: 'If I gave you a letter to him, it is a guarantee that you will never see the exhibition.'*[50]

However strained its implementation, the Barnes Foundation admirably fulfils, in Cret's words, 'the needs of painting exhibitions in a novel manner, yet simply and economically constructed and practical in plan'.[51] The circuit of rooms, which begins and ends in the grand hall, and the variety of lighting function exactly as Cret intended. Yet the tension between the architect and the collector is sometimes apparent. Barnes once complained that Cret was 'a man with only one string to his bow', probably referring to the Frenchman's scrupulous adherence to classicism.[52] The doctor made several efforts to liven up what he considered Cret's overly severe design. He commissioned Matisse to paint a 14-metre-long mural

---

*   In 1930, Cret received the prestigious Philadelphia Award. Although the nominators included public figures such as Edsel Ford and Gifford Pinchot, prominent architects such as George Howe, Raymond Hood, Albert Kahn, and John Russell Pope, contractors, educators, engineers and politicians, as well as clients, Albert Barnes's name is notably absent.

in the large gallery, though the result appears somewhat out of place and, according to Henry Hart, 'Barnes was never completely satisfied with it.'[53] For the exterior, Barnes invited Jacques Lipchitz to make five bas-relief panels. The sculptor at first demurred, thinking his modern art and Cret's classicism would be at odds, but that is precisely what Barnes wanted, and he instructed Cret that Lipchitz should be given complete freedom. The result is surprising but not disagreeable. Two contrasting sensibilities are also evident in the central portico, whose walls and apse are lined in brightly coloured mosaic. Barnes personally instructed the Enfield Pottery and Tile Works to incorporate motifs based on African art works in the collection, and expressed himself delighted with the exotic result. Cret was noncommittal.

Barnes died in 1951, when his Packard roadster was hit by a truck after the doctor had driven through a stop sign. He had lived at the foundation for twenty-five years, running classes, writing about art, and rearranging his paintings. Following his original intention, the collection served chiefly for teaching, members of the public being allowed in by special permission only. The forbidding admission card, which was issued only after a personal request in writing, read: 'The Barnes Foundation is not a public gallery. It is an educational institution with a program for systematic work organized into classes which are held every day and conducted by a staff of experienced teachers. Admission to the gallery is restricted to students enrolled in the classes.' Salvador Dalí, Thomas Mann and Albert Einstein got in, so did Bob and Lisa Sainsbury. In 1957 they were in Philadelphia seeing their daughter Elizabeth, who was studying at Swarthmore College. Bob had heard of 'the fabulous Barnes Foundation' since the first time he visited Paris as a young man, but nothing had prepared him for what he described as 'one of the great aesthetic experiences of my life'.[54] On the other hand, T. S. Eliot, Alexander Woollcott and Le Corbusier were turned away. So was Jacques Lipchitz, with whom Barnes had a falling out. This exclusivity did not serve Barnes well; it fed gossip, prompted resentments, and resulted in a flood of largely apocryphal stories about the abrasive millionaire collector. His own, often outrageous, public statements – he regularly issued inflammatory pamphlets and press releases – didn't help.

Although Barnes assembled an extraordinary art collection, and housed it in a fine museum, he failed to create an effective and long-lived institution. The Barnes Foundation did not achieve the scholarly reputation of, say, the Courtauld Institute of Art in London, or of the Dumbarton Oaks Research Library and Collection in Washington, DC, founded in 1940 by collectors Robert and Mildred Bliss. But Courtauld and the Blisses placed their collections in the hands of established institutions, the University of London and Harvard University respectively, while Barnes, who feuded publicly with the University of Pennsylvania and scorned the Philadelphia Museum of Art, never forged an institutional alliance that would have provided long-term stability and continuity.

In his will, Barnes stipulated that his paintings could not be moved or shown elsewhere. Many collectors place peculiar restrictions on their bequests. Margaret Desenfans left money to fund an annual memorial dinner in the Dulwich gallery – Soane attended the first one in 1817. The famed Boston collector Isabella Stewart Gardner mandated that her collection could never be moved or replaced, so that when thirteen paintings were stolen the museum was obliged to leave the empty frames on the wall. When the Austrian collector Count Antoine Seilern left the Courtauld Institute his collection of old masters in 1978, he specified that pre-1600 works could not be shown outside the museum, and the rest could travel only within the London region. Shortly before his death, Barnes changed the terms of his foundation's indenture so that in 1989 control passed to Lincoln University, a small college in the Philadelphia suburbs.[55] Thanks to his requirement that the bequest invest only in government bonds (which was a liability in inflationary periods) – and to administrative mismanagement – by 2000, the Barnes Foundation had reached the brink of bankruptcy. The 'art circles of Philadelphia', which the doctor so hated, intervened; Lincoln University agreed to cede control of the board, and a year later a Pennsylvania judge ruled that the collection could be relocated to a new museum in downtown Philadelphia.[56] The Barnes collection would survive; Barnes's idiosyncratic vision would not.*

The Kröller-Müller Museum

Hélène Emma Laura Juliane Müller (1869–1939) was the daughter of a wealthy German industrialist. She grew up in Düsseldorf and married one of her father's Dutch employees, Anton Kröller. On her father's death, her husband assumed control of Wm H. Müller & Co., moved the head-quarters to Rotterdam, and turned the company it into an international powerhouse, operating mines, docking companies and a fleet of cargo ships. Hélène Kröller-Müller had four children, and led a leisurely, luxurious life. As a hobby, she collected Delftware. In 1907, she met Hendricus P. Bremmer, a charismatic Dutch art critic, lecturer and collector, whose invitation-only 'Bremmerclubs', with their art-appreciation sessions and lantern-slide shows, were a singular feature of Rotterdam society. Soon Bremmer was giving weekly private lessons at the Kröller house. He introduced Hélène Kröller-Müller to the work of contemporary European painters, such as Picasso, Braque, Léger and Van Gogh, and became her guide and mentor, eventually gaining a place on the company's payroll as art consultant. Just as Barnes was enamoured of Renoir, Hélène Kröller-Müller was especially taken with the work of Van Gogh; in one year alone, she acquired twenty-eight canvases (she eventually owned ninety-seven paintings and 185 drawings).[57] She was a small, handsome woman with large appetites, but like Barnes she was not merely accumulating art. She developed her own original ideas, influenced by Bremmer but, according to many art historians, eventually overtaking her teacher.[58] She had a didactic streak, and collected not just to suit her taste, but to demonstrate

---

* The story of how Barnes's will was overturned is amusingly told in the documentary film, *The Art of the Steal*.

her theory that the history of painting represented an aesthetic evolution culminating in Van Gogh's expressionism.

In 1910, inspired by a visit to the Uffizi Gallery in Florence, Hélène Kröller-Müller decided that, like Cosimo de' Medici, she would build a museum. 'Then, in a hundred years' time, it will be an interesting cultural monument, proof of the extent to which a merchant family at the turn of the century could achieve intrinsic refinement,' she wrote.[59] Her vision was of a grand country villa, where she and her family could live surrounded by art, and which in due course she would leave to posterity as a public museum. The site would be their recently acquired coastal estate at Wassenaar, north of The Hague.

A decade earlier, when the Kröllers had moved from Rotterdam to The Hague, they had hired a local architect, L. J. Falkenburg, to build their house, and they now asked him to draw up plans for a villa–museum. But after he submitted a preliminary design, Hélène realized that she should set her sights higher. By this time, thanks to her reading and conversations with Bremmer, she had been exposed to more adventurous currents in contemporary European architecture, such as the well-known Belgian architect and designer Henry van de Velde, and the leading Dutch architect H. P. Berlage. Van de Velde and Berlage had each designed a striking villa in The Hague, not far from Hélène Kröller-Müller's home, but she was drawn to her countryman Peter Behrens. Behrens (1868–1940) had a background that appealed to Hélène Kröller-Müller – he was trained as a painter. He had been a member of the Jugendstil ('youth style') movement, the German equivalent of art nouveau, and acquired an architectural reputation when he designed his own house, including all the furnishings and interior appointments.

In February 1911, Kröller-Müller and her husband went to Berlin, met Behrens, and toured several of his projects. A month later, after visiting the Dutch site, Behrens accepted the commission. He was forty-three and in his creative prime. His office was busy with several residences, the new German embassy in St Petersburg, and projects for AEG, the giant

German electricity company, for whom he designed not only factories but also appliances, fans and lamps. By now, Behrens had abandoned the flowery style of his earlier Jugendstil years, and his designs, whether they were buildings or products, were sober and austere. This attracted Hélène Kröller-Müller, who said of her villa, 'I want no decorative embellishments.'[60] She had very definite ideas about her new house. She wanted a low, spread-out building on the edge of the dunes, with a conservatory and, of course, an art gallery. 'By which I mean a pleasant, top-lit room closed off from the outside world, with a few tables and chairs, where one can happily sit and read and where, if one looks up, one's eye will fall upon something beautiful.'[61]

Behrens's design consisted of a flat-roofed central block containing a family room, a study, a sun-room and the top-lit painting gallery. On one side was a wing with the main public rooms overlooking a paved court; on the opposite side, another wing housed the family quarters around a landscaped atrium. The exterior is reminiscent of the great nineteenth-century architect Karl Friedrich Schinkel, although simpler in its details. Except for a loggia of Doric columns, there is no classical ornament, and the flat, stone-faced exterior is relieved only by a single cornice moulding. Behrens had taken his client's request for 'no embellishments' to heart.

Hélène Kröller-Müller was not sure she liked the scheme, and her husband had a full-size wood and painted canvas mock-up constructed on the site. The mock-up was mounted on a system of rails so that it could be moved to different locations. A surviving photograph shows a large blocky building, sitting awkwardly in the landscape. It is not Behrens's best work: the exterior is stiff, while the sprawling composition, perhaps because he was instructed to follow Falkenburg's floor plan, is undistinguished. The result feels institutional and lacks the intimacy that Kröller-Müller sought.

Behrens's assistant on the project was an architect-in-training named Ludwig Mies, who had been with him for three years.* Mies was

---

* This was a decade before Mies adopted his mother's maiden name, 'Rohe', and the Dutch-sounding 'van der' as additions to his surname.

one of several bright young men attracted to Behrens – at one time or another, Walter Gropius, Adolf Meyer and Le Corbusier all worked in the office. Mies (1886–1969) was born in Aachen to a family of modest means. His father, a stone carver, made mortuary monuments. The business was unsuccessful and the young Mies was obliged to leave school at fifteen to work. After learning a variety of practical skills as a building trainee, he left Aachen for Berlin, where he attended architecture classes and worked for the architect Bruno Paul as a draughtsman. From there he moved to Behrens's office.

Behrens could sometimes be a bully, and Mies was stubborn. During the Kröller-Müller project, the two men fell out and the twenty-six-year-old architect found himself jobless. Hélène Kröller-Müller, who had decided she didn't like Behrens's design, offered young Mies, who had engaged her sympathies, the commission. He accepted, moved to The Hague, and set up a drawing table in Müller & Co.'s offices. For six months he worked on the villa, Mrs Kröller-Müller paying daily visits to monitor her protégé's progress. Mies's design was not radically different from Behrens's, but was enhanced in a number of subtle ways. Only the residential block, which served as the central focus, had two storeys; the subsidiary wings were lower, establishing a clear hierarchy. He gave the art gallery its own identity in a separate wing, windowless and illuminated not by skylights but by a ribbon of openings just beneath the ceiling. Like Behrens, Mies used courtyards, but he enclosed the largest with a Schinkelesque pergola that overlooked a vast water basin. The interlocking composition masterfully balances symmetry and asymmetry, a remarkable performance for a novice whose only previous independent commission had been a four-bedroom house.

When Mrs Kröller-Müller engaged Mies, Bremmer, who considered the young architect too inexperienced, convinced her husband that the Amsterdam architect, H. P. Berlage should be commissioned to prepare an alternative design.* The fifty-six-year-old Hendrik Petrus Berlage (1856–1934) was a link between the historicist styles of the late nineteenth century and the contemporary currents represented by younger architects such as Behrens, but the design he produced for Kröller-Müller looked backwards rather than forwards. With broad sloped roofs, courtyards that resemble cloisters, and even a small belfry, it has often been likened to an abbey.[62] To modern eyes, it appears ponderous, and rather grim. Nevertheless, Berlage's proposal had Bremmer's unqualified support. 'That is art,' he proclaimed, and then pointing to Mies's project: 'That is not.'[63] Hélène Kröller-Müller, devastated by her trusted advisor's dismissal of her protégé, wavered. Her supportive husband had a full-size mock-up of Mies's design built on the site. The building looks splendid in the surviving photograph, but Bremmer was adamant and Mrs Kröller-Müller gave in. Mies returned to Berlin.

Berlage's design was never built. Later that year, the town council approved a tram line next to the Kröllers' property that would spoil their view, and they abandoned the project. Their relationship with Berlage continued, however. Kröller offered the architect a ten-year contract to work exclusively for the firm and the family. The villa–museum project was temporarily set aside while Berlage designed an office building in London, a farm for their son, and a palatial hunting lodge for Anton Kröller. Meanwhile, Hélène Kröller-Müller continued to add to her collection. The Netherlands was neutral during the First World War, and Müller & Co. prospered. By 1916, she owned several thousand paintings and drawings, as well as a collection of art furniture and applied-art objects. She had not forgotten her idea of building a villa, although now she referred to it as a 'museum house', reflecting the growing importance of the collection. Berlage produced a new design. This time the site was a dramatic hilltop on Hoge Veluwe, her husband's vast, 16,000-acre hunting estate in the province of Gelderland. But Berlage's monumental

---

* Coincidentally, Mies was a great admirer of Berlage, whose work in the Netherlands he had just discovered.

museum–house, which resembles a stepped fortress, piled up on the hill, did not appeal to Mrs Kröller-Müller. Sensing his client's misgivings, and having been offered the commission to design a new municipal museum in The Hague, in 1919 Berlage resigned his post with Müller & Co.

Kröller-Müller never warmed to Berlage, which may have been a matter of temperament, or perhaps she never forgave him for ousting Mies. In any case, she found a soulmate in her next architect. 'Berlage forces walls to rise for you,' she once said. 'Van de Velde builds music.'[64] Henry van de Velde (1863–1957), seven years younger than Berlage, was born in Antwerp and, like Behrens, studied painting, which he pursued in Paris and Barbizon. He was greatly influenced by the pointillism of Seurat and Signac and was also an early admirer of Van Gogh.* After returning to Brussels, van de Velde abandoned painting in favour of applied art, and became one of the leading figures in the Belgian art nouveau movement. Like Behrens, he began his architectural career by designing his own house, and like Behrens he was a 'total designer', responsible for interiors, furniture, porcelain, cutlery, even women's dresses. His architectural practice blossomed, and he built many residences, including a private museum for the German collector Karl Ernst Osthaus, a friend of the Kröllers. In 1905, van de Velde had been invited to establish – and build – the Grand Ducal School of Arts and Crafts in Weimar (which later became the Bauhaus), though as a Belgian national he was forced to leave Germany at the outbreak of the First World War. Van de Velde was at a loose end when Osthaus introduced him to Hélène Kröller-Müller, who took to him immediately and offered him the museum commission.

Starting afresh, Hélène Kröller-Müller decided that she did not want to live in the wilds of Hoge Veluwe, and chose Groot Haesebroek, another suburban location in Wassenaar.[65] The site proved too constricted for the now vast museum–house, so it was decided that van de Velde would design the family a new villa in The Hague, and the museum

---

* Van de Velde helped Kröller-Müller to acquire Seurat's great painting, *Le Chahut*.

itself would be built in Hoge Veluwe as originally planned, near the town of Otterlo. Hélène Kröller-Müller was intimately involved in the design: 'Oh, the museum will be beautiful,' she wrote to a friend.[66] Van de Velde's concept was simple: a large central gallery, with two flanking wings ending in hexagonal pavilions. He made extensive use of top-lighting, which might have made the windowless exterior bunker-like, but in his skilled hands the imposing volumes have a Mayan solidity that recalls Wright's Hollyhock House of the same period. It was the largest building of van de Velde's career.

In 1921, work commenced on the foundations. Then disaster struck from an unexpected quarter: the great post-war depression of 1922. The global economic slow-down had a serious impact on the operations of Müller & Co., and the company suffered its first ever loss, coming close to collapse. Construction of the museum was halted. Hélène Kröller-Müller asked van de Velde to complete the construction drawings – there would be 600 of them – so that the building could be completed once the economy improved. In the meantime, the architect returned to Brussels. The depression continued. Since Müller & Co. was family owned, there was a real danger that in the event of a business failure creditors would seize the art collection as well as the estate. In 1928, Anton Kröller established a foundation to safeguard the integrity of both, and in 1935 he sold his hunting preserve to the Dutch state, which turned it into a national park. The art collection – 800 paintings, 275 sculptures, 5,000 drawings, and 500 applied-art objects – was donated to the nation, on the condition that van de Velde's design be completed within five years.

It was soon apparent that the financially strapped Dutch government would be unable to honour its agreement. A compromise was struck. As early as 1925, when it already appeared unlikely that the museum would be built, van de Velde had designed a greatly reduced version of his grand design, to serve as temporary quarters for the collection. The government agreed to build this version as a stopgap measure. Van de Velde, now seventy-five, returned to oversee the construction. The temporary museum used the same planning idea but with smaller rooms, and a landscaped sculpture court instead of a central gallery. Some of the top-lit rooms were self-contained and some were interlocked, with corners overlapping, which created the effect of a single, continuous space. On the exterior, the flat-roofed, one-storey building was extremely plain, with undecorated, windowless, buff-coloured brick walls.

What was now called the Rijksmuseum Kröller-Müller was finished in only fourteen months, and Mrs Kröller-Müller was appointed its first director in 1938. Responsible for the installation of the collection, she was not without experience, having converted a building next door to the Müller & Co. offices in The Hague into a temporary, semi-public gallery in 1913. In that gallery, she had hung the paintings in tiers, but in the new museum she followed the more modern practice of hanging paintings in a continuous line at eye level. Like Dr Barnes, she had a didactic streak, formed by her studies with Bremmer, and she organized her collection as a chronological progression. The entrance area contained works of non-Western art – a sort of overture – then old masters and the positive realism of Corot and Fantin-Latour, followed by symbolist, impressionist and post-impressionist painters. Finally, the visitor arrived at the galleries surrounding the court, which were devoted solely to Van Gogh. The second series of rooms contained post-Van Gogh artists such as Picasso, Braque and Gris, and terminated in the abstractions of Mondrian. She made some of the galleries room-settings, with her Delftware and art furniture. Throughout, she placed Persian carpets on the floors and furniture pieces by Berlage against the walls, which heightened the museum's domestic atmosphere. Her entire collection was together at last. She died a year after the museum opened.

Van de Velde's stopgap solution is not as imposing as his original design, yet it has turned out to be a very good place to exhibit art. The light in the galleries, for example, is exceptional, and is said to have influenced Louis Kahn (who visited the Kröller-Müller in 1959) in his design of the Kimbell Art Museum in Fort Worth.[67] Van de Velde struck exactly the right balance between the building and its contents. 'At no point does the art look overpowered by the architecture, but neither does the architecture disappear into the background,' observes Wim de Wit, a curator at the Getty Research Institute. 'It is no exaggeration to say that the Kröller-Müller is one of the few museums in which architecture and art coexist without tension. This is why the temporary museum building became so popular and remains today as a permanent building.'[68]

THE COLLECTORS AND THE ARCHITECT

Choosing Norman Foster. A study tour. Identifying a site.

ROBERT SAINSBURY, A CAREFUL BUSINESSMAN, liked to plan things in advance. Two months before notifying Frank Thistlethwaite of his intention to fund a museum at the University of East Anglia, he had had his solicitors draw up a draft of a deed of gift – with the name of the university left blank. A key provision of the deed was that, while the university would be responsible for building the museum, 'the selection of site and architect, choice of plans and equipment, and acceptance of costings shall be subject to the approval of Sir Robert Sainsbury during his life, failing him of Lady Sainsbury during her life, and failing her of David Sainsbury during his life.'[1] It is common for a university donor to exert some influence on a building erected in his name, but is unusual for the influence to be so total and long-lived. '*That* is *my* drawing, *my* object – the one that I like.'

'My father wasn't an architecture buff at all,' says David Sainsbury. 'He would have said "I want to display the collection," not "I want an iconic building, a memorial to myself."' Bob turned first to his friend Kho Liang Ie. In early November 1973, three weeks before the public announcement of the gift, he invited Kho and his wife, Hetty, to Smith Square and offered him the commission to design the interior of the new museum. They agreed that the work would be done jointly with an architect, yet to be determined. 'Lisa and I are delighted at your willingness to co-operate in the East Anglia scheme,' Bob later wrote to Kho, 'and shall be most interested to hear your reaction to the site etc. after you have visited the university.'[2] Kho went to Norwich a month later, on a visit that the vice-chancellor's office described as 'confidential'. 'We have had a very satisfactory half-day with Ie who impressed me greatly,' Thistlethwaite reported to Sir Robert.[3] Discussing the matter of an architect with the vice-chancellor, Kho proposed a Dutch practitioner (unnamed), whose work he thought would suit the University of East Anglia campus. Thistlethwaite had no objection, and left the decision to Sir Robert, but he emphasized to Bob that 'I feel that the most essential point is to enable a firm and understanding relationship to develop between him [Kho] and the architects to be appointed.'[4] Having spent the previous decade overseeing the creation of the most architecturally prominent of the new universities, Thistlethwaite understood the importance of the human factor in the design process. Moreover, he had a keen appreciation of buildings. 'I had always taken a serious interest in architecture,' he once wrote, 'and indeed as a schoolboy wished to become an architect.'[5] Before returning to the Netherlands, Kho visited Sir Robert at Smith Square, and they must have decided that it would be more practical if the architect were British, for there was no further mention of a Dutch collaborator.

A week before Kho's visit, Bernard Feilden, a Norwich practitioner who was the university's consulting architect, spoke to the vice-chancellor about possible architects for the new building.[6] After contacting the Royal Institute of British Architects in London, Feilden provided Thistlethwaite with the names of firms that had experience of designing museums. The list comprised: Sir Basil Spence, probably the best-known British architect of that period; Chamberlin, Powell & Bon, which was building a new home for the Museum of London in the Barbican; Renton, Howard, Wood Associates, which had designed an arts centre at the University of Warwick; Barry Gasson, John Meunier and Brit Andresen, who had recently won a competition to design the Burrell Art Gallery in Glasgow; the established firm of Cruickshank & Seward, which had built at the University of Manchester; and two younger architects, Michael Brawne and Peter Lowe. Thistlethwaite also consulted Gordon Marshall, the head of the Estates Office, which operated and maintained the university's buildings, and Marshall provided half a dozen additional names, mostly of younger firms.

Before forwarding the list to Sir Robert, Thistlethwaite added several names of his own: Denys Lasdun, the eminent architect whom the vice-chancellor had hand-picked a decade earlier to design the East Anglia campus (though the architect and the university had since parted ways); Edward Cullinan, who had been Lasdun's chief assistant on the much admired student residences at East Anglia and was now on his own; and Thistlethwaite's favourite, the London architecture and engineering firm Arup Associates, which had just finished the university's School of Music, a modest but thoughtfully designed building. After alerting Arup's chief architect, Philip Dowson, who introduced himself to Sir Robert and also contacted Kho, Thistlethwaite forwarded the seventeen names to Sir Robert. 'By now you will have talked to Dowson,' he wrote, and suggested that three other firms 'merit special consideration': Lasdun, Cullinan, whom Thistlethwaite described as 'highly regarded as one of the up-and-coming architects,' and Foster Associates.[7]

Foster Associates, a fledgling London firm, barely six years old, had no previous connection to the University of East Anglia, had not built a museum, indeed, had never built any sort of campus building. Norman Foster was not one of Feilden's recommendations, so how did he come to be on Thistlethwaite's list? In his memoir, Thistlethwaite generously credits 'our knowledgeable and discerning Estates Officer, Gordon Marshall' with suggesting Foster, and Patricia Whitt, who was the vice-chancellor's personal assistant, believes that Foster's name was on Marshall's list.[8] On the other hand, the Foster firm (misidentified as Foster and Associates) does not appear among Marshall's choices, but is second to last, among the names that Thistlethwaite added.[9] It is possible that Foster's name was brought up by Kho in his meeting with the vice-chancellor, for the Dutch designer had met Foster three years earlier, and knew and admired his work.[10] 'From talking to Kho, I gather he knows Foster extremely well and no doubt he would discuss Foster with you,' Thistlethwaite wrote to Bob.[11]

This was the only explanation that he gave as to why Foster should 'merit special consideration'.

Although Foster had never built a museum, that would not necessarily have counted against him, for neither had Lasdun or Cullinan.* In truth, no British architect had distinguished himself in that field and, as the *Sunday Times* art critic, John Russell, observed, 'There is not in the whole of the British Isles a major museum building that is modern in the sense that museum buildings by Mies van der Rohe or Philip Johnson are modern.'[12] Perhaps that's why the architect that Bob and Lisa had first considered was a foreigner, the Finnish master Alvar Aalto, who had just completed an acclaimed art museum in Denmark. But, as they later told an interviewer, they decided that 'his advanced age [seventy-five] and geographical remoteness disqualified him.'[13]

Despite his interest in Aalto, Bob was not knowledgable about modern architecture. His extensive library of art books at that time contained a scant ten architectural titles, of which only two dealt with modern architecture: an illustrated anthology by Hoffmann and Kultermann, and a monograph on the Sydney Opera House.[†14] Thus, Bob would not have been familiar with most of the names on Thistlethwaite's list. He turned to Corin Hughes-Stanton (the son of his old friend Blair Hughes-Stanton), who was the editor of *Design*, an influential magazine that reported on contemporary architecture as well as graphics and industrial design. They went over the list together, and Bob's annotated copy indicates that, while he did not add any new names, he did highlight six of the firms. He passed over Dowson – the two men had not hit it off – as well as Spence and Lasdun, but he starred Chamberlin, Powell & Bon, noting (probably after a conversation with Hughes-Stanton) '1950 reputation'; Ahrends, Burton & Koralek, which had designed buildings at Trinity College, Dublin ('v. good'); Gollins Melville Ward & Partners ('good'), which had built the

---

*   Curiously, Foster's final-year student thesis had been an anthropological museum.
†   Most of the eighty-four architecture titles in Sir Robert Sainsbury's extensive library of art books date from after 1973. The oldest title is John Betjeman's polemical history of British architecture, *Ghastly Good Taste* (1933).

University of Sheffield; as well as Shepheard, Epstein & Hunter ('main-stream good firm'), which had planned the new University of Lancaster. He also starred Howell, Killick & Partridge, which had built colleges at Oxford and Cambridge; and Edward Cullinan. Later that month Bob and Hughes-Stanton visited several buildings in London. 'I spent two days looking at buildings by different architects,' Bob later told the *Architects' Journal,* 'and when I got to a certain building I decided that the man who designed that building was the man for me.'[15]

For some reason Bob did not star Foster Associates, but did add 'very able' next to the name, and jotted down 'To see. Docks. Norman Foster' on the back of the sheet.[16] The Foster-designed buildings in London's Millwall Dock belonged to Fred Olsen, a Norwegian shipping line, and included a passenger terminal for cruise ships – basically a long, ribbed, aluminium tube – and, sandwiched between two cargo sheds, a small two-storey block containing administrative offices and a canteen for workers – an unusual mixture. Bob, who had actively promoted enlight-ened labour relations at Sainsbury's, visited the building and talked to the managers and the workers. He was impressed by the unconventional combination of uses, as well as the general appearance of the building; its steel-and-glass façade recalled Mies van der Rohe, a designer whom he admired – 'one of the century's undoubtedly great architects', he called him.[†17] Foster's dramatic façade – reflective glass with no visible means of support – was lighter and more attenuated than a typical Mies building, appearing at once elegant and tough. According to Steven Hooper, 'Bob remembers immediately being struck by the appearance of a black glass-wall, and he sensed that their quest was over.'[18]

Bob and Lisa were scheduled to leave London on 8 January, for a six-week trip to New Zealand and Fiji; Bob was a member of the Arts

---

*   According to a friend of Bob and Lisa's, 'For Bob, UEA were more or less spectators to the process, and he certainly never credited them with original initiative vis-à-vis Foster. As he told it, Bob took the responsibility and credit for the choice.'
†   Bob had earlier supported Mies's controversial design for Peter Palumbo's Mansion House Square project in London.

Council, and he had agreed to visit museums to choose objects for a possible Oceanic exhibition. That left little time to meet the architect of the Olsen building. Foster has described the encounter. 'It was the morning of New Year's Day 1974 and I was standing in front of the door of number 5 Smith Square, for what I was told would be a brief meeting with Sir Robert Sainsbury about a possible museum project. Before ringing the bell I remember feeling apprehensive, nervous.' He was also slightly under the weather from the festivities of the previous night. He did not bring a portfolio of his work. 'We did not discuss my professional attainments,' he says. 'We talked about museums in general, and it turned out we had a lot of similar views. The meeting went on longer than Sir Robert expected. At one point he asked his wife to come down and we had lunch.' There was much for Foster to absorb: the house itself – 'surprisingly modest, intimate and discreet', but crammed with art of every sort. Foster was struck by the contrast between this elegant couple and their radical collection.[19]

The first meeting of an architect with his client is a delicate moment, for it is an encounter of personalities, sensibilities and, equally important, tastes. The architect must quickly determine what sort of people his clients are, what they really want, and how far they might be prepared to go, architecturally speaking, and how far he might be prepared to go with them. 'I was getting early clues about their way of looking at things and I do not mean visually: it was as radical as those progressive artists they had encouraged,' Foster later said.[20] At the same time, the Sainsburys were sounding out the architect. 'I was asked what I felt about works of art,' he recalled. 'I was asked what I felt about galleries – it was a very personal exchange.'[21] He told Bob and Lisa that he was interested in seeing works of art as a spectator, but that he wasn't really interested in catalogues. About galleries he said that he was unhappy in a building that was monumental or pompous, and that what he enjoyed were buildings that were nice places to be in. The conversation, which did not finish until after three o'clock, was marked by a growing awareness of shared attitudes.

At one point Foster overheard Bob say to Lisa, 'He's young enough to be our son.' (At the time David Sainsbury was thirty-three, Foster was thirty-eight.)

Foster left Smith Square feeling optimistic. 'I thought things had gone well,' he says. 'In hindsight, knowing the kind of people they were, it is likely that they made the decision then and there.' In any event, Foster called Thistlethwaite's office the following Monday to say that he had met Sir Robert, had spoken with Kho, and that he and Kho would like to make an appointment to visit the vice-chancellor. The pair had lunch with Thistlethwaite on 28 January, met Gordon Marshall, and saw the university's preferred building site, which was next to the music school. Thistlethwaite was impressed that Kho and Foster clearly had a close rapport. 'Kho and I hit it off,' says Foster. 'There was a shared respect. I didn't know him well before that but I was definitely aware of him as a designer. I admired his work, and I even used the suspended metal ceiling he designed for Schiphol airport when we built our office.'

From this point, things moved quickly. Ten days later, Thistlethwaite informed Feilden, the university architect, that Foster was being considered for the Sainsbury project, subject to a review of his portfolio and references.[22] Thistlethwaite could not have taken this decision without Sir Robert's approval, and since no correspondence survives, at some time between New Year's Day and his departure for New Zealand, it is likely that Bob telephoned his friend and said something like, 'Lisa and I have spent a day with Foster and as far as we're concerned, he's our man. He and Kho will work well together. Of course, you must meet him, but please proceed with the appointment process in our absence.' It is possible that there was a further, long-distance telephone conversation, but I prefer to think that Bob and Lisa, who had made their decision, brought a certain amount of pressure to bear. As a member of the university's Estates Office staff told me, 'Sir Robert was good at leaving people without options.'

The appointment process was largely a formality – none of the other candidates was interviewed. Foster had named Sir Hugh Casson, in whose office he had worked as a student, as a referee. Casson, who had made his mark as the architectural director of the epochal Festival of Britain, was an influential figure on the British architectural scene, a member of the Royal Academy (the first architect since Sir Edwin Lutyens to hold its presidency), and a close friend of the royal family, for whom he designed the interiors of the royal yacht *Britannia*. It is said that Casson taught the young Prince Charles watercolour painting. Thistlethwaite asked Casson for his opinion of Foster, particularly with respect to how well a building of his might fit into the Denys Lasdun-designed campus. Casson's reply is worth quoting at length, since it is a telling description of the young architect:

> I know a little about Kho Liang Ie and the splendid Schiphol airport, and think he would be an excellent choice for the interior presentation. I am also a great admirer of Norman Foster. He worked in our office for a short time, but I have known and worked with him on many projects and committees for some years now. As you have already met him, you need not be told that he is a man of great energy, drive and enthusiasm, with enough granite beneath the charm to ensure consistency in any project to which he lays his hand. He is also a 'lateral thinker' who instinctively queries the true nature of the problem before dreaming up its solution. This is a rare quality in an architect, who tend to be the prisoners of images long before they have studied the parameters. He would, I am sure, be respected by Denys which is an important issue, and in my view, could be trusted to produce the most adventurous, efficient and magical building.[23]

Who was this architectural magician? Like Mies, an architect he revered, Norman Foster's social origins were humble. He was born in 1935 into a working-class family in the industrial suburbs of Manchester. An only child, he left school at sixteen, worked in the city treasurer's office, and after completing his national service in the Royal Air Force (as a technician, not a pilot) gained admittance to the University of Manchester to study architecture. His talent was recognized early and, on graduating in 1961, he was awarded both a Fulbright scholarship and a Henry Fellowship. He chose the Henry, and enrolled at Yale, where the architecture school was directed by Paul Rudolph, an up-and-coming architect who was then designing the university's Art and Architecture Building (Foster would briefly work in Rudolph's office as a draughtsman). The master class met on the top floor of the Yale University Art Gallery, newly designed by Louis Kahn, and among its teachers were not only the charismatic Rudolph, but also James Stirling, Vincent Scully and Ivan Chermayeff. It was a heady environment for a young man from Manchester. After receiving his degree Foster worked for a year in Massachusetts and California. America had a formative influence. 'In England I was the odd one out. Working-class background, early-school-leaver, a place in the university but no grant. I was an outsider,' Foster recalled later. 'But when I came here I felt that I had come home. There was pride in working and serving. I felt liberated. It is no exaggeration to say that I discovered myself through America.'[24]

One of Foster's classmates at Yale was a fellow Englishman, Richard Rogers. Both were talented designers, though very different personalities: Foster, intense and somewhat withdrawn; Rogers, two years older, handsome and with his continental background (born in Florence and the cousin of Ernesto Rogers, a well-known Italian architect) somewhat glamorous. The unlikely pair teamed up at Yale – Foster was a superb (left-handed) draughtsman, Rogers, dyslexic, hardly drew at all – and became friends. On their return to London in 1963, they formed an architectural partnership with two wealthy architect sisters whom Rogers knew: Georgie Wolton, who was a registered practitioner (at the time the only one in the firm with this qualification), and Wendy Cheesman, whose

Hampstead flat served as their office. They called themselves Team Four.[*] Over the next four years the firm completed several award-winning projects, including an elegant electronics factory for Reliance Controls, before amicably breaking up in 1967.

Rogers went on to garner international acclaim by winning the Pompidou Centre competition with Renzo Piano. Norman and Wendy, now married, founded Foster Associates. Despite a national building boom, they had difficulty attracting commissions, and at one point even considered moving to the United States. Eventually, by focusing on industrial buildings, a field neglected by British architects, they found clients – first Fred Olsen, then others. The early commissions were simple, low-budget suburban buildings, but were executed with precision and considerable panache. The schemes were published in architectural magazines, won awards, and led to a major commission, an office building in Ipswich for the insurance giant, Willis Faber & Dumas. (The Willis Faber building, which gained Foster a national reputation, was not completed until 1975, after the Sainsbury project had begun.) At the time of the Sainsbury commission, the firm had grown to about fifteen employees and occupied a space in Fitzroy Street in central London, next to the Post Office Tower. The Fitzroy Street studio was designed, as Foster put it, with 'the conviction that the practice should itself practise what it preaches.'[25] The architectural historian and critic Reyner Banham, a friend of Foster, caught the flavour of the place: 'Inside you'll see a fully carpeted open-plan office à la mode, divided into work spaces by Herman Miller system furniture, in a colour gamut that tends to yellows and greens. A green wall down one side is punctuated by snub-cornered spaceship doors, giving access to kitchen, lavatories and the usual etceteras. On the other wall leans the boss's racing bike (yellow, naturally).'[26]

In mid-February 1974, Bob and Lisa returned from New Zealand. In March, Foster went to Amsterdam for his first working session with Kho. 'Although Kho was to design the interior, and I the building, it was intended to be a true collaboration,' says Foster. Six weeks later, Sir Robert convened a meeting at Smith Square. Although the University Council had not yet approved his selection of the architects, he wanted to get started. Kho and Foster were there, as well as Gordon Marshall, representing the university.[27]

The first order of business was to fix the sizes of the different parts of the building. Sir Robert had told the vice-chancellor that he did not want his collection to be isolated in a museum, but to be part of the everyday life of the university, just as it was part of everyday life at Smith Square. Thistlethwaite, in complete agreement, suggested adding space for the School of Fine Arts, which did not have its own building. He also proposed that the building include the university art collection, the Senior Common Room (the faculty club) and, since East Anglia did not have traditional dining halls, a restaurant for students and faculty. The cost of building these additional premises would be borne by the university.[28] The complex was to be called the Sainsbury Centre for Visual Arts.[29] Foster calculated the total building area to be about 5,000 square metres, two-thirds devoted to the collection (including an area for special exhibitions and a library), and one-third to university uses.*[30]

At the same meeting it was decided that three art museums would be visited for study purposes: the Kröller-Müller in Otterlo, the Whitney in New York, and the Gulbenkian in Lisbon. Although almost forty years old, the Kröller-Müller had been the scene of Sir Robert's and Kho's first collaboration in 1966. It is unclear why the Whitney, a relatively new American museum, was chosen, since it is a five-storey building in dense urban surroundings. The Gulbenkian was a more understandable

---

*   As the detailed briefs were developed, the building grew to 5,600 square metres, although the proportion between gallery and university uses remained roughly the same. The non-exhibition spaces (administration, storage, workshops, etc.) represented about a quarter of the total gallery, which is a low ratio for an art museum. This would cause problems later (see Chapter 8).

selection. The museum, a one-storey building of comparable size to the proposed Sainsbury Centre, designed by Pedro Cid, Alberto Pessoa and Ruy d'Athouguia, had opened in 1969. Bob admired the Calouste Gulbenkian collection, which included European, Islamic and Oriental art, furniture, silverware, jewelry and coins; moreover, as an exhibition designer, Kho would have been familiar with the building, which was one of the first museums whose design reflected the recent finding by conservators that excessive daylight was injurious to organic artefacts. According to the minutes of the Smith Square meeting, the group decided that the Sainsbury Centre would likewise have 'no natural lighting for works of art'.[31]

At the end of April, the university issued a press release announcing the appointment of Foster and Kho as 'joint architects' for the Sainsbury Centre.[32] Foster's office sent Kho topographical maps of the site and, during the summer, Foster again visited Amsterdam. This time he brought along one of his assistants, Ian Ritchie, who had been with him for a couple of years. They met at Heathrow airport. Ritchie, twenty-seven with long hair and an unruly beard, arrived wearing a salmon-pink suit. 'What's this?' asked Foster. 'You told me to get a suit,' Ritchie replied. It was the only comic moment in what turned out to be a sombre visit. They went to Kho's house, a narrow Amsterdam row house; Hetty let them in and told them that her husband was unwell. 'Kho was sitting up in his bed being very chirpy, and he showed us a sketch of the building,' recalls Ritchie. As the conversation continued, Kho revealed that he was seriously ill, having been diagnosed with cancer of the liver (he had already notified Sir Robert). Ritchie recalls that the usually voluble Foster said very little during the meeting. Besides his concern for Kho, whom he liked and admired, Foster must have been wondering who would replace him if he died and whether, as Kho was the Sainsburys' friend, the project itself would be in jeopardy?

Kho's sketch, which Ritchie remembers as a delicately coloured pencil drawing of three overlapping squares, was for a site at the east end of the campus, near the music school and the arts building.[33] The best site in this area was occupied by a brand new gymnasium, and Kho's initial idea had been to demolish the gymnasium and build the Sainsbury Centre in its place. Sir Robert quashed this impractical suggestion, and when Foster began working on the project the first thing he did was to make a systematic study of possible sites. 'I wasn't satisfied that the music school site was really the best one,' he says, 'so we looked at other alternatives.' The oldest Sainsbury Centre drawing in the Foster office archive is by Birkin Haward, one of the senior associates.* The large axonometric of the entire campus shows potential growth points, car parks, the chief landscape features, and other elements that might influence the selection of a site.[34]

Haward's drawing is titled 'Problems', and, indeed, the University of East Anglia offered a prospective builder many challenges. When the master plan was designed in the early 1960s, the architect, Denys Lasdun, was asked to produce 'a single unified concept, so that the University would become a consistent whole.'[35] The bucolic site was a 165-acre golf course on the outskirts of Norwich, overlooking the River Yare. The campus planning of the British new universities was dominated by two different approaches: quadrangles (on the Oxford and Cambridge model), and free-standing buildings surrounded by open space (following the arrangement used by Mies van der Rohe at the Illinois Institute of Technology in Chicago).[36] Eschewing these planning strategies, Lasdun conceived East Anglia as a dense linear arrangement of connected six- and eight-storey buildings. 'It's like a little city,' he explained; 'it's probably the most urban modern university in the country.'[37]

Lasdun's plan, which is laid out along 45-degree diagonals, closely resembles Candilis, Josic, and Woods's contemporaneous urban plan for Toulouse–Le Mirail in France. The guiding concept of that project, which was influenced by the ideas of Le Corbusier (for whom Georges Candilis and Shadrach Woods had worked), was the vertical separation of pedestrians and cars. At East Anglia, Lasdun, who also admired Le Corbusier,

---

* By coincidence, the building that Kho recommended demolishing had been designed in 1970–71 by Johns, Slater & Haward, the firm of Birkin Haward's father.

created a similar system of raised pedestrian decks. The decks were flanked by a long building containing the classrooms, and terraced student residences. The students nicknamed the residences the Ziggurats, and the classroom building – less affectionately – the Teaching Wall. Ground level was reserved for roads, parking and service vehicles. Lasdun's concept was what architects call a 'megastructure', a self-contained complex, conceived as a single, continuous built form.

Norman and Wendy Foster identified six potential sites for the Sainsbury Centre: one near the music school; another near the entrance to the university, where Lasdun had proposed locating an auditorium; and a third in the centre of the campus. Another three possible sites were dotted around the campus, including a critical one on the western edge. The choice of a site is a crucial early decision in the design of a building, since it is difficult to design a really good building on a poor site. It was as yet unclear exactly what form the new building would take, and how it would relate – or not relate – to Lasdun's megastructure, but the western site offered the most options. The other sites were hemmed in by existing buildings, whereas the west end of the campus was open, and being on the edge of the university it was next to an attractive wood. It also offered a striking view down to the River Yare and to a manmade lake then under construction. 'Bob liked the location because of its closeness to the science facilities,' says Foster. 'I also liked it for several reasons, in particular the views to open countryside. We also had a tight budget, and since the services, roads and so on, were all there, it meant we could use more of the money on the building.'

On 29 September 1974, Norman and Wendy Foster set off with Bob and Lisa Sainsbury on a four-day study tour of European art museums (Kho, now bedridden, was unable to travel).[38] As Foster later described it: 'We visited a number of museums, and we wanted to get a feel from the buildings around the way that they worked, the way that they would work if you were going to visit them and see works of art, the way that they would work if you were guarding the works of art, the way that they would work if you had the job of erecting the exhibitions.'[39] The three museums originally identified – the Kröller-Müller, the Whitney and the Gulbenkian – were not the ones that they visited, however. As Foster puts it, they chose more suitable models: Aalto's recently opened North Jutland Art Museum at Ålborg; the Louisiana Museum of Modern Art, also in Denmark, which Foster had visited as a student; and Mies van der Rohe's New National Gallery in Berlin, which Foster had read about and wanted to see. The two couples flew to Copenhagen, whence they made excursions to Ålborg and the Louisiana Museum on the North Zealand coast, then continued to West Berlin. The brief tour was an opportunity for Foster and his clients to get to know each other better – after all, they had only met nine months earlier.

Alvar and Elissa Aalto had won an international competition to design the North Jutland Art Museum in 1958, but construction had been delayed for a decade and the museum did not open until 1972. Foster had not seen the Ålborg museum before, although he had been to Finland as a student and visited many of Aalto's buildings, including the Säynätsalo Town Hall. 'I especially appreciated Aalto's use of top light in various buildings,' he says, 'so I was keen to see how he used it in a museum.' In Ålborg, some galleries are lit from above by diffused north-east light, and others by direct sunlight, reflected by curved ceiling baffles. The Fosters and the Sainsburys arrived at the museum in the late afternoon as the sun was setting, yet the quality of the light inside was superb – not just diffused light but streaks of direct sunlight on the floor. Foster pointed out that all the light came from skylights, there were few windows. Another feature that impressed him was that the main exhibition area could be subdivided into smaller rooms by means of sliding screens, or left open to create one large space. The curators they met described this flexibility as extremely useful. According to Foster, it was in Ålborg that he and Wendy and the Sainsburys decided that the site of their building should be at the west end of the university.[40] It was an interesting coincidence that the Ålborg Museum was close by a similarly wooded area.

The Louisiana Museum of Modern Art is located in Humblebæk, a half-hour's drive from Copenhagen. Unlike the North Jutland Art Museum, this is a private museum, founded by Knud W. Jensen, who as a young man inherited a wholesale cheese business from his father, sold it, and in 1958 bought the 25-acre estate overlooking the Øresund strait. He then commissioned two young Danish architects, Vilhelm Wohlert and Jørgen Bo, to transform an existing nineteenth-century country house into a museum for his collection of Danish art. They added a gallery and created a building that was widely admired as a masterpiece of modern Danish design – low-key, unpretentious, human in scale. Wohlert and Bo had enlarged the museum twice since Foster had seen it as a student, and Jensen's collection now included an international cross-section of contemporary art – Bacon, Giacometti, Ernst, Picasso – displayed in a series of pavilions linked by glazed corridors. Foster was struck by the casual atmosphere; 'What was also very exciting were the displays, which were not over-protected ... somehow you had this feeling of vitality and exuberance.'[41] The older galleries of the Louisiana Museum had the domestic scale of large living rooms, but Foster noticed that the most recent addition was a tall, column-free space that could accommodate large works as well as small objects. Although he found much to admire, Foster thought that Louisiana, which had grown in phases, had drawbacks in terms of servicing and moving exhibition materials in and out of the buildings.

The study tour ended in West Berlin. The New National Gallery, which had opened in 1968, was Mies van der Rohe's last major building (he died the following year). His ideas about museums had evolved considerably since the Kröller-Müller project. 'The ideal museum is one large area, allowing complete flexibility,' he observed, and his design in Berlin consists of a large glass-walled pavilion containing a single vast space for special exhibits.[42] The pavilion stands on a low podium that contains galleries as well as a so-called 'open reserve', a storage area that is accessible to the public. The Berlin museum was an odd choice to visit, since it is much larger than the planned Sainsbury Centre, it is a national rather than a personal collection, and it is in distinctly urban surroundings. Moreover, the glass-walled pavilion (which Mies had originally conceived as an office building for Bacardi in Cuba) had been criticized by curators as inhospitable to art – too large, too difficult to light, too much glare, and Bob thought the hall 'most unsuitable'. The day they visited, the hall was being used for an audio-visual performance with multiple projection screens. 'Whether or not it works in gallery terms is really quite irrelevant,' Foster said later, 'but the lesson that it seemed to offer, was that the benefit of a generous multi-purpose space in anticipation provides the possibility of something that is more usable in the future.'[43]

The collectors and the architects drew important lessons from the tour. The experience of Aalto's museum convinced them of the importance of well-designed skylights. Although the Sainsbury collection had been assembled in domestic surroundings, and everyone agreed that the galleries should be accessible and relaxed, the Louisiana Museum demonstrated that while a museum could be casual it was different from a private house, both in scale and function. Finally, Foster's instinctive preference for large open spaces, which had marked most of his earlier projects, was confirmed – museums needed to be flexible. Bob agreed that the exhibition space of the Sainsbury Centre should be open and without columns.

The standard procedure at the University of East Anglia was to have a building sub-committee oversee major building projects. The Sainsbury Centre sub-committee, which met every six months, had four members: the vice-chancellor as chair; Andrew Martindale, the senior professor in the School of Fine Arts; W. Rowan Hare, the university treasurer and a trustee; and Sir Robert.[*][44] It was not unusual for a building committee to have an outside member, but it was unusual for this to be the donor – and for meetings to take place in his home. Typically, Thistlethwaite and Sir Robert would have lunch together at Smith Square, and then at two-thirty the rest of the committee would arrive. They met in the wood-panelled

---

[*] According to Frank Thistlethwaite, 'the sub-committee met rarely ... it is fair to say that the effective decisions were taken by Sir Robert and me.'

dining room, under Soutine's *Lady in Blue.* Also in attendance were the university registrar, George Chadwick, and, to answer operational questions, Gordon Marshall. Peter Yorke of the Estates Office acted as secretary. 'I would write up the minutes of the meeting,' he recalls. 'The vice-chancellor would simply sign off on them, but Sir Robert would make copious notes to reflect all the changes that had happened since the meeting.' (In fact, Bob sometimes sent his edits to Foster for his comments.)

The subject of the sub-committee's first meeting, which occurred shortly after the study tour, was Foster's report on a possible site for the building. He described six alternative locations in terms of ease of access, parking, services and the visual impact on the surroundings. Bernard Feilden, the university architect, had recommended a so-called 'gateway' site near the entrance to the university, on the grounds of public accessibility.[45] Foster firmly voiced his disagreement. 'The suggestion that the gateway site would help the University's ambivalent relationship with the outside world would be more appropriate if the University was on an urban edge rather than straddling open country and the outer suburban fringes of Norwich,' he later explained.[46] Instead, he proposed a site at the west end of the campus, arguing that, unlike some of the more remote locations, it already had roads, drainage, gas, electricity, water and steam heat, so there would be no need to spend money on new infrastructure. He added that the proximity to the science buildings was another advantage, since it would avoid creating what he called an 'arts ghetto'. Another factor – perhaps unacknowledged – was that the site had the potential to offer dramatic views outside.

A spirited discussion followed. Hare thought the remote location was not ideal for the Senior Common Room. Professor Martindale didn't like his school being so far from the centre of the campus and felt that the museum would be too remote to attract casual visitors. Thistlethwaite, who had been briefed on Foster's recommendation before the meeting, countered by saying that the siting of the Centre should not be driven by considerations about the SCR, and he was sure that in time the centre of gravity of the university would shift towards the west. Then Sir Robert weighed in. Since he did not consider the primary role of the Centre to be a public museum, he was not concerned about attracting visitors, he said. He supported his architect's choice. He understood that others might not agree, but in that case he preferred that the sub-committee re-examine the siting question entirely, rather than simply choose one of the alternatives. In other words, if they didn't like the west end, they should go back to square one. 'It was a polite way of saying that the project might not proceed,' recalls Yorke. The minutes record that the sub-committee voted unanimously to approve the architect's recommendation. Foster had his site.[47]

FOUR

THE SHED

*The design of the Sainsbury Centre. A last-minute change drastically
alters the concept.*

KHO LIANG IE'S HEALTH STEADILY DETERIORATED; he spent his last weeks
in his country house in the northern Netherlands and died on New Year's
Day 1975. Foster joined the Sainsburys to attend the funeral. 'Since I
understand that the contract required the personal attention of the two
principals, I am assuming that as from the death of Kho Liang Ie the
services of Kho Liang Ie Associates will no longer be used,' Sir Robert
informed Thistlethwaite, 'but that any new arrangements with Norman
Foster Associates [*sic*] will provide for the payment of specialists in the
field of design either in the employ of Norman Foster Associates or otherwise.'[1] Sir Robert consulted Sir John Pope-Hennessy, director of the British
Museum, as well as Andrew Ritchie at Yale, and asked Foster to prepare a
list of designers. Ian Ritchie remembers that the five or six names included
Ettore Sottsass, Jr., and Gae Aulenti. 'I put together a list,' Foster recalls.
'But first I told Bob and Lisa, "I have to say that I believe we are the best
persons to do it [the interior design]. I have prepared a small presentation
of our work. I will show you this, although you probably won't agree, and
you are, of course, free to decide. But I feel obliged to do it." After I finished, they decided that our firm should do it, and I never showed them
anybody else's work.'

   Meanwhile, the design of the building was under way. How does
an architect arrive at a concept? Foster had secured a site to his liking,
but he faced several challenges. For a museum building of fifty thousand
square feet, the construction budget of £1.5 million was barely adequate.
That didn't scare him; his firm had a reputation for getting good results

on tight budgets. Five years earlier, he had been approached by IBM to design a temporary office building in Cosham, a village near Portsmouth. Foster convinced the corporation that for the same money, and in the same short time – less than twelve months – they could have a permanent building. IBM, who would normally have allocated two and a half years to such a project, was sceptical, but not only was the 10,700 square-metre building delivered on time and within the budget, its handsome design also won several awards – and led to a second, larger IBM commission for the firm. A more worrying challenge was the state of the British economy, which was experiencing a period of steep inflation, manifested in the building industry by rapidly escalating prices. Foster told the building sub-committee that it was critical to begin construction without delay. That meant a simple building – simple in design and simple in construction.

It was common practice in the Foster office to explore a variety of options. Foster liked to have several alternatives ready, if only to elimi-nate them. Sometimes he had different designs prepared in order to introduce a less desirable option first, paving the way for what he really wanted to do.[2] Under Foster's direction, Birkin Haward and Bodo Zapp, a German architect at the firm, developed several designs that extended Lasdun's stepped profile and connected to the pedestrian deck system.[3] Anthony Hunt, a structural engineer who regularly worked with Foster, independently studied a building on piers that stepped down the hill and continued partway into the waters of the lake. Based on a sketch by Foster, Ian Ritchie made a drawing of a museum that was three-quarters under-ground, with glass skylights set flush into a grass-covered roof. Foster had recently designed an (unbuilt) underground theatre for St Peter's College, Oxford, but while burying a building made sense in a historic quadrangle, it seemed too discreet for East Anglia, which of all the seven new universi-ties had the strongest architectural image.

From 1964 to 1968, while he was the architect for the university, Denys Lasdun not only devised the master plan, he also put his personal stamp on the place by designing all the buildings. Lasdun had been an apprentice with the first generation of British modernists – Wells Coates, Berthold Lubetkin and Maxwell Fry – and like them was a devotee of Le Corbusier and reinforced concrete. The buildings at East Anglia were built of pre-cast concrete, a choice that was the result of a limited budget but was also an aesthetic decision. Because he used exposed concrete, Lasdun's style is sometimes described as 'brutalist', but his architecture is quite different from that of Paul Rudolph, say, whose Art and Architecture building at Yale predates the University of East Anglia by several years. Lasdun's concrete is generally smooth rather than textured, and his buildings have the scaleless, abstract look of giant architectural models. A book on the architecture of the University of East Anglia describes his approach: 'There is nothing that can be called attached art or ornament. Lasdun does not wish to differentiate between zones with a primarily decorative or symbolic character, as being opposed to those of a primarily utilitarian character. There is no axiality, no symmetry, no façade of any kind, no general contrast between "front" and "back" … reinforced concrete serves as the chief unifying element.'[4] This makes his architecture sound bleak – which it is – but it is also extremely assertive, like a public speaker pounding on a lectern, repeating the same slogan over and over.

One way to build beside an aggressive building is to design something entirely different. That was probably inevitable anyway, since Foster generally avoided exposed concrete, which he believed was unsuitable for the damp British climate.[*5] The idea of extending Lasdun's planning concept was not appealing either, for while the stepped residences presented a memorable architectural image from the front, the rear service area was distinctly less successful. As Haward wrote on his 'Problems' drawing: 'Fronts great! But the backs … visual squalor, rubbish bins, disorganized parking, stained concrete, compromised service bays, no landscaping, no colour or clear signing systems, not much weather protection either.'[6] More of the same didn't seem like the right solution.

---

[*] When Lasdun was asked to leave his post as the university's architect in 1968, dissatisfaction with the weathering of his concrete buildings was cited as a reason.

Peter Yorke of the Estates Office prepared detailed briefs for the School of Fine Arts, a 300-seat restaurant and the Senior Common Room. 'Foster poured scorn on the briefs for their old-fashioned and conventional thinking,' Yorke recalls. 'I had written a section on "Contents of Corridors", and Foster was adamant that his building wouldn't have any corridors.' Yorke, a genial man and a Cambridge classicist by education, felt chagrined, although in time he couldn't help but be impressed by the calibre of the Foster team. 'They were obviously capable and knew what they were doing,' he says.

There was no brief for the museum, since Sir Robert insisted on leaving Foster the maximum degree of flexibility when it came to the galleries, and did not want to burden his architect with a list of rooms and floor areas. 'Architecturally Norman Foster was given only two guidelines, we did *not* want a monument to ourselves nor to him, and we *did* want a positive statement,' Bob said.[7] This somewhat philosophical directive did not mean that the architect was working without any functional guidelines, however. The study tour had provided a number of insights into how a museum should be designed, which Foster summarized:

> an awareness of the positive qualities of tuneable natural top lighting; the importance of flexibility for change and growth; the need for effective but not labour-intensive security; the value of usable storage space – most museums seemed to have as many works of art closeted away inaccessibly as on display; the need to service a gallery without disturbing either exhibits or users – changing and adjusting lamps and air filters, for example; a desire to respect and integrate social elements; and a need to understand the furniture and installation of exhibits as integrated elements of the design.[8]

The concept for the building was arrived at gradually. 'When we started the design development, it was regarded as inevitable that there would be at least two buildings,' Foster remembers, 'a Sainsbury building and a university building, or perhaps even three or four buildings.' An early schematic design had four separate blocks, corresponding to the four main uses: the collection, the special exhibitions, the School of Fine Arts, and the restaurant and SCR. As the design was refined, the blocks drew closer together, forming a cluster, then lining up along the access road, and finally becoming a single building. At one point, Foster explored an organic composition in which the individual parts were angled according to the contours of the site and connected by glass conservatories (which would later become a feature of the final design). 'Putting everything in one building was considered very radical at the time,' says Foster, but that is precisely the solution that emerged. In fact, the possibility of a single building had come to him early, and he remembers discussing it with the Sainsburys during the study tour.

The site was on the edge of the flat plain on which most of the university was built, at the point where the ground began to slope down to the lake. One way to avoid the complication and cost of building on the slope was to make the plan long and narrow, about 30 by 150 metres. The alignment of the building followed the diagonal geometry of the rest of the campus, a solution that was probably influenced by Foster's decision to consult Denys Lasdun at the beginning of the project. An early sketch plan shows a long rectangle with the service functions, such as truck docks, mechanical rooms and entrances, lined up on the north side, along the existing road.* The interior is a large open space with the collection at one end and the more public uses, such as the restaurant and the special exhibitions area, at the other. Later sketches show the building opening up to an outdoor sculpture terrace on the south side. The single tube of a building was a recurring theme throughout Foster's many exploratory sketches, and it finally resolved itself on the axis of the views and the overall geometry of Lasdun's adjacent megastructure.

---

* Actually the northeast side, since the orientation of the building is northwest–southeast, but for convenience the building is generally referred to as being on an east–west axis.

Architects often explore an idea in successive projects. In 1974, Foster Associates had finished a small building for Modern Art Glass, a company that specialized in installing glass curtain walls, and earlier had worked on the Olsen and IBM Cosham projects. The Modern Art Glass company was located on an industrial estate in Thamesmead, near Woolwich on the south bank of the Thames; Foster's warehouse was a long shed with roof and walls wrapped in corrugated aluminium, no windows, skylights in the roof, and a big overhead door for lorries. What distinguished this mundane industrial building from its neighbours was the care with which it was built, the all-glass end wall, and the colour of the metal cladding – bright blue. The building received a Financial Times Industrial Architecture Award, cited as 'an excellent example of a low-cost industrial building, of ordinary materials, handled in all its detailing as if it were the most significant construction possible, a most distinguished achievement assembled from a basic vocabulary of corrugated sheeting, steel and glass'.[9] The glazed end of the Modern Art Glass building contained a showroom and company offices on a mezzanine; the rest was a warehouse. The Foster office often combined several uses within a single structure. This was more than simply a question of making buildings that were flexible and adaptable to change: it also reflected an egalitarian ideal. At IBM Cosham, for example, the spaces for managerial offices, clerical work, a restaurant and the mainframe computer area, were architecturally undifferentiated. The Olsen building combined a recreation centre for dock-workers, offices for administrative staff and a twenty-four-hour canteen for everyone. Even an early Team Four project such as Reliance Controls placed the manufacturing and office workers side by side in what Foster called a 'democratic pavilion'. So, combining students, professors, the public and art within a single space was an easy, if not instant, decision for Foster.

The immediate concern was to establish the correct relationships between the different uses. Bob wanted his collection to be an intimate part of the university, but he didn't want it mixed up with non-teaching functions such as the Senior Common Room and the restaurant. The

BUILDING A NEW MUSEUM

Bob and Lisa Sainsbury decided to build their
museum at the University of East Anglia. The
striking campus, designed by Denys Lasdun
in 1962–8, consisted of a linked series of
buildings based on 45-degree diagonals. The
stepped forms in the foreground contain
student residences.

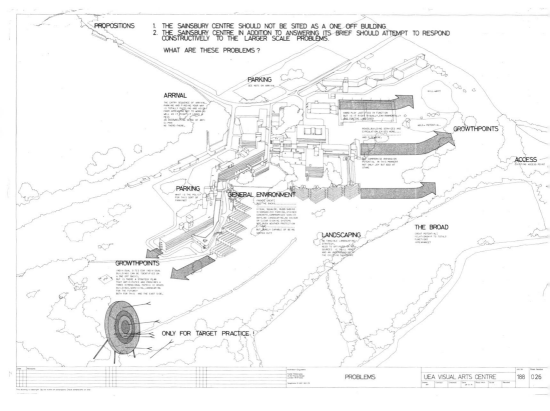

Adding on to Lasdun's assertive architecture (*opposite, top*) was a challenge for architect Norman Foster. An early drawing (*bottom*) shows the chief directions in which Lasdun's campus could be extended. Foster's team often annotated such preliminary studies 'Only for target practice'. On a visit to the University of East Anglia, Sir Robert and Lady Sainsbury and Foster are shown the possible sites for the new museum by Gordon Marshall, the university estate's officer. A rough sketch (*below*) indicates six of the potential sites for the Sainsbury Centre. Number 1 was the university's first choice, but Foster successfully argued that number 3 offered more advantages.

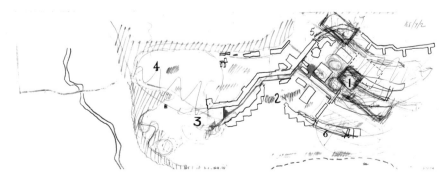

Client and architect engage in conversation on opening day, 7 April 1978 (*above*). The so-called 'Living Area' is animated by streaks of light coming from overhead skylights (*opposite, top; below*). The exhibition space is unlike a conventional museum, since the moveable panels and cases can be easily rearranged. The 'kit of parts' (*centre*) consists of bases and plinths for sculptures, glass cases and free-standing panels. The ceiling structure supports the louvres that control the natural light, and also carries the exhibition lighting; George Sexton focused more than a thousand fixtures in the weeks before the building opened.

The shimmering Sainsbury Centre has been compared to a streamlined express train; with its open ends, it reminded the architectural critic Reyner Banham of an airship hangar.

School of Fine Arts wanted its own identity, too. The alternatives piled up as the architects explored now one option, now another. By this time it was April 1975, seven months since Birkin Haward had produced the 'Problems' drawing. That had been Sheet No. 26; they were now up to No. 120. 'Norman had a great talent to get people to work hard,' says Haward. 'He might come in and announce that he had decided – overnight – that a six-storey building should be four storeys. But people were excited to work for him.' Haward remembers Foster as being heavily involved in every aspect of the design of the Sainsbury Centre. 'Norman was very hands-on and did many of the drawings. He had an amazingly fertile imagination and just churned them out.'

The architectural creative process unfolds in three different places: in the studio, on the building site, and during meetings with clients. Bob and Lisa took a particularly active role in the design process. According to Foster, they demanded explanations and asked a lot of awkward questions. 'Not because they were trying to be difficult, but because they took the project very seriously,' he says. They met regularly in the dining room at Smith Square, as often as once or twice a week. 'That was where all the important decisions were made,' Foster says. 'Lisa could read drawings, but Bob couldn't, so I often brought models. It was usually just the three of us, for this was not something I could delegate.' Bob once explained to Foster that when he had been responsible for setting up Sainsbury's pension fund he did a lot of research before making up his mind. This was also Foster's method; he would describe several alternative solutions before presenting his recommendation. He remembers one occasion when Lisa, who could be impatient, said, 'Oh Norman! Just tell us what you want.' Another time, when he proposed a plan that situated the restaurant near the main entrance, Lisa objected that the smells and noise would intrude on the museum experience. 'She took a sharp knife to it in the first sixty seconds,' Foster recalls, adding that she was absolutely right. 'You could not have built the Sainsbury Centre without both of them,' he says. 'It needed his artistry and her practicality, his ambition and her strength.'

Foster describes the Sainsburys as fast-moving; once they had made a decision, they expected everyone else to fall in behind it. This is not the way that universities work, however, which led to more than one contretemps. The situation was complicated by the fact that the building combined museum and university functions, yet there was a considerable discrepancy between the funding available to the university and the Sainsbury budget. 'Bob and Lisa could never understand this,' says Foster. A rift grew up between the Sainsburys and Gordon Marshall, a gruff Liverpudlian, whose demands they found frustrating. 'At one point it got so bad that they couldn't be in the same room together,' says Foster. 'Marshall could be heavy-handed, but he was key to getting the project done, and I had to find a way to work with him. He became an ally of the project and we ended up respecting each other.' Foster increasingly found himself cast in the role of intermediary between his clients and the university. He calls this 'being at the coal face'. 'A big part of my role on the project meant I had to go beyond being an architect,' he says. 'My daytime job was the design; my night-time job was keeping everyone happy. The architecture couldn't have occurred otherwise.'

By May 1975, Foster felt that the design was far enough advanced to be presented to the building sub-committee. At the meeting, Sir Robert described the evolution of the gallery area, and the close connection that had developed between the collection, the open reserve and the special exhibitions area. Foster explained the concept of housing all the functions under one roof, and presented two options, one in which the collection and the School of Fine Arts overlapped within the same space, and a second – his and Sir Robert's preference – in which they were separate. The sub-committee approved the second option.

Not everyone was happy with Foster's radical design. Andrew Martindale had reservations about the faculty offices. The School of Fine Arts' first home in the Village – a complex of temporary buildings that originally housed the university – had been spacious and sunny. Its present temporary home was a dreary and cramped basement, and the faculty had been hoping for an improvement. Martindale was disappointed with Foster's proposal to provide offices with no outside views. Bernard Feilden, who disagreed with the western location of the building, felt that a metal shed was unsympathetic to Lasdun's architecture and wouldn't fit well into the university. Although Foster had consulted Lasdun, the relationship of his design to the rest of the campus 'could most kindly be described as tangential', as a later observer put it.[10] Lasdun's architecture was fragmented, angular and concrete, while Foster's was streamlined, linear and metallic. Feilden advised the vice-chancellor that 'the layman will imagine that Norman's building is like a large agricultural building with its tubular shape'.[11] Nor did Feilden have confidence in the ability of a metal building to withstand the elements, and he thought that maintenance and operating costs would be high. He felt so strongly about this that he asked to have the Sainsbury Centre excluded from his responsibilities as university architect.

The Sainsbury Centre was assuming its final form: a 150-metre-long shed, functionally divided into slices. Moving from east to west, the first slice, with a view down to the lake, was the special exhibitions area. Since the land at this point was sloping, the floor stepped down from the rest of the building, the steps doubling as seating for lectures. Next was a glass-roofed conservatory, housing the entrance lobby and a café. The third slice was a large open space for the collection. The School of Fine Arts was planned around an open space containing the slide collection and a library. Beyond it was the university collection and a second conservatory containing another café. The west end of the building housed the restaurant, the kitchen and the Senior Common Room.

While the interior of the shed was being planned, Tony Hunt was designing the structure. Hunt, who had been apprenticed to the legendary British engineer Felix Samuely before starting his own firm, had collaborated with Foster since the Team Four days. He remembers the day that Foster called him when he was first approached by IBM in 1970. Foster wanted Hunt to attend the meeting, but he didn't want to receive the IBM representatives in Wendy's apartment, which still served as his office. Hunt had just leased a small office building in Covent Garden in London's West End. On one empty floor, they created a make-believe studio, painted the door acid green with a 'Foster Associates' sign, and borrowed some office furniture. The meeting took place, they got the job, and Foster Associates moved into the office for real. Foster and Hunt had a close working relationship: the engineer would participate in the design from the very beginning of a project, so that structure and architecture developed in tandem (this accounted in great part for the success of IBM Cosham, as well as Reliance Controls). Once Foster had fixed on the shed solution for the Sainsbury Centre, Hunt started working on the structure. To make the interior column-free, he used portal frames, in which the vertical and horizontal elements form a continuous arch. Hunt had used similar portal frames in the Modern Art Glass building, although the span at the Sainsbury Centre was three times larger so the frames were proportionately deeper. The proposed structure was approved by the building sub-committee, and Hunt proceeded to make the required calculations, work out the details and even get preliminary cost estimates.

Design, as Foster was fond of saying, is not a simple linear process. Function, structure and appearance have to be brought into balance, and this often means exploring dead ends, questioning one's initial assumptions, and changing direction, sometimes late in the day. As the building took shape, Foster grew dissatisfied with the interior. 'It was becoming clear our concept of an open shed was an illusion,' he says; 'there was too much stuff compromising the space.' The 'stuff' included toilets, cloakrooms, vestibules, storage rooms and darkrooms, as well as spaces for mechanical and electrical equipment. At the same time, the design team was wrestling with the question of whether the building skin should be on the inside or the outside of the portal frames. The obvious solution was to put the skin on the outside, making the building into a smooth tube, but since the steel portals were more than a metre deep they tended to overwhelm the interior. On the other hand, when the skin was inside the structure, the exposed frames gave the building a heavy industrial appearance. In September 1975, out of these two problems – where to put the services, and how to handle the structure and skin – emerged what Foster describes as a 'giant breakthrough': not one skin but two, one on the inside of the structure and one on the outside, far enough apart to create a space that could house ancillary service rooms and mechanical equipment. Put that way it sounds obvious, but it had taken more than twelve months of design work to arrive at this solution.

'At the next of our regular design team meetings with all the key individuals involved – architects, engineers and cost consultants – we unveiled the new proposals. As the full implications of the change became apparent, the mood of the meeting became very strained,' Foster recalled. 'Everybody accepted that it was an infinitely better scheme. But dare we put the completion date at risk and threaten the goodwill and confidence of the client by proposing such far-reaching changes at such a late stage?'[12] There were good and practical arguments for not changing course – the construction schedule was fixed, preliminary cost estimates had been solicited, planning permission was already secured, and such a radical redesign would eat up a further portion of the firm's fees. But Wendy Foster's argument that they could not proceed with a design that was second-best carried the day.

It was up to Foster to explain the radical change to Bob and Lisa. 'Their first reaction was one of anxiety: "Not again!" – how could we propose more changes just as everyone had grown accustomed to the scheme?' he later remembered.[13] This was a delicate moment, since it would have been perfectly reasonable for the Sainsburys, rattled by the last-minute change, to put their foot down and insist that their architect continue on the original approved course. After making his case, Foster asked them not to decide immediately. The three met again the following day and went through the ramifications once more in great detail.

Finally, Bob and Lisa agreed that Foster should pursue the new direction. This intense dialogue was the furthest thing possible from the client who simply approves whatever their architect suggests. 'I was later to describe them as the toughest clients that I had ever worked for,' Foster wrote of the Sainsburys, 'and I hasten to add that as an architect that was the highest compliment I could pay. Nothing came easily because everything was worked at hard. They made extraordinary efforts to research, to challenge and to support.'[14]

The member of the team most affected by the change was Hunt, who now had to redesign the structure from scratch. 'My office was rather unhappy,' he recalled.[15] His first thought was a space frame. Space frames are light-weight, rigid structures, consisting of triangulated interlocking struts and capable of very long spans. What makes space frames extremely efficient is their great depth, which would be perfect since the Fosters wanted a space 2.4 metres deep inside the thick wall. Hunt considered that the best space frames were manufactured by Triodetic, a Canadian company. 'But by now time was pressing,' he recalls, 'and we felt there was not enough time to go to Canada and talk to the experts.' Under pressure to find a solution, he developed a hybrid structure that resembled a space frame but consisted of deep prismatic lattice trusses made out of welded steel tubes, simply supported by prismatic columns. 'If it had been a portal frame, then the column–beam junction would have needed to be stiffened in some way, and the junction would have ended up rather clumsy, so we elected to make the columns cantilever up from the foundation and have the beams simply supported,' Hunt explains. This structurally 'impure' solution also had the advantage of extreme simplicity in fabrication and erection.

Meanwhile, the architects redesigned the building, moving the small service functions into the thick wall space. In the process three changes were made that further simplified the plan. The stepped section at the east end was eliminated, making the floor level throughout the entire building. Two mezzanines, one for the open reserve and the other for the Senior Common Room, were introduced, which shortened the building by 15 metres. Third, a basement was added to accommodate storage rooms and museum workshops. Lisa had long advocated a basement, but the architects had resisted – none of Foster's earlier projects had basements. 'This was another breakthrough,' says Foster. At first, the basement was along the north side, running the full length of the building and half the width, but when cost-cutting measures were put into effect it was reduced to a quarter of the width (a decision that was later to be regretted, however financially prudent at the time). The basement was connected at intervals to the main floor and the mezzanines by staircases and lifts, and by a hydraulically operated platform that lifted art works into the special exhibitions area. The problem of vehicular access for deliveries proved vexing. 'One day Norman came in with the idea of a long ramp, something he had just seen in Paddington Station,' recalls Haward. At first the ramp was on the north side of the building, but it was Wendy Foster's idea to move it to the west end, with the basement running down the centre of the building. This was an important decision, since it meant that the Sainsbury Centre no longer had a traditional service side, or, as Foster put it, 'We reject the notion that buildings cannot escape having "clean and dirty" sides.'[16]

One of the key functions of the double-skin wall was to accommodate heating and ventilating equipment. Integrating architecture and building services was an important part of Foster's design philosophy. Unlike most architectural firms, Foster Associates was an integrated practice, with environmental engineers alongside architects.[17] The key engineer was Loren Butt, who had worked for a services contractor on two Foster projects, and was invited by Foster to join the firm in 1970. 'I did some work on IBM Cosham,' he says, 'the truth is that the original services concept for that project was never right, but I came into the office too late to get it changed.' That was not an issue with the Sainsbury Centre, which was an early example of what has come to be known as integrated design.[18] According to Leonard R. Bachman, the author of *Integrated Buildings*, integrated design affects three aspects of a building: physical, visual and performance. 'Components have to share space, their arrangement has to be aesthetically resolved, and at some level, they have to work together or at least not defeat each other,' he writes.[19] The thick walls of the Sainsbury Centre are a good example of integrated design, since they look the way they do because of the structure, and they combine useful spaces with mechanical services. All the ducts and machinery are in the walls; heated air is supplied by forty fan-coil units, distributed throughout the building.

The decision that the Sainsbury Centre would not be air-conditioned was made early on. As Loren Butt has put it, 'Bob Sainsbury questioned the need for air-conditioning on the basis that the collection had been in his Georgian London house for many years, living with what one might call quixotic English central heating and manually opening windows – a small-scale version of what art collections in English country houses had been experiencing for centuries and not apparently in much worse condition for that.'[20] Butt points out that in houses that have poor heating and leaky sash windows, the damp British climate produces remarkably stable relative humidity – the holy grail of art conservation, after all. He once described:

> a strong feeling on the part of the benefactors, shared by Norman Foster, that art should be exhibited in a building which would encourage relaxed but active enjoyment, rather than be essentially a hermetically-sealed preservation vault. This led to the fundamental decision not to provide full air conditioning to the whole building, but to establish the concept of local conditioning of objects within showcases, where necessary or appropriate. The considerable area and height requirement of the exhibition spaces dove-tailed well with the absence of mechanical cooling, in that the natural

buoyancy of warm air in summer would be able to rise, and thereby alleviate discomfort at floor level. Air conditioning, apart from being unavoidably costly to install is also costly to operate: two years after the opening of the building, university financial cut-backs created a situation in which the university would have been forced to close the building if it had relied on the operation of a full air-conditioning system, because they could not have afforded it.[21]

Butt adds that the insulation performance of the Sainsbury Centre cladding far exceeded the standards of the day, an advantage that was influenced as much by the structural stiffness requirements of the panels as by their thermal performance. 'It was what we did all the time – making the most of everything we did,' he says.

In fact, the exterior skin of the Sainsbury Centre was its most unusual feature. Traditionally, buildings have walls and roofs made of different materials; Foster wanted to make them out of the same material. A Boeing 747 has a metal top, he used to say, why not a building? The Modern Art Glass building, like most warehouses, had been clad in continuous corrugated aluminium sheets that wrapped around the roof and walls, and, according to Ritchie, Foster was preoccupied with the idea of using a factory-produced panel system to build the entire walls and roof of a building – something that had never been done before. The cladding concept for the Sainsbury Centre consisted of a system of standardized and interchangeable panels – solid, glazed and louvred, curved (to turn the corner between the roof and the wall) as well as flat. The glazed panels could function as windows or skylights. The silver-coloured surfaces reflected the sun's rays and reduced heat gain, while the core of the panels was 10 centimetre-thick foam insulation. For stiffness, the panels were ribbed, which gave them the appearance of the sides of a Citroën van. The automobile metaphor was not accidental, but referred to the age-old architectural dream of using mass-production in building construction.

The panels fitted into a continuous grid of neoprene gaskets, which sealed the joints and also acted as gutters, leading rainwater to a collection trough at the base of the wall.* The gaskets were manufactured in long sections, but had to be welded and vulcanized on the site – that had never been done before, either. Since each panel was attached to the structure by only six machine screws, it could be easily and quickly replaced or changed. According to the architects, 'external entrances can be "popped out" and moved to new locations as required'.[22] While it is unclear that such extreme flexibility was required, in fact the panels' demountability did later turn out to be an advantage, though not quite in the way that was anticipated.†

The material of the panels was superplastic aluminium, which was heated and slowly stretched over moulds, using compressed-air presses, a process developed for the aircraft industry but never before used in building construction. The size of the panels, 1.8 by 1.2 metres, was the maximum possible at the time. 'People think we are always on the leading edge, using untried technology. It's not true. We are a belt and braces outfit but nobody believes it,' Foster later told an interviewer. 'On Sainsbury we had a plastic, recessed-gutter roof we could have used if quality control on the superplastic aluminium panels had turned out to be too much of a risk.'[23] The aluminium panels were developed in collaboration with TI Superform, a subsidiary of British Aluminium. 'Norman always said that buildings were made by manufacturers, not contractors,' recalls Loren Butt. In traditional building projects there is a single general contractor, who coordinates numerous subcontractors, who in turn deal with manufacturers. 'We developed a different way of working, where all the contracts were done individually with manufacturers and installers, each one doing only the things that they did really well,' says Butt. 'For example, one company might develop and manufacture a glazing system, while

---

* The idea of panels sitting in a neoprene grid had been conceived – though not implemented – in an early roof design for the Willis Faber & Dumas project.
† See Chapter 7.

another would install it. The general contractor was usually a local firm that acted as a manager, but didn't actually build anything. Since there was no single overall contract, it meant that we could fast-track the construction and modify the design to meet the cost. Thanks to this process, we developed a reputation for on-time and on-cost, which was important for a young firm.' This novel approach meant that the manufacturers and installers – who were, after all, the experts – were also legally responsible for their part of the work. In the case of the Sainsbury Centre, the general contractor built only the concrete basement, while various manufacturers and installers handled the rest.

At the beginning of November 1975, only two months after the switch to the thick wall scheme, Foster was ready to present the revised design to the building sub-committee, which approved the change. He also submitted an estimate of the construction cost. The building was the same size as originally planned, but inflation had driven up the cost to £3.3 million (as Foster had anticipated). Sir Robert was strict about costs. For example, he would not allow the architects to have a contingency allowance in the budget; '"If I give it to you, you will just spend it," he used to say.'[24] But in this case, he decided that he liked the new design and the endowment would simply cover the extra expense. The day before the meeting, David Sainsbury added 286,000 J. Sainsbury shares, worth £1.5 million, to the gift. Since almost £1 million pounds of interest had accrued to the original gift between the date it was set aside and the date it was transferred to the university, the total now stood at almost £5.5 million. In addition, the university was contributing more than £600,000 to the project, so that, even after the increase in building cost, there was £2.7 million left in the endowment.[25]

Cost estimating was the responsibility of John Walker, a quantity surveyor and a key figure on Foster's team, since he coordinated the contracts of the various manufacturers and installers, and kept a finger on the economic pulse of the project. Like Hunt, Walker, who worked with the Hanscomb Partnership, had collaborated with Foster since the

Team Four days. Another member of the team was Tony Pritchard, an industrial designer, who did much of the early research and development on the cladding panels. The landscape architect was Lanning Roper. An American who had settled in England after the Second World War, Roper was a garden journalist as well as a distinguished landscape designer, and was responsible for scores of gardens in Ireland, France, Italy and Britain (including the Sainsburys' garden at Bucklebury).[26]

The Foster in-house team included Loren Butt and Chubby Chhabra, another mechanical engineer, as well as architects Arthur Branthwaite and Richard Horden. The team leader was Roy Fleetwood, who had joined Foster Associates two years earlier. As an architecture student at the University of Liverpool, Fleetwood had spent summers on construction sites, and had become interested in that part of the building process. On the Willis Faber building he had worked closely with Bovis Construction's Mike Stafford, who was also the project manager for the Sainsbury Centre.

The design team was small, which was the usual practice in the Foster office. 'Norman had like-minded people who were able to work very closely with him to realize his vision,' says Fleetwood. 'At that time, compared with any other architect, from a technical innovation point of view Norman was really pushing back the boundaries. Remember that there were no computers, no fax machines, no mobile telephones, no Powerpoint. The way of working within this regime demanded tremendous discipline and rigour of thought. Putting together a report or a presentation, for example, required preparation and planning, not like today when everything can be done at the last minute.' According to Fleetwood, there was a very strong design ethos in the office. 'We sometimes had client lunches in the office, and Wendy prepared a manual for the staff that described in detail how food should be prepared and presented.' This sounds excessive, but it reflects the desire not only to control the process – a hallmark of the Foster firm – but also to raise the standards for even mundane activities. That is why Fleetwood remembers it as an 'elite office'.

Foster Associates at this time had grown to two dozen. Architectural offices often increase uncontrollably in size in response to new commissions, and can quickly become unwieldy – and unprofitable. Foster wanted to expand in an orderly fashion, and he asked Loren Butt to look into the matter. 'I was the only one in the office who knew how to work a calculating machine,' explains Butt. 'Balancing fees and salaries, I figured out that we needed to expand to fifty-five. Norman said that was ridiculous, and that the office would never exceed thirty-five, more than that and you lose control.' This echoed the view of Foster's teacher, Paul Rudolph, who once said that a good office must remain small, 'or its leader becomes nothing more than a critic of his draftsmen'.[27]

As work on the Sainsbury Centre intensified, one of the first new hires was David Nelson, who was put to work on interior planning. He was impressed by the close communications between the members of the team. 'Norman's habit was to come in for only part of the day. People would gather around, and he and Fleetwood and the senior associates would talk in a kind of shorthand. There was genuine discussion; Norman would listen to others' opinions. At the end, nothing appeared to have been decided, but everyone knew what to do. That was the advantage of shared values.' Walker, Hunt, Butt and Foster had worked together for years. 'We were similar in age; we were at a similar stage in our careers; and each of us had a greater than average interest in disciplines other than his own,' Walker later wrote.[28] That was the key to Foster's approach to teamwork: the ability not only to bring together different specialists, and keep them together, but also to attract exceptional individuals – engineers who were interested in architecture, and architects who were interested in engineering.

'The way that Norman set the office up was so different from any other office in the UK at that time,' says Fleetwood. 'We stressed the high priority that was placed on cost and programming disciplines as a framework within which to control quality and attempt innovation,' Foster wrote in an introduction to a special issue of *Architectural Design* magazine devoted to the firm's work. 'We were also aware of the broadening range of skills necessary to realise truly integrated design solutions and the vital importance of teamwork to that end.'[29] That sounds dry and technocratic, but the important word is 'innovation'. If Foster's aim had been merely quality control and efficiency, his firm would have been a smaller British equivalent of Skidmore, Owings & Merrill, the giant American firm that produced well-designed though rarely revolutionary commercial buildings. But Foster had set his sights higher, and he was intent not only on radically rethinking how buildings were built, but also on questioning the social relationships they contained, as the Sainsbury Centre was about to conclusively demonstrate.

Despite the last-minute redesign of the building, construction started on schedule at the end of 1975. That was only twenty months after the formal appointment of the architect, which was a short gestation period, given the complexity of the brief. The concrete floor slab and the basement were the most conventional parts of the building. Foster later calculated that the unit cost of the basement was about twice as much as the unit cost of the rest of the building, and although the basement represented only eight per cent of the volume of the building, it constituted eighty per cent of the building's weight. Once the concrete work was done, the steel went up quickly. 'I've always hated conventional building sites,' Hunt told an interviewer. 'Working on them is sheer misery, bloody depressing, but the building industry isn't geared up to making components to fine tolerances off site. I try to engineer buildings so that they can be pre-assembled and pieced together with the least possible fuss.'[30] The structural elements for the Sainsbury Centre were prefabricated in Warwickshire by a company with whom Hunt and Foster had previously worked. The seventy-four columns were delivered to the site completely assembled and painted, and were tilted up and bolted to the foundation; the trusses, which arrived in two sections, were hoisted into place, welded together, and pinned to the columns. Because of the light weight of the tubular-steel elements, large cranes were not required. It took only three weeks to erect the entire structure. Once the neoprene gaskets were laid down, installation of the aluminium panels began. To speed things up, Bovis enclosed the entire building in temporary plywood panels, so that indoor work could start; the plywood sections were gradually replaced as the permanent cladding was delivered. Inside the watertight enclosure, the installation of the mechanical systems and finishing of the interior began. The end walls of the shed were fully glazed. 'At first they were to be supported by metal mullions, designed as vertical trusses,' says Fleetwood. 'We worked with the manufacturer to develop an all-glass wall with structural silicon.' Twelve huge sheets of 2-centimetre-thick annealed glass, 7.5 metres high and 2.5 metres wide, and each weighing more than 450 kilos, were stiffened by glass ribs, which gave an impression of total transparency, especially from a distance. It was the largest self-supporting glass wall of this type ever built in Britain.

Loren Butt remembers Sir Robert visiting the building site when the structural frame first went up. 'Norman, what on earth have you done?!' Bob exclaimed. He had seen drawings and models, but like most non-architects he had a poor appreciation of building scale, and seeing the huge shed came as a shock. But he soon came round. 'Lisa is worried – more than I am – about the size, particularly the height, in relation to the objects to be displayed,' he later wrote to Haward, and added 'I know that Norman and the rest of you are quite happy on this score.'[31]

'Throughout the process, the design was intentionally overlapped with the construction,' says Foster. While the building of the enclosure continued, a second team – Birkin Haward, David Nelson and Tomm Nyhuus, a Norwegian architect and Foster associate – worked on the interiors. The collection and the special exhibitions area were open spaces with movable display panels and cases; the restaurant was likewise an open area; and, while the Senior Common Room had a partially enclosed bar and television room, the rest of the mezzanine was undivided (a snooker room was in the basement). The School of Fine Arts, on the other hand, was more complicated, and included a dozen faculty offices as well as a library for

90,000 slides and 180,000 photographs, a seminar room, a dark-room and administrative offices.

According to John Onians, an architectural historian in the school, 'When we heard of the Sainsbury gift, we thought the collection would be paintings in gilt frames, and that we would get a building with columns on the front.' They were quickly disabused of this notion. During their first meeting with the architect, Foster asked the faculty members how they imagined their offices. There was a consensus that the rooms should be spacious, perhaps with a view down to the lake, and that windows should be openable. One person said that ideally he would like to choose the flowers that grew outside his window. Foster, not an architect associated with flowerbeds, diplomatically answered that he didn't yet know what the building was going to look like, but that they should keep an open mind. Perhaps the school would be in a large open space, he said. Maybe offices would be moveable, like carriages in an underground railway, able to be relocated in different parts of the building. They might even be transparent spheres suspended over the collection. Foster's lateral thinking did not go down well. 'His ideas were off the wall, from the faculty's point of view,' says Onians. 'From then on it was one surprise after another.' Transparent spheres sound far-fetched, but Foster was serious about mobile offices; he and the design team had visited an aircraft maintenance hangar at Heathrow to examine the hover palettes that were used for moving heavy pieces of equipment. He later described the concept: 'a whole series of moveable study rooms, enclosures for individuals, which could be, as it were, completely mixed up with the gallery spaces'.[32] This idea was finally set aside, especially when it turned out that neither the faculty nor Sir Robert were keen to integrate the school with the collection.

The truth was that the fine arts faculty felt lukewarm towards the Sainsburys and their art. Like most British academics at that time, they had little experience of wealthy donors. The art history that they taught

– Romanesque, Gothic, Renaissance, Baroque – was very little represented in the collection, and they were not interested in tribal art. Alastair Grieve taught modern art, but his speciality was abstract art, quite different from the representational works of Moore, Bacon and Giacometti. Peter Lasko, the senior professor in the school, was more sympathetic to the idea of the Sainsbury Centre, and to modern architecture in general, but at the time of the initial consultations he was about to leave East Anglia to assume the directorship of the Courtauld Institute. Lasko's leadership role was taken over by another Courtauld art historian, Andrew Martindale. A distinguished scholar specializing in the art of the Middle Ages and Renaissance, Martindale was an accomplished harpsichordist, and an old-fashioned person of traditional tastes, active in the preservation of local historic buildings. Not someone who could be expected to warm to Foster's minimal modernism.

The design process for the School of Fine Arts began inauspiciously. The university emphasized seminar teaching, and the school required faculty offices large enough to accommodate eight persons around a conference table, with facilities for projecting slides. The government space allowance was 156 square feet, but the school requested 170 square feet, suggesting that a 'Sainsbury contribution' pay for the additional space.[33] This was a vain hope. The government's share of the construction cost of the academic spaces of the building – never generous – had not kept up with inflation, and the Sainsburys were already obliged to pick up the difference, about £500,000, which did not make Bob happy. 'With his accounting background he was very methodical,' remembers Foster. 'He kept track of costs on little index cards that he would keep in his pocket. Then months later, he would pull them out and confront you with what you had said earlier.' Thus, while Foster fulfilled the university's requirements, he was in no position to provide extras.

Foster's approach to office design was demonstrated by his Fitzroy Street studio.[34] There were no enclosed offices; instead the workspaces were laid out according to the concept of 'office landscape' or *Bürolandschaft,* an idea developed in Germany in the 1950s. The loft-like room was sub-divided by low, moveable screens, with everyone, from the newly hired junior to the boss, sitting in the same kind of chair, at the same kind of desk and drawing table, and working out in the open-plan space. Scattered conference tables provided places for impromptu meetings, and much of the furniture was on casters so that it could be wheeled from one area to another. The entire studio, which was at street level, was fully visible from the pavement through a floor-to-ceiling plate-glass wall. The effect was functional, coolly efficient, and chic in a futuristic way. Photographs call to mind the spaceship interiors of Stanley Kubrick's 1968 film *2001: A Space Odyssey*.

The fine arts faculty soundly rejected Foster's proposal for a similar open-plan arrangement. The reason was not so much practicality, accord-ing to one faculty member, but because 'they didn't like the feeling of working in typing pool'.[35] Besides, the confidentiality required for super-vision – and filing – would have made teaching in an open environment difficult. Foster's alternative was two rows of enclosed offices, beneath the mezzanines. In the end, each office was 160 square feet. The individual rooms were larger than the existing offices, but long and narrow, with low ceilings and no windows; instead the all-glass end-walls looked onto a common area that the architects called the School Court. The court had glazed walls at each end in response to Martindale's request for external views. The airy, top-lit space extended the full height of the building, and contained an open administrative work area and a students' study area. The central feature of the court was the slide library (replicating an arrangement in the school's original home in the Village), which was sur-rounded by low partitions for privacy.

Foster's approach to architecture has been described as 'extremely thorough, even cautious'.[36] He had a full-size mock-up of an individual office built, and invited the faculty to visit and comment on different fur-niture arrangements. In one option, the tables and desks were attached to the walls, but at the faculty's request they were made moveable. Foster showed them models and large-scale drawings of the School Court. His staff designed a special drawer system for the slide library, with built-in viewing stands.

In October 1976, Foster presented the final design for the school to the building sub-committee. After he finished explaining the plans, Andrew Martindale expressed his dissatisfaction with the layout, singling out the narrow offices and their lack of windows. He added that there was a basic difference of opinion between him and the architect about the entire concept. He clearly wanted the offices to be redesigned. Peter Yorke remembers Sir Robert's quiet response: 'Well, Andrew, if that's your view, I shall just withdraw the gift.' In the event, the sub-committee approved the final plan, while noting 'Prof. Martindale's reservations'. According to Yorke the episode was 'a display of naked power, used quite ruthlessly', but it was also an indication of Sir Robert's – and Foster's – frustration. It was late in the process to be bringing up such concerns, especially since windowless offices had been part of the design from the beginning, and Foster had been led to believe that the school was open to the concept. He reminded Bob that the meetings with the faculty in his office 'have an almost set pattern of enthusiastic response and open-mindedness, not-withstanding lively critical debate on most issues affecting the design of the School … In every case the group leaves this office in an apparent mood of enthusiastic approval.'[37] It was only later that objections were raised in the form of critical memos from the school's senior professor.

There was not much that the Foster team could do at that stage in any case, since the thick wall concept did not allow for perimeter offices with windows. The only parts of the building that had direct views to the outside were the special exhibitions area and the restaurant, which were at the two ends of the building, and the two conservatories, one of which already housed the School Court. Once the faculty opted for private offices, the die was cast – the rooms could not have outside views. It is unclear if this trade-off was clearly understood. The truth was that the faculty had not seen the Sainsbury collection and the new building as an opportunity to explore different ways of organizing itself. Instead, like most institutions, the school simply wanted an improved – that is, larger – version of the set-up it was accustomed to.

The brief had specified that since the faculty offices were used for teaching, 'the less "office-like" they look in architecture and furniture, the better.' But what did that mean? Bay windows? Wood-panelling? Wing chairs? The problem with Foster's approach, as far as the faculty were concerned, was that transparency, flexibility and adaptability to change, and his rather austere style, were precisely what they *didn't* want. 'It was an almost C. P. Snow-land academia,' Foster later observed.[38] It was also, in the end, a matter of taste.

FIVE

THE LIVING AREA

*Creating a setting for the Sainsbury collection. Light, lighting
and display.*

JOHN JAMES SAINSBURY WAS KNOWN FOR PROVIDING his customers with
not only good-quality produce at reasonable prices but also attractive
surroundings. He developed a 'house style' for his shops that included
decorative wall tiles, made especially by Minton Hollins, mosaic floors,
white marble counters, polished brass fixtures, mahogany screens and
bright lighting. The atmosphere combined prestige with hygienic spot-
lessness. Once he had perfected this scheme, he standardized the shop
layouts, always giving the interior precedence over the exterior. That was
how Robert Sainsbury saw the Sainsbury Centre: the interior came first.
'I think it's a marvellous building but it wasn't a building created and
then we had to put the objects in,' he said. Like Albert Barnes and Hélène
Kröller-Müller, Bob had definite ideas about how his collection should be
displayed, and he gave Foster very strict instructions. 'You had to be able
to walk round the objects, and the cases had to be so designed that if it
was a small object you could see it without it being propped up on three
things.'[1] This approach was innovative, even revolutionary, at a time when
most museums simply placed objects and cases against the wall. But Bob
and Lisa didn't want a conventional museum, and, while they knew better
than to try and recreate the domestic surroundings of Smith Square, they
wanted people to experience the collection in a casual and relaxed way,
and to have a sense of intimate engagement with the objects as individual
works of art, not as specimens or types. They requested the architects to
provide study tables for reference materials, and plenty of lounge chairs

so that people could sit and read a book.* According to Bob, 'It will be so arranged that any individual in the University, or group of people, can sit there either reading, working, or talking, be used for small seminars and, I hope, continuous slide displays.'[2] The students' experience of art as part of their everyday environment gave rise to the name 'the Living Area'.

Foster described the Living Area as 'an anti-monumental and informal area where you can read books, where you can relax, where you can look quietly at objects.'[3] An early sketch resembles a department store interior, but with easy chairs and coffee tables scattered among the display shelving, and paintings hanging on walls. However, after analysing the extremely varied collection, Foster reached a startling conclusion: 'The one thing you don't need in an art gallery are walls to hang paintings on because you are never going to know how much wall area you are going to need,' he said.[4] Instead, Birkin Haward and Tomm Nyhuus devised a system of hinged, moveable screens for displaying the drawings and paintings; the sculptures were on bases or plinths and in free-standing cases. They called it a 'kit of parts', the exhibition equivalent of the Herman Miller office system in the Fitzroy Street studio, whose design they had earlier overseen.

In the spring of 1976, Claude R. Engle, a lighting consultant based in Washington, DC, joined the team. In Europe, most architects got their lighting layouts directly from manufacturers when they bought the fixtures, but in America it was common practice among leading architects to engage an independent lighting consultant. The generally recognized pioneers in this field were Richard Kelly and Edison Price. Kelly, who had studied architecture at Yale, worked for many of the premier post-war architects, including Mies van der Rohe, Eero Saarinen, Philip Johnson and Louis Kahn. It was Kelly who designed the lighting – and Price who manufactured the fixtures – for Kahn's Kimbell Art Museum in Fort

---

* The idea of incorporating comfortable seating in an art gallery hardly sounds radical today, when many museums have copied the Sainsbury Centre's example; but at the time, gallery seating – if it was provided at all – generally consisted of hard benches with no backs.

Worth, Texas, widely considered an exemplary modern gallery in terms of lighting.

Foster, with his admiration for American ways of doing things, went to New York to approach Edison Price about working on the Sainsbury Centre. Price, a manufacturer not a consultant, recommended Claude Engle, with whom he had recently collaborated on I. M. Pei's East Building of the National Gallery in Washington, DC. Engle, a Princeton engineering graduate, belonged to the second generation of lighting consultants. One of his first clients had been Philip Johnson. 'When Johnson first telephoned me, he asked me a question out of the blue,' Engle recalls. '"I'm doing two buildings separated by a slot, with an atrium between them. How would you light the atrium?" I said that I would use mainly natural light, to make the transition between inside and outside. "Right answer," said Johnson, and invited me to work with him on Pennzoil Place in Houston.'

Lighting consultants do much more than merely pick light fixtures. 'I think of myself as the architect's consultant on all things involving light,' Engle says. He stresses that the important thing is to control the quantity and quality of the light entering the building, and to effectively manage the light within by providing reflective surfaces. He also points out that, while architects are fascinated by skylights, natural light always needs artificial light to enhance it. When Foster visited Engle's Georgetown office, he brought drawings of the Sainsbury Centre with him. 'What should light do here?' he asked the lighting designer. 'We talked a lot about museums and light,' says Engle. 'We both admired Soane's Dulwich Gallery, where light bounces from one surface to another.'

A month after meeting Foster, Engle went to London. 'The back wall of his studio on Fitzroy Street was a large whiteboard, on which you could draw in Magic Marker crayon. The architects made a full-scale drawing of the trusses, then the services guy would draw in his stuff, I would draw in my stuff, and so on. We went on for hours, developing the details right there on the wall,' he says. 'At six o'clock we would open a bottle of wine.' The trusses, 2.4 metres deep, presented an interesting opportunity. 'I figured that if you could walk along the bottom of the truss, you could adjust and service the lights without using ladders or scaffolding,' says Engle. 'We laid out the catwalks on the floor to see how far you could reach to actually adjust the spotlights.'

The roof of the Sainsbury Centre is pierced by four strips of glazed panels over the entire length of the Living Area. 'You don't need a lot of top-light area,' says Engle. 'What you need are reflective surfaces below to expand the light.' The reflective surfaces were two sets of louvres, orientated at right angles to each other to create the maximum scattering effect. The upper set, immediately below the skylights, was motorized – a technology adapted from greenhouses – and connected to light sensors that automatically adjusted the angle of the louvres to control the *quantity* of daylight entering the building. The lower set, attached to the bottom of the trusses, was fixed, and controlled the *quality* of the light by reflection. The metal slats of the louvres were perforated with tiny holes. 'The result was like a pin-hole camera,' says Engle. 'At a distance you could actually see the sky.' The same perforated slats, which resembled giant venetian blinds, were used on the walls, where they were also adjustable. Thus, both the quantity and quality of the natural light could be controlled. Foster called it 'tuning the building'.

When Engle arrived on the project, the design of the Living Area consisted of a relatively small number of screens and lots of seating and study tables. This arrangement, which reminded Engle of a library study hall, was radically different from a conventional gallery. 'The art work was placed within the seating groups at seated eye level to be viewed casually over a period of time.'[5] This layout changed as the design of the display area evolved to accommodate the growing collection. At the time of the original Sainsbury gift to the university, there were just over four hundred objects but, since Bob and Lisa had continued to acquire works, in the intervening two years the number had increased to over five hundred, including large works such as John Davies's *Bucket Man* (1974). By the time of the opening in 1978, the collection numbered almost six hundred works. A much denser arrangement was called for to accommodate the additional pieces, which meant that, while the seating areas remained, most of the Living Area consisted of screens and display cases – more like a conventional exhibition space. And this meant that more lights were required.

In early 1976, during a dinner at Smith Square, Foster and Engle discussed the lighting system with the Sainsburys. 'Bob and Lisa thought that seeing paintings in natural light without sun streaks was boring,' says Engle. 'We agreed that there should be some sunlight on the floor. Bob said that fragile objects could be hung facing north, or on the north side of the building.' Engle explained to the Sainsburys that only after the collection was in place could the exhibition lighting be installed and focused, a delicate operation that could take several months. Engle said that focusing was not his speciality, but that he had someone in mind to do it – a young American architect, who had once worked for him and was currently employed by the National Gallery of Art in Washington, DC, as an exhibition designer.

George Sexton, twenty-eight years old, had come to lighting more or less by accident. He was studying architecture at the Virginia Polytechnic Institute in the late 1960s, and since he couldn't find a summer job with an architect he took one in the newly formed office of a lighting consultant – Claude Engle. 'Claude became my mentor,' says Sexton. 'I found I really liked lighting, and I ended up working for him every summer, during Christmas holidays, and for two and a half years after I graduated.' During this period Sexton learned about design and hardware, and also about lighting exhibitions. It was while he was working on the East Building of the National Gallery that he met Gil Ravenel, an art historian who coordinated the design and installation of exhibitions at the gallery. Sexton started moonlighting, designing lighting and exhibits for Ravenel; when Ravenel was charged with creating a new department to handle the design and installation of special and permanent exhibits, George Sexton was the first person he invited to join him. Engle wanted Sexton to stay, but the young architect demurred. 'At that point I was not so interested in lighting,' he says, 'I wanted to design shows.'

Following meetings with Engle and Foster, Sexton was invited to come to England for an exploratory visit. When he arrived in Europe in late January 1977, his first stop was Paris and the Pompidou Centre. Engle was designing the lighting for that building, too, and he wanted Sexton to focus the exhibition lights. According to Sexton, two things are essential in museum lighting: 'having lights in the right position to be able to light the objects, and having the right equipment'. He wasn't satisfied with either at the Pompidou, but since the building was already finished, he didn't think he could have much effect, so he refused the assignment.[6]

Sexton's next stop was London. 'I arrived at Smith Square at nine o'clock in the morning, knocked on the front door, and after a long time it was finally opened by a flustered servant,' he recalls. 'It turned out that Sir Robert was stuck in the lift, and it was some time before he emerged.' Sexton was shown around the house. He was impressed both by the Sainsburys' collection, and by the way that it was displayed. 'I thought that Kho's work at Smith Square was very successful,' he says. 'Looking at art is an intimate conversation between the viewer and the object, and also between the objects themselves. The designer's job is to remove any obstacle to that experience. All the artifice in the method of display should be directed to putting the focus on the work of art.'

Sexton and the Sainsburys discussed how objects should be displayed, and discovered they shared a taste for simplicity – all three agreed that the design of the Pompidou Centre was too busy. Sexton spoke the language of art and museum display. It dawned on Bob and Lisa that in this voluble young man with shaggy hair and a George Harrison moustache they might have found a worthy successor to Kho. Before Sexton left, late that evening, Lisa asked him, 'What else might you do for us?' Sexton remembers that the idea of him helping with the design of the cases was raised at this first meeting.

When Sexton visited the Foster office, he was shown models and drawings of the building. The concept of servicing the exhibition lighting from above appealed to him. Sexton also met Haward and Nyhuus, who explained the general idea of the kit-of-parts display system. Before returning to Washington, Sexton travelled to Norwich. The building was under construction, and only a quarter of the structural frame was up, but it was enough to give him an impression of the space. He knew that lighting small objects from a tall ceiling so that they maintained their individuality would be a challenge, but it was something he had done before in the high rooms of the National Gallery.

The following month, Bob and Lisa flew to Washington, DC, to see Sexton's handiwork in the 'Treasures of Tutankhamun' exhibition in the National Gallery.* The visit confirmed their feeling that Sexton was the right person to install the collection. Bob and Thistlethwaite had earlier discussed the possibility of appointing an acting keeper (or acting director) of the Sainsbury Centre for a year or two, while the building was being put into operation.[7] Bob knew that in the long run the university wanted an academic as keeper, but he had always been wary of art historians – he used to say that they looked at photographs instead of the objects themselves – and he wanted someone more practical, especially in the early days. He proposed the acting keeper position to Sexton. Sexton, who was growing to like the Sainsburys, admired Foster's design and was interested in broadening his horizons. 'Bob was apologetic about the "acting" title,' says Sexton, 'but I didn't care – I considered myself an exhibition designer, not a museum director.' After the Sainsburys returned to London, Sexton received a formal communication from the University of East Anglia, inviting him to serve as acting keeper for eighteen months. He resigned his position at the National Gallery and left for Norwich in May.

Shortly after arriving in England, Sexton attended a meeting in the Foster studio to discuss the design of the display cases. Bob and Lisa were

---

* The Tutankhamun show, which originated in the British Museum in 1972 and travelled to the United States and Canada, is generally considered to be the first 'blockbuster' art exhibition.

there. Haward and Nyhuus presented the current design with the help of a full-size mock-up. 'Well, George, what about it?' asked Foster. Sexton, who thought that the case, which was on a sculptural pedestal, drew too much attention to itself, gave a scathing critique. 'George spent the next two minutes completely demolishing [the case design],' recalled Bob, who described the situation as 'one of the more embarrassing moments of one's life.' Foster – to his credit – reacted immediately. 'Right,' he said, 'we start again, get rid of them all.'[8]

So Haward and Nyhuus simplified the design of the display cases. In the new version the 60-centimetre-square base, made out of stove-enamelled mild steel, was surmounted by an all-Plexiglas case without a metal frame, following Sexton's dictum that 'the trick is to minimize the hardware'. Since the building would not be air-conditioned, Sexton worried that humidity might affect the art works, so the cases were made airtight; the micro-environment inside was controlled by silica gel, engineered to humidify or dehumidify the case, depending on its contents. Different plinth heights accommodated different-sized objects.

A photograph from that period shows five prototype cases (manufactured by a Swiss company) standing on a rectangular piece of carpeting inside the unfinished Sainsbury Centre. Norman Foster, accompanied by David Nelson, is presenting the cases to Bob and Lisa, who are sitting in low, chrome-and-leather lounge chairs. Building materials are stacked on the concrete floor. The unfinished walls, with mechanical equipment exposed, are visible in the background; the east end of the building is shrouded in scaffolding, in preparation for the installation of the glass wall. It is late afternoon, judging from the shadows cast by the sunlight streaming through the skylights (the louvres are not yet in place). Foster has positioned the prototype cases in what will be the Living Area. The lounge chairs that the Sainsburys are sitting in and an accompanying ottoman are furniture that Foster and Wendy have chosen.* The carpeting

---

* The choice of furniture led to the Fosters' visiting Finland to meet the designer Yrjö Kukkapuro and the manufacturer.

is a sample of the final fabric. It is all part of Foster's working method – examining many alternative solutions through sketches, drawings, models, mock-ups, prototypes and finally the real thing.

Once the design of the cases was finalized, it fell to George Sexton to organize their contents. He spent July and August of 1977, while Bob and Lisa were at their country house, working at Smith Square. He set up three different cases in one of the top-floor guest rooms; then he brought the objects up from Bob's bedroom and the study and decided what would go in which case. The larger pieces had their own cases, and smaller objects were placed in groups. In addition to the standard cases, there were also what Sexton calls 'specials' – wall-mounted shelf cases and larger cases for odd-shaped objects. There would be more than seventy cases in all.

Sexton came every morning from his flat in Chelsea and worked alone in the house. Occasionally, Bob and Lisa stopped by. 'I think they were curious,' he says. 'I talked to them a lot about the installation before I started, so I knew what they wanted. I usually showed Lisa the fabrics that would cover the floor of the case, since she had a very good eye for colour. There were a few instances when Bob didn't like the way objects were grouped, but he usually agreed after I explained the rationale to him.' Since some of the collection was at their country house, Sexton spent several weekends there, sketching and photographing objects. 'The Sainsburys were very generous to me,' he recalls. That summer, Bob had a cataract operation, and Sexton helped him to edit the text for the opening exhibition catalogue.

The Sainsbury Centre was nearing completion. Work proceeded smoothly, although the bridge and the spiral stair were briefly a cause for concern. A delicate footbridge connected the Sainsbury Centre to Lasdun's elevated walkway. The original idea had been for the bridge to terminate in a dog-leg, stepped ramp inside the building. Late in the day, it was determined that the lightweight wall trusses were not strong enough to support the ramp, and an alternative solution was devised: the bridge was carried through the wall to a supporting column with a spiral staircase wrapped around it. This was engineered by Tony Hunt, with the treads and risers welded to the column, forming a continuous folded spiral. Because of the precision required, the stair and column had to be prefabricated off site in one piece. This work took longer than expected and, by the time the stair was ready, the glazed end walls of the building were already in place. 'It looked as if there was no way to get the ten-foot diameter spiral stair into the building,' recalls Hunt. 'At the last minute, the stair fabricator figured out that it might be possible to thread the stair through the double doors of the restaurant entrance if the stair was rotated like a corkscrew. It worked in model form, and that was the way that the stair was brought into the building.'

The spiral stair was the source of another problem. The footbridge was supported eccentrically by the stair column and, a day after the building opened, one of the engineers noticed that when three or more people walked on the bridge odd vibrations occurred in the stair treads. Tests showed that the column needed stiffening. The column was reinforced by cutting slots in the treads and welding two half-tubes to the column, which required removing several roof panels and lowering the long half-tubes into the building using a very large crane. The Endowment Fund paid the cost of the modification, though Sir Robert experienced 'a feeling of very considerable irritation and upset every time I visit the place,' as he wrote Hunt.[9] 'Bob and Lisa were very prudent about spending money,' Foster recalls. 'They could be quite outspoken when something went wrong. It might be someone else's fault, but they would say to me, "We don't care about that. You brought this person into the project, it's your responsibility."'

Landscaping is one of the final phases of work in a building project. Lanning Roper belonged to the naturalist school of English gardening, and favoured ground cover and planted beds, which produced some friction between him and Foster, who like many modern architects preferred extremely simple landscaping. 'Generous areas of grass with fine tree groupings would constitute the best possible setting for the building,' he advised Roper.[10] Roper thought that the building would look too stark with only grass. 'There are people who are saying that the building looks like Sainsbury's warehouse,' he wrote in a letter to Roy Fleetwood. 'I must say that what is in mind for the exterior finish of the road and the approaches certainly is in character with that epithet. I don't mean this unkindly but I do want to bring the point home.'[11] Although Bob and Lisa (especially Lisa, who was an accomplished gardener) were sympathetic to Roper's views, Foster convinced them of his approach. Thus Roper's interventions at the Sainsbury Centre were untypically minimal. He had undergrowth in the existing stand of trees thinned out, planted new trees along the north side of the building and, most important, reshaped the meadow leading down to the completed lake – called The Broad – fitting the building comfortably into its surroundings.

On 3 January 1978, the contractor formally handed over the building to the university, two years after construction began, and four years, almost to the day, since Foster first presented himself at Smith Square. The interior was still incomplete, however: furniture and fittings had to be moved into the school area and Senior Common Room, fig trees placed in the conservatory and the School Court, and the lifts completed. Above all, the art had to be installed. The inauguration of the building was scheduled for the beginning of April, when the entire Sainsbury collection would be on display, occupying not only the Living Area but also the special exhibitions area. That left only three months to install the cases and panels, hang paintings, mount objects and focus the lighting.

The Foster workshop built a large-scale model of the building's interior, which was set up on the mezzanine overlooking the Living Area. The model, the size of a ping-pong table, included Plexiglas blocks representing cases, moveable screens, model furniture, even tiny human figures. Sexton started by laying out a preliminary plan, with the moveable screens defining rectangular 'rooms' that replicated the domestic arrangement at Smith Square. 'Norman and Birkin were horrified,' he recalls. 'They wanted a more unified design, with an angular flow of space throughout the entire area.' The screens were rearranged on the diagonal, carving the space up into overlapping areas. Initially, Bob wanted the objects mixed together, as they were in Smith Square, but he was finally convinced that some general organization was required. After form, size and colour were discarded as organizational devices, the objects were grouped according to major cultural regions (Egypt, the Cyclades, Oceania, Africa, Central and South America, and so on), with the nineteenth- and twentieth-century European art distributed throughout. The horizontal plane and the absence of route meant that no hierarchy or precedence was given to any group, European or non-European. Visually stimulating juxtapositions and dramatic inter-object sightlines were the principal aims of the display. Paintings and drawings were hung on the moveable screens; larger canvases were mounted on taller, free-standing panels that served as vertical accents in the space. The colour scheme was monochrome, recalling Kho's treatment of the interior of Smith Square: dark-grey plinths, white screens, dark-grey taller panels, a greyish custom-made carpet. As the cases and screens were delivered, the tiny cases on the model were translated into reality on the floor below. The collection arrived in several vans with a police escort and was moved to a storage area in the basement. Sexton's team, which consisted of a conservator, a mount-maker and two technicians, set up a workshop in the basement, where they fabricated the wire mounts that held or cradled the individual objects. When the mounts were ready, the objects were brought up and placed in the cases or hung on the panels.

Once individual art works started appearing on the floor of the Living Area, Sexton could begin to focus the lights. Engle had planned to use the same lighting system at the Sainsbury Centre as at the Pompidou, but Sexton was not satisfied with the fixture design, and together with Fleetwood he designed a new flexible lighting system, with fixtures that could be serviced from the rear. 'We had all the parts manufactured in

England, and we assembled them on site,' he says. Focusing lights is a crucial step in mounting an exhibition. 'Lighting should be integrated seamlessly into the environment. If you notice it, you've done something wrong.' Focusing is usually done at night, when the shadows are most pronounced. Staying behind in the empty building, Sexton would climb up to the catwalk and focus a dozen spotlights on the cases and screens nearly 8 metres below. Then he would climb down and judge the results. Small adjustments were usually required, and he would either climb back up and make them, or take notes and leave it until the next evening. He was the only one with lighting experience, so he worked alone. Since there were more than a thousand spotlights, the focusing took most of the final two months.

SIX

LIFE AND LUX

The building opens and the critics react.

THE SAINSBURY CENTRE WAS INAUGURATED OVER THREE DAYS, 6–8 April 1978. Sir Robert invited a thousand people to the opening – the entire London art world, it seemed to him – many of whom travelled to Norwich from Liverpool Street Station on a specially chartered train.[1] Peter Yorke remembers crowds of people on the platform when British Rail's new high-speed train arrived: 'They were not well-wishers but trainspotters, who would never again see an Inter-City 125 in Norwich.' This being the 1970s and a university event, there was, of course, a demonstration. During the last three years, the Conservative government had cut back on university funding, resulting in reduced student grants, higher fees, a freeze on faculty posts, and reductions in support staff. This was the climate in which the Sainsbury Centre – which, compared to Lasdun's drab concrete buildings, looked especially opulent – opened. The actress Vanessa Redgrave, a member of the Workers Revolutionary Party and committed Trotskyite, threatened to bring busloads of protesters to East Anglia, which caused the university to post round-the-clock security. No busloads appeared, but student members of the local Communist Party picketed the entrance to the Centre and distributed pamphlets attacking the university, the vice-chancellor, the Sainsburys ('the grocers') and their collection ('imperialist plunder').[2] Sir Robert good-naturedly accepted a copy of the pamphlet at the door, though George Sexton remembers that he and Lisa were upset by the incident. Yet nothing could dampen their spirits on that momentous occasion. Bob expressed his elation to Frank Thistlethwaite: 'If before any of this started, someone had told me that I would one day – as I did on Saturday evening – stand in a building containing our collection and be completely happy in all respects, I would have said it was not on – this semi-miracle has in fact happened and I really could not be myself more thrilled.'[3] According to Steven Hooper, Bob had on more than one occasion told him that he considered architecture the greatest of the arts. 'Although he loved painting and music, sculpture was Bob's great passion, and great architecture was for him the greatest sculpture. In working on the Centre, he could genuinely be a creative partner with the architect,' observes Hooper. 'This was a gift that Norman probably didn't realise he was making at the time, but there can be no doubt that it enormously enriched Bob's life.'

The Marxist pamphlet denounced the Sainsbury Centre as a 'monument to the bourgeoisie' and a 'costly white elephant', which was inaccurate on all counts. Foster's hard-nosed minimalism was anything but bourgeois, and the building was not monumental – as *The Burlington Magazine* observed, 'The Centre is mercifully without pretension, either of style or scale.'[4] Nor was this a particularly expensive museum. The total cost, including fees, fittings and furniture, had crept up to £4.2 million.[5] This was more than the projected budget, yet Foster had managed to keep the construction cost remarkably low: £375 per square metre compared favourably with the £650 per square metre then being spent on the Burrell Gallery in Glasgow, and the more than £800 per square metre that the French government had lavished on the Pompidou Centre, which had opened the previous year.[6]

Once inside, the guests found themselves in another world. Whether one entered through the ground-level doors, or by the upper-level bridge, one was immediately thrust into a vast, dramatic space. 'The interior, silvery-grey like the outside, is restful and light in feeling,' observed one visitor. 'It is a setting for works of art that communicates that particularly modern kind of exhilaration one feels in the presence of a piece of graceful yet expert precision engineering.'[7] The distinguished landscape architect Geoffrey Jellicoe was one of the guests. Like many of the visitors, he did not know what to expect. 'I had had doubts about the building when seen in photographs, but on entering I was quite overwhelmed,' he wrote to Bob and Lisa. '[Foster] has taken an ordinary box and by proportion only lifted it into the sublime.'[8] The art critic and historian Edward Lucie-Smith thought that the building 'will force a lot of very necessary new thinking about the nature and function of the museum. I thought the collection looked wonderful *in* the building, and I was more than ever struck by the fact that it seemed to be totally personal, a joint self-portrait.'[9] Novelist Malcolm Bradbury, who led the renowned East Anglia creative writing programme, found the building 'an admirable contrast to Lasdun, who has always seemed to me a bit too massive, and so was apt to confine internal space. Forster [*sic*] has opened it up, and this gives a wonderful sense of expansiveness, of having enfolded a variety of different functions in an always vigorous space, so that everything interfuses with and illuminates everything else, and the user expands to the spaciousness he has provided.'[10]

The professional critics were more guarded. Charles McKean, writing in *The Times*, recognized the advantages of flexibility and openness but seemed uncomfortable with Foster's spare approach. 'There must surely be more to architecture than the efficient enclosing of usable space,' he wrote.[11] The American journal *Progressive Architecture* was likewise ambivalent. The reviewer praised the technical attributes of the building – the light structure, the sense of weightlessness and transparency, the precisely prefabricated parts – but concluded that 'because the building as the Modernist response par excellence comes at a time of serious questioning of architectural values and attitudes, the Sainsbury Centre has to be measured not only on its own Modernist terms but also against a background of emerging expectations about architecture's role'.[12] 'Emerging expectations' was a veiled reference to what was starting to be called 'postmodernism', exemplified by architects such as Robert Venturi, James Stirling and Aldo Rossi. Measured against their concerns with history, symbolism and context, the unbridled technological optimism of the Sainsbury Centre seemed, at least to *Progressive Architecture*, out of step.

The British magazine *Architectural Design* devoted a special issue to the Sainsbury Centre – a rare honour. The editor, Monica Pidgeon, who regularly published Foster's work, invited a variety of architects to comment. 'It is good to see an English architect muscle-flexing and producing work that is tough, obsessive and wilful, amongst so much that is reasonable, sensitive and contextually proper,' wrote Ron Herron, one of the founders of the 1960s architectural group Archigram.[13] Derek Walker, the chief architect of the new town of Milton Keynes, was likewise fulsome in his praise: 'The building is surely East Anglia's Parthenon and the most completely elegant component building ever produced in this country.'[14] 'Let us not be mealy-mouthed,' wrote Foster's old partner Richard Rogers. 'By dint of sweat, imagination and superb control Norman Foster, during the past five years, has produced two great buildings [the Willis Faber building and the Sainsbury Centre] which stand proudly and lonely amongst the mediocrity that surrounds us.'[15] Even Philip Dowson, who might have been excused a degree of sour grapes, allowed that 'The uncompromising nature of the solution, rigorously worked through, itself reflects a will and conviction on the part of both client and architect that we've come to associate with a different age.'[16] Speaking to an audience in London, Philip Johnson, who had been one of Foster's studio critics at Yale, singled him out for praise: 'There isn't anyone in America who could do something as good as the Sainsbury Centre. England has at once become the leader in the engineering and technology game.'*[17] Architects focused on Foster's technical skill, but art historian Peter Lasko, by now at the Courtauld, applauded the Sainsbury Centre's function as a gallery. 'The aesthetic of the building is in tune with the collection, not in scale but in kind: an aesthetic stripped to essentials, with concern for texture and surface, simplicity and purity.'[18]

---

* But Johnson also waspishly called Foster 'the last modern architect.'

Architectural criticism in Britain is a blood sport, and the *Architectural Design* issue included many opposing views. Léon Krier, a vocal proponent of traditional architecture, considered an industrial shed to be an inappropriate setting for art. 'Foster is forcing us to eat soup with a fork, and with a very well-designed fork at that,' he observed.[19] The architectural historian Robin Middleton deplored the lack of connection to the rest of the university, felt that the art objects were lost in the vast space, and criticized what he considered a simplistic design solution. The architectural critic Charles Jencks, author of *The Language of Post-Modern Architecture* (1977), described the style of the building as 'Late Modern' and referred archly to technological 'hocus-pocus', whatever that meant.[20] Doug Clelland, an architect and author, was derisive, finding nothing of value in either the collection – 'does not rate placement in the first or second divisions in terms of either size, range or excellence of types' – or the building, whose technical accomplishments he characterized as 'fetishist expressionism'.[21]

A more balanced reaction to the building came from Sir Hugh Casson, who in a small way had contributed to its existence. He visited the Sainsbury Centre two years after the inauguration, on the occasion of the opening of an exhibition of medieval sculptures. He had not seen the building before, and found it 'smaller and greyer than expected, not a glittering monster, just a quiet silver shed. Once inside the light takes over, clear as water. Humming machines, grey floor, white walls, silver slatted ceiling. Two end windows frame and command the view.' Like many others, Casson was impressed by how well the small and precious objects of the collection looked in the building; 'the space is vast, but it doesn't bully'. He was an even-handed critic: 'Does it matter that [the architecture] is already dated, that its objectivity is mythical and that the arrangement of uses is not as flexible as it appears? (No.) Does it matter that the residents work permanently by artificial light? (It would to me.) Is it unfair to say that any space that can be comprehended in a single glance ceases, after repeated visits to amaze? (Yes. Look at the Pantheon in Rome or King's College Chapel, Cambridge.)' His chief misgiving concerned the future. 'All buildings decay from the day they are finished,' he noted in his diary. 'The streak of rust, the jammed louvre, the bashed-in skirting – endurable in a conventional building – are unendurable in a structure where precision and immaculacy are all.'[22] A wise observer, he had put his finger on the single frailty of the Sainsbury Centre – its apparent perfection.

Norman Foster had no illusions about perfection. 'There are a few things that you can guarantee about a building – what you can guarantee is that it won't be perfect,' he candidly admitted during a public lecture delivered at the University of East Anglia shortly before the Sainsbury Centre opened. 'The reasons why it's not perfect, and why no building could ever be perfect, are the people who use them, who design them, who build them are not perfect, and so it follows that it will be imperfect.'[23] It did not take long for complaints about imperfections at the Sainsbury Centre to surface. A week before the official opening, the *Sunday Times* published a three-page spread in its colour supplement titled 'The Sainsbury Collection: Private Taste Made Public.' After praising the 'serenity, soft light and quiet' of the Living Area, the article described a less than happy fine arts faculty. 'Many are already complaining that it won't work. The building cannot be blacked-out, so how can they show the slides to fine arts students? It is so sound-absorbent that they won't be able to have lectures without sound amplification; and students are also uneasy about the level of noise and lack of privacy because of the open-plan layout. Eleven of the 12 faculty members dislike their studies, feeling they are stereotyped and claustrophobic.'[24]

'The twelfth person was me,' says John Onians, now an emeritus professor. 'I think it's a great building, not least because it exerts a powerful positive influence on those who work in it, encouraging them to raise their game in creative ways.' Another faculty member, Jane Beckett, found the building to be an 'unlikely but marvellously stylish juxtaposition of coffee bar, galleries, common room, restaurant and School of Fine Arts [that] makes up for the limitations of stuffy faculty teaching rooms, the noise from batteries of fans, typewriters and television, the curious siting of locks at floor-level, and the overheated atmosphere.'[25] The 'noise' came from an air-supply system that had been engineered to provide a masking sound level throughout the building, especially in the Senior Common Room; the typewriters were in the open secretarial area of the School Court; the television set was in the SCR, which overlooked the court. The 'locks at floor-level' were on the faculty office doors, a not uncommon arrangement in all-glass store fronts, but one that made it necessary for the tutors to go down on their knees to lock and unlock their offices.

Some of the school's complaints were valid. The interiors of the studies were silver-grey, although in the mock-up that the faculty had been shown they were white; it is unclear when and why the colour changed, but the result makes a somewhat dull effect. And kneeling down to unlock one's office *is* undignified. But other irritations were the result of normal teething problems. 'I've been the client and I've been the designer, and there is usually a clash of cultures between the two,' says Sexton. 'Most clients have unrealistic expectations, and are usually unhappy when they first move in to a new building. It takes at least six weeks for them to settle in.' It took longer than that for the faculty to come to terms with their new quarters. Many months after the building opened, some were still complaining about their offices, and about 'the indignity of such permanent public scrutiny' from people on the mezzanines.[26] The University Health Service was enlisted to write a report on the psychological burden of the lack of privacy, and the potential health problems associated with floor-level locks. It all got rather overheated – an academic tempest in a teapot. At one extreme point, the school even proposed that the university take legal action against Foster for 'fundamental negligence for which he alone is responsible'.[27] No action was taken.

'We were of two minds about the building,' says Stefan Muthesius, an architectural historian and long-time faculty member. 'It was a wonderful building, but we didn't like our offices, which were stuffy and hot in the summer. Soundproofing was a problem, and we had no lecture room.' Sound insulation was eventually increased between the offices, but the lack of a lecture room remained a sore point. That was unfair to the architect; no lecture room had been included in the brief that had been given to Foster, since lecture rooms in the university were part of a common pool. The problem was that the lecture rooms were at the other end of the campus. An improvised classroom, with sixty folding chairs, was set up on one of the mezzanines, but viewing slides in the bright light proved awkward. Foster converted a section of the Living Area into an open classroom, and installed a back-projection unit inside the service wall. 'It was like lecturing on a street corner, since people were also in the gallery,' says John Mitchell, a faculty member. 'It fazed visiting lecturers, although I rather liked it.' Since the masking sound of the air supply also masked the speaker, it was necessary to install an amplified sound system, which intruded on the peacefulness of the gallery. After a year, this unpopular solution was abandoned and an enclosed lecture room was created under the first mezzanine. But the acoustics were poor and eventually the lecture room found a permanent and satisfactory home in the basement, in a large space originally occupied by the SCR's snooker room.

The causes of the complaints about stuffiness and overheating are difficult to pinpoint. After a two-hour seminar, a small space with twelve people and a slide projector throwing off heat will feel stuffy, especially if people are smoking cigarettes, as they may have done in the 1970s. According to Loren Butt, 'The internal environment provisions were simple but adequate, essentially in line with project objectives, standards and cost.' But he adds that, when he has been called to investigate complaints on other projects, he has often found that equipment was not fully understood, or properly operated and maintained. The air-handling system in the Sainsbury Centre, for example, consisted of individual units distributed throughout the building, rather than a single plant. According to Peter Yorke, after the building was put into operation, the university engineers turned off many of the units, considering them redundant. That would have affected the internal environment. Stuffiness became a critical issue during one particularly hot summer, when the catering and security staff walked out, protesting about high temperatures in the building, especially in the kitchen.[28] The air supply nozzles were readjusted to send fresh air further into the building, and mechanical ventilation was improved in the kitchen.

In time, people adjusted to their new home – as people generally do. The maintenance staff learned how to vary the adjustable louvres to greater effect, although on exceptionally warm summer days the building still heated up. 'When I first visited the Centre with Bob and Lisa in June 1982,' recalls Steven Hooper. 'I remember standing on the mezzanine, with sweat pouring down Lisa's brow, but nothing being said about the heat problems in the building.' When the *Architects' Journal* critic Martin Pawley saw the building two years later, he concluded that the decision not to install air-conditioning accounted for the building's most severe operational weaknesses, although he noted that the thick wall concept meant that air-conditioning could be introduced at any time in the future without changing the building's appearance.[29]

These start-up problems did not prevent the Sainsbury Centre from being widely acclaimed. The building was showered with honours: the Structural Steel Finniston Award, the Royal Institute of British Architects Award, a British Tourist Board Award, the Ambrose Congreve Award, the Sixth International Brussels Prize for Architecture, and the American Institute of Architects' premier building design prize, the prestigious R. S. Reynolds Memorial Award, which the year before had been won by Philip Johnson's Pennzoil Place.* The architecture prizes recognized outstanding

---

* Foster was the first architect to win the Reynolds Award twice – the first time for the Willis Faber building.

design, but Bob and his architect must have been particularly satisfied when, in 1980, the Sainsbury Centre was named Museum of the Year.

Shortly before the building opened, Alan Borg, an art historian and medievalist, was appointed keeper of the Sainsbury Centre. Borg, who had been assistant keeper in the Royal Armouries of the Tower of London, was interested in attracting first-rank visiting shows to the Centre, and he pointed out that the special exhibitions area would need to be modified to meet the stringent lighting standards demanded by most lenders. The effect of environmental conditions on works of art in museums had been scientifically studied only since 1950. Garry Thomson, a chemist and conservator at the National Gallery in London, was a pioneer in this field, and his influential handbook, *The Museum Environment*, was published the same year that the Sainsbury Centre opened. Thomson argued that excessive humidity, dust, pollutant gases, and especially natural light, could degrade art objects. The lighting levels he recommended – 250 lux for paintings, and 50 lux for works on paper – were drastically lower than anything found in traditional museums. Not everyone agreed with his recommendations. 'Those were different times when it came to lighting levels,' says Claude Engle about the new standards. 'At the National Gallery [in Washington, DC], Paul Mellon had his own conservator, who was much less categorical. And at the Pompidou Centre, the French were not much concerned with excess light. "Pictures need natural light," they used to tell me.'

In September 1978, *Building Design*, a leading industry weekly, published an article with the headline 'Too much daylight at Sainsbury Centre could damage exhibits'. The newspaper quoted a senior lecturer at North East London Polytechnic, Dr Nick Baker, who claimed to have recorded light levels in the building of 450–700 lux. 'The values of lighting are totally at variance with accepted standards,' he told *Building Design*. 'I doubt very much whether this design can provide adequate light control

– the simple Venetian blinds are just not good enough.'[30] What made the public airing of this issue a particular embarrassment to the university was that Baker had been invited to evaluate the lighting by one of Borg's assistants.

Foster and Engle were aware of the daylighting issue, which is why the louvres in the wall and ceiling were adjustable, but on the whole they came down on the side of the debate that favoured more rather than less daylight. Early photographs of the building's interior show streaks of sunlight enlivening the walls and floor. As Foster reminded Sir Robert, 'The pros and cons were discussed in depth at the design stage and a conscious decision was taken not to duplicate the standard, highly-serviced, hermetically sealed, darkened gallery box.'[31] To achieve the quality of light that visitors to the Centre universally admired, Foster and Engle had resisted using tinted glass, although Loren Butt, for one, thinks that the glass on the east wall could have been tinted. 'A dark green tint preserves the colour balance of the light,' he says, 'even though it makes the glass almost dark.' However, Butt was sceptical of 'the scientists or quasi-scientists who give conservation questions blinkered numerical solutions', and he reasonably pointed out that most paintings and sculptures were created in strong natural light, so if they were presented in reduced lighting conditions they would not appear as the artist intended.[32]

A number of remedies were considered, including adding black-out roller blinds on the east wall, reducing the number of skylights, and using a temporary enclosure within the special exhibitions area.[33] Finally, less drastic measures were implemented. Louvres were added to the curved section of the roof, where sunlight occasionally entered; the light sensors activating the automatic louvres on the roof were recalibrated to lower levels; the wall louvres were kept in a closed position; and the window blinds at the east end were permanently lowered (much to Foster's chagrin for this blanked out the magnificent view of The Broad). These measures did not reduce lighting levels to the minimal 50 lux but, as Lisa sensibly pointed out, not all exhibits required extremely low light levels.

The inaugural special exhibition featured the graphic material, furniture and films of the American designers Charles and Ray Eames, and during the Centre's first decade special exhibitions included medieval sculptures, posters, photographs, ceramics, and Chinese bronzes, all of which could tolerate a higher level of daylight.

One of the exhibitions mounted by Borg was 'Treasures from the Tower of London', featuring arms and armour, which proved immensely popular. 'I remember that the Sainsburys were appalled by the Tower show,' says Onians, who served on the Centre's board. 'There were too many people! Sir Robert explained that great art was extremely difficult, so if too many people came, it must mean that the exhibit was too easy.' Onians also recalls that Sir Robert expressed the opinion that the collection should be less a tool for teaching art history than a way to develop students' sensibilities. Bob wanted the gallery to open early in the morning, before the general public was admitted, to allow students to actually handle the objects. The curators vetoed that idea. 'The Sainsburys were individuals who had strokes of genius,' explains Onians, 'assembling the collection the way they did, giving it to the university, building a huge steel shed in the middle of a field. They formed their collection in a personal, eccentric fashion, and they went on doing things that way. It was all part of their powerful inner drive.'

When Sir Hugh Casson attended the opening of the 'Medieval Sculpture from Norwich Cathedral' exhibition in spring 1980, he observed Bob and Lisa Sainsbury 'blissfully hugging the place to their hearts'.[34] The couple retained a close personal connection with the management of the Centre, participating in board meetings, regularly attending openings, and suggesting subjects for special exhibitions. At one point, Bob proposed to Thistlethwaite that he and Lisa build themselves a house – to be designed by Foster – on the campus. They even bought some Amish quilts to decorate its anticipated white walls. The house would be their personal gift to the university. Here the vice-chancellor drew the line, pointing out that locating a personal residence within the university grounds was problematic in the light of recent student disturbances (the vice-chancellor's own official residence, Wood Hall, was some distance from the university). Despite Thistlethwaite's claim that 'to have you as our neighbours would be temptingly attractive', one senses that he was uneasily starting to realize the perils of having such energetic donors so close at hand.[35]

'It was not long after the initial Gift when we first realized that the ways of Universities – at any rate of UEA – are indeed strange,' Bob wrote to his friend the vice-chancellor, 'with a standard of behaviour all their own – a standard requiring much tolerance to be acceptable.'[36] Bob was used to the hierarchic structure of the corporate world, but within the university, dealing with administration, faculty, staff and students, it was often difficult to know who was in charge. Conversely, Bob's rapid decision-making often struck academics as high-handed and imperious. After the building opened, a number of incidents further strained the relationship between the Sainsburys and the university. Bob felt that he had been intentionally misled when the university hired Alan Borg, who was a Courtauld art historian of medieval arms and armour, and did not share the Sainsburys' taste in art, nor their interest in the strengths of the collection – the modern and the tribal.[37] Another irritant was that none other than Gordon Marshall had assumed the position of general administrator of the Sainsbury Centre, and in Bob's estimation he was not following their agreement as to how the building should be managed and maintained. Bob was particularly upset by Marshall's attitude towards George Sexton; at one point, Marshall told his staff that there was nothing particularly difficult about lighting since he (Marshall) had experience, having participated in amateur theatricals in Norwich.[38] There was also the affair of the catering pamphlet. In an attempt to generate income, Marshall produced a pamphlet promoting the catering facilities of the Centre. Bob discovered a stack of the pamphlets on the information desk during one of his regular visits. 'The first impression on anyone opening the pamphlet is that the Sainsbury Centre for Visual Arts is primarily a restaurant,' he complained. 'I did the only thing open to me. I collected them and threw them in the waste paper basket.'[39] Matters were made worse when the university, without consulting the Sainsburys, produced a series of postcards of works from the collection with garish coloured backgrounds that destroyed the subtlety of the objects depicted. According to Sexton, such incidents also strained relations between Bob and Lisa, for at times she wanted to withdraw from the project altogether, while he – despite his complaints – was more circumspect.

Eventually, Bob and Lisa took themselves out of active involvement with the everyday management of the Centre, although they continued to oversee the acquisition of objects for the collection.* The greater amount of space in the Living Area, compared to Smith Square, allowed them to acquire larger works, such as the sculptures of John Davies – another in the long line of their protégés – and they were also able to indulge special interests, such as Lisa's passion for contemporary ceramics. Thanks to the friendship with Frank Thistlethwaite, who in 1980 was completing the final year of his term as vice-chancellor, their connection to the university remained strong, a stability that would soon prove to be of paramount importance.

---

* By the time that the collection was 'closed', there were 1,200 objects, three times as many as at the time of the original gift.

FOSTER'S FORTUNE

The evolution of lightweight modernism. American influences and the British engineering tradition.

ONE OF THE MOST PERCEPTIVE CRITIQUES OF THE SAINSBURY CENTRE appeared in the journal *Architectural Review*. The author, Peter Cook, a founding member of the Archigram group, found much to admire in the Sainsbury Centre. 'It has panache,' he wrote. 'It has that special Foster quality that is so rare – even uncharacteristic in English architecture – which is strength of will.' Cook was unconcerned about Foster's 'cavalier lack of contextualism', and judged the Sainsbury Centre a successful attack on 'tweedy provincialism and technical mediocrity', an implicit criticism of the state of British architecture. Cook liked the idea of an all-purpose shed. 'A strong object can take the addition of crap, high jinks, or inconsequentiality on the inside, without the destruction of the idea or the atmosphere,' he wrote. But he didn't consider the Sainsbury Centre a complete success, judging it a little too self-conscious about displaying its technical prowess, too carefully composed, too anxious to impress. 'The Foster Ultimate will happen elsewhere,' he wrote. 'And when [that has been] built, the Sainsbury Centre will have its correct position in history as the building that did the spadework, that made its last obsequities to the English picturesque tradition, and introduced us to the idea, if not the reality, of the shimmering tube.'[1]

In the same year that the Sainsbury Centre opened, Norman Foster was on a list of architects being considered to design the new headquarters of the insurance giant Lloyd's of London. That commission went to Richard Rogers, still basking in the international acclaim accorded to the Pompidou Centre, but Foster's presentation impressed Lloyd's architectural adviser, Gordon Graham, president of the Royal Institute of British Architects. Graham admired Foster's work and considered the Sainsbury Centre to be 'one of the three most outstanding buildings created this century.'[2] When the Hongkong and Shanghai Banking Corporation was planning a high-rise headquarters in Hong Kong and asked Graham to serve as its architectural adviser, he recommended that Foster be considered for the commission. Among the seven names on the shortlist were Skidmore, Owings & Merrill, the world's leading designer of high-rise office buildings; Hugh Stubbins and Associates, another American firm that had just completed a major bank building, the well-regarded Citicorp Center in New York; Harry Seidler and Associates, the top Australian firm, recently responsible for a sixty-seven-storey office tower in Sydney; and the venerable Hong Kong firm of Palmer and Turner, the bank's architect since 1886. As the youngest firm on the list, Foster Associates faced long odds: it had never built outside England, never designed a bank, and never built anything taller than four storeys. Foster's team made up for its lack of experience by hard work. They studied the bank's operations, interviewed its employees, and analysed its requirements; of the seventy-odd questions formally submitted during the selection process, fifty came from Foster Associates. The bank was so impressed with Foster's energy, the quality of his team, the depth of his research, and the clarity of his sketch design that it chose him after only two days of deliberation – there were no other finalists. According to Graham, 'Foster's submission was in a league of its own.'[3]

Foster's design was unveiled in January 1981. Ever since the late 1940s and 1950s, when Mies van der Rohe had invented the modern skyscraper with the Lake Shore Drive Apartments in Chicago, architects around the world had been content to follow the American model of a steel or concrete frame supporting a standardized floor-plate, with a central elevator core, and the exterior wrapped in a steel and glass curtain wall. With the Hongkong Bank, Foster showed how an office tower could be designed differently. To maximize flexibility, he located all the functions normally found in the central core (elevators, stairs, washrooms, mechanical rooms, air-handling ducts) on two sides of the building. The floors of the forty-three-storey tower hung like the decks of a suspension bridge from a series of huge trusses, dramatically exposed on the exterior. Suspending floors from overhead trusses is hardly the simplest way to construct an office building, but it produced unusually open floors. High-speed elevators whisked people up to 'sky lobbies', from which escalators led up and down to intermediate floors. The main banking hall was surmounted by a ten-storey atrium and, in the final version of the design, was dramatically raised up in the air, leaving an open pedestrian plaza below. It was an extraordinarily innovative building, whose construction cost – almost £500 million pounds – made it the most expensive office tower in the world at the time. Even before the construction was complete, the American magazine *Progressive Architecture* wrote that the Hongkong Bank 'may well be the building of the year'.[4]

The design was finalized in 1982, but construction took more than another three years. In the meantime, Foster Associates was busy with other projects. The first major building completed after the Sainsbury Centre was a 24,000-square-metre warehouse for the Renault automobile company. That sounds mundane, but it turned out to be Foster's showiest building to date. The structure consisted of self-supporting modules that resembled upside-down umbrellas, with the roof suspended from masts by thin metal guy rods. Since all the steel was exposed and painted bright yellow, Renault's corporate colour, some architectural critics observed that Foster was turning playful.[5]

The Renault building and the Hongkong Bank marked a decided shift in Foster's style. Commenting on the bank, architecture critic Jonathan Glancey contrasted its design with the 'slick enveloping aluminium skin' of the Sainsbury Centre, and described the bank as 'highly stylized, somewhat Gothic and almost Expressionist. This is Foster moving into a new phase in terms of visible massing and articulation. The intense search for new building techniques, materials and searching for God in the detailing continues, but when before would Foster allow himself to reveal so much structure and workings?'[6]

This judgment turned out to be premature. In 1981, Foster Associates were appointed architects for a new terminal for London's third airport, Stansted. This project turned out to be the 'Foster Ultimate' that Peter Cook had predicted. As at East Anglia, Foster went back to first principles. 'Without denying that the realities that lie behind international airports are complex,' he wrote, 'it seemed important to challenge the assumption that they would therefore produce a complicated building.'[7] His solution, which drew on ideas that he had first explored in the Sainsbury Centre, was in effect a very big shed – 50,000 square metres – a flexible, multi-purpose space, covered by a roof that similarly incorporated skylights. All the mechanical services, as well as baggage handling, were housed below, an arrangement that would become the standard for air terminal design worldwide. Stansted demonstrated conclusively that the expressionistic aspects of Renault and the Hongkong Bank were anomalies in Foster's work. It was the silver, monochrome, multi-purpose tube of the Sainsbury Centre that had signalled the architectural direction that Foster would henceforth follow, just as Cook predicted.

Stansted cemented Foster's reputation as one of Britain's leading architects, and the Hongkong Bank raised his international profile. In 1983, the Royal Institute of British Architects awarded him its highest honour, the RIBA Gold Medal – only sixteen years after the firm was founded in Wendy's flat. There had been setbacks along the way. Foster Associates lost an invited international competition for the Humana headquarters in Louisville, Kentucky, to a postmodern design by Michael Graves. A mixed-use development in New York and a stadium in Frankfurt, the result of an international competition, fell by the wayside. So did two large projects in London: the Hammersmith Centre and the BBC Radio Centre. The competition-winning BBC project, on which Foster Associates had worked for three years, was a particularly galling loss, since it represented a new type of building for the firm – a large urban complex, integrated into a dense, historical fabric.

But there were also successes. In 1985, Foster beat a collection of leading international architects that included Jean Nouvel, Frank Gehry, César Pelli, Alvaro Siza, Aldo Rossi and Arata Isozaki to win a commission for an art gallery and public library in Nîmes. The Carré d'Art was to face the Maison Carré, a famous Roman temple, and tested Foster Associates' ability to build on a site of great historic significance, as did the firm's first public building in London, the Sackler Galleries at the Royal Academy of Arts. Here, Foster remodelled the Victorian wing of Burlington House, a Palladian mansion designed in the eighteenth century, and, without altering his design style, showed an unexpected sensitivity and lightness of touch in dealing with the historic building. The renovation was a great success, and more than one critic observed that the project marked an important moment – the general acceptance of modern architecture by the British public.[8] With the Carré d'Art and the Sackler Galleries, Foster, who might have remained a technical specialist – a latter-day Joseph Paxton or Gustave Eiffel – moved into the architectural mainstream. 'This was a new Norman Foster,' Martin Pawley observed, 'still an architect with attitude, but an architect with respect, too, a respect for the past that, like his vision of the future, has opened doors all over the world.'[9]

'Both the Sainsbury Centre and Willis Faber were positive statements at a time when British architecture was marked by stylistic slanging matches and not much conviction,' observes Foster. The 1970s was a period of ferment in the architectural world. The giants of the modern movement – Le Corbusier, Walter Gropius, Mies van der Rohe and Alvar Aalto – who had dominated the scene for fifty years, were gone; Louis Kahn, whom many considered their natural successor, died in 1974. The brutalist style, advanced by architects such as Lasdun in Britain and Paul Rudolph in America, had petered out – owing in no small part to its unpopularity with the general public. To many, conventional modernism seemed to have run its course, its long-held dogmas having lost their compelling urgency. Influenced by the writings of Robert Venturi in the United States, Aldo Rossi in Italy, and Oswald Mathias Ungers in West Germany, architects began tentatively experimenting with ornament, exploring historicist references, and looking for ways to incorporate signs and symbols – that is, *meaning* – into their designs. These tendencies (they never quite coalesced into a movement) came to be known as 'postmodernism', a term coined by Charles Jencks. In a contemporaneous 'history' of postmodern architecture, published in West Germany in 1984, Heinrich Klotz described an array of built postmodernist works in the United States, Germany, Italy and Austria, though not in Britain. Klotz puzzled over why the world's leading postmodernist, James Stirling, who had lately been invited to participate in several architectural competitions in West Germany, and had completed an acclaimed extension to an art museum in Stuttgart, had received only one recent commission in his native country. 'What stands in the way of postmodernism in Great Britain', Klotz complained, 'is not so much a lack of commissions as a continuing faith in the virtue of modernism.' He singled out Foster and Rogers as the dominant British architects, and referred to England as 'the country of High Tech.'[10]

The term 'high tech', which came into popular use in the 1960s, originally referred to industries such as aerospace, silicon chips and computer software, but it was also used to describe a style of architecture that incorporated advanced industrial materials and techniques, and whose forms were influenced by engineering rather than by the plastic arts. As Klotz pointed out, architects who demonstrated a continued faith in modernism were almost exclusively British, and included, in addition to Foster and Rogers, Nicholas Grimshaw, Michael Hopkins, who had been a partner at Foster Associates, and younger practitioners such as Eva Jiřičná, who had worked for Rogers, and Ian Ritchie, Richard Horden and Jan Kaplický, who had all been apprenticed with Foster. Not that these architects saw themselves as belonging to a school. Creative people dislike being pigeon-holed, and Foster for one rejects the 'high tech' tag. 'The structure of the Sainsbury Centre, for example, is only exposed at the two ends, otherwise it is suppressed,' he points out. 'Similarly, the mechanicals are hidden, except for a hint in the conservatory. This is very different from high tech.' Like many architectural labels, 'high tech' does not bear close scrutiny. Nevertheless, Klotz was right to observe that there was something different going on among certain British architects. They shared a tendency to favour lightweight steel structures, to be partial to industrially produced components, to design generalized spaces that could be used flexibly, and to emphasize a building's performance rather than merely its appearance. More to the point, they showed not the slightest interest in any of the ideas that Klotz identified as the core of postmodernism: contextualism, metaphorical meaning, ornament and historical allusion.'[11]

The architecture that emerged in Britain in the 1970s belonged to a European tradition that dates back to early pioneers such as Bruno Taut, whose pavilion at the 1914 Werkbund exhibition in Cologne used glass in an adventurous way, and Erich Mendelsohn, who built some extraordinarily light glass façades in Germany in the 1920s. The tradition continued in the 1930s, with the Dutch architect Frits Peutz, who designed the Modehuis Schunck, a department store in Heerlen that was locally nicknamed the Glass Palace, thanks to its delicate all-glass façade, and the Parisian Pierre Chareau, who was responsible for the remarkable Maison de Verre, a building greatly admired by Foster. In the immediate post-war era, the French engineer Jean Prouvé turned out a variety of designs: furniture, curtain walls, and a series of lightweight, prefabricated steel buildings.[†]

Architects such as Taut, Mendelsohn, Peutz, Chareau and Prouvé exploited the lightweight possibilities of steel and glass, and incorporated

---

* Robert Sainsbury once described postmodernist architects as 'those who decorate buildings with all sorts of bits and pieces'.

† Foster met Prouvé – they discovered a mutual interest in gliding – and invited him to consult on the curtain wall of the Willis Faber building. 'You don't need me,' the Frenchman said, after examining the drawings.

industrial materials to a much greater extent than their Bauhaus-influenced contemporaries. However, thanks to the proselytizing writings of art historians such as Sigfried Giedion and Nikolaus Pevsner, and Henry-Russell Hitchcock and Philip Johnson's famous 1932 'Modern Architecture – International Exhibition' at New York's Museum of Modern Art, the work of Taut and the others was marginalized, and the prominence accorded to that of Le Corbusier, Mies and Gropius ensured the dominance of Bauhaus-style modernism.

The next chapter in the history of what might be called 'lightweight modernism' unfolded in faraway southern California. It began in the 1920s with the arrival of Richard Neutra in Los Angeles. A Viennese who had worked for Mendelsohn, Neutra married the International Style with lightweight American construction technology, and produced a series of hybrid houses, consisting of extremely slender steel frames filled in with glass and prefabricated panels. His two masterpieces, the airy Lovell house in Los Angeles and the Kauffman house in Palm Springs, are replete with what Reyner Banham called 'skinny details', which became one of the hallmarks of the southern California style.[12]

Neutra's early work in California influenced the post-war generation of Angeleno architects such as Raphael Soriano (who was Neutra's apprentice), Pierre Koenig (who was Soriano's apprentice), Craig Ellwood (a self-taught designer of great talent), and Charles Eames (a designer, who had worked under Eliel Saarinen at the Cranbrook Academy of Art). Although obviously influenced by Mies as well as Neutra, their steel-frame buildings, assembled from off-the-shelf building components such as ordinary I-beams and open-web joists, corrugated metal sheets and fibreglass panels, had a distinctive character: pragmatic, extremely light, industrial-looking and – compared to Mies – distinctly unmonumental. The steel-frame house and studio that Charles and Ray Eames built for themselves was probably the best-known example of southern California modernism. According to Reyner Banham, the Eames house 'had a profound effect on many of the architects of my generation in Britain and

Europe. It became the most frequently mentioned point of pilgrimage for intending visitors to Los Angeles among my friends.'[13] Among the pilgrims was the young Norman Foster, who visited the house when he was working in California after finishing at Yale.*

Seventeen years – and five thousand miles – separate Reliance Controls, with its kit-of-parts approach, thin steel frame and steel cross-bracing, from the Eames house. Why did lightweight modernism re-emerge in Britain, rather than taking root in the United States? The second part of the question is easier to answer than the first. Neutra-inspired California modernism had a short run. Perhaps, as Banham speculated, the rather ascetic style was at odds with the hedonistic culture of Los Angeles.[14] By the mid-1960s, interest in minimalist houses had dried up, and *Arts & Architecture* magazine, published in Los Angeles, which had popularized the work of the southern California architects and sponsored a series of experimental houses – the so-called 'Case Study Houses' – ceased publication. Soriano stopped building, Koenig moved into teaching, and Charles and Ray Eames focused on furniture, film-making and exhibition design. Only Ellwood continued to build, but he seemed more like a survivor than the harbinger of something new. In addition, southern California modernism had only a slight national impact. Eero Saarinen, who had collaborated with Eames on furniture, designed a lightweight, prefabricated house-building system for *Arts & Architecture* magazine in the 1940s, and later incorporated 'skinny details' into several industrial projects, moved to a heavier, more expressive style. So did Skidmore, Owings & Merrill (SOM), which had produced some extremely light steel designs in the 1950s. Paul Rudolph, who had started his career with a series of lightweight steel-frame houses in Sarasota, Florida, in the late 1940s and early 1950s, shifted to concrete and brutalism. East Coast architects such as Rudolph, Philip Johnson, I. M. Pei, Louis Kahn, Gordon Bunshaft and Kevin Roche

---

* Foster's admiration for Eames, is attested to by his consistent use of Eames-designed furniture, starting with Reliance Controls. Eames died in 1978, two months before the opening of 'Connections: The Work of Charles and Ray Eames', which Foster organized to launch the Sainsbury Centre's special exhibitions programme.

(Saarinen's successor), favoured concrete, and produced buildings that were heavy, monumental and distinctly *not* industrial-looking.

The answer to the question why lightweight modernism surfaced in Britain in the 1960s is more complicated. To the generation of British architects who came of age surrounded by the grim, heavy concrete style that dominated post-war British architecture, lightweight California modernism had a special appeal. 'There was a romantic idea about American technology, which represented a clean break with the past,' says Birkin Haward. 'Norman was very keen on SOM, especially the early work.' Haward remembers a large photograph of a steel-and-glass façade – SOM's Gunner's Mate School in Great Lakes, Illinois (1952) – hanging in the office. Foster was hardly alone in his admiration for lightweight American architecture. Reyner Banham, who was based in London but spent much of his time teaching in the United States, dedicated *Los Angeles: The Architecture of Four Ecologies* (1971), still the best book on the modernist architecture of southern California, to the British architect Cedric Price, whom he credited with directing his attention to the subject. Price built little, but his theoretical projects and writings on adaptable architecture were influential (his Fun Palace project is said to have inspired the Pompidou Centre). Peter Cook and his colleagues in Archigram, who taught, lectured and published widely in the 1960s, likewise advocated a lightweight architecture that incorporated flexibility and change. Their theoretical projects, such as Plug-In City and the Walking City, incorporated prefabricated capsules and robots, combining images from science fiction with American aerospace technology. The projects of Price and Archigram appeared in the pages of *Architectural Design*, which also published Foster's work. All were a part of 1960s Swinging London – Carnaby Street, Twiggy, the Beatles – and the combination of brash futurism, irreverent gadgetry, and stylish, youthful glamour seemed like the perfect architectural analogue for the age.

Another American influence on Foster in the 1960s was a California project known as SCSD, School Construction Systems Development. This was the brainchild of architect Ezra Ehrenkrantz, who convinced thirteen school districts in the state to pool their building programmes and adopt a standardized construction system. The components, which included structural, mechanical and electrical systems (though not façades), were produced by manufacturers according to performance specifications developed by Ehrenkrantz's team.[15] Foster's later integration of services with architecture owed a debt to Ehrenkrantz's systematic approach to building. So did the idea of working directly with industry to develop innovative components and products based on building performance.

Building performance was an obsession of the many-faceted Buckminster Fuller. Fuller had been a fixture on the American scene since the 1930s, designing cars, prefabricated houses and, most notably, geodesic domes. He preached the need for a fundamental revolution in building construction, and his Dymaxion House, which used aircraft technology and lightweight materials, looked more like a flying saucer than a dwelling. Although he was considered a marginal figure by most American architects, Fuller appealed to groups like Archigram, which peppered its projects with tensile and pneumatic structures and geodesic domes.[*][16] In 1970, Foster designed an air-supported structure as a temporary office building for Computer Technology. The following year, Foster met Fuller, who had been commissioned to design an underground theatre at St Peter's College, Oxford, and who invited him to be the architect. That project remained unbuilt, as did several more collaborations, including a design for a dome house that was to be built in two versions, one in Los Angeles for Fuller, and one in Wiltshire for Foster. The two became close friends. When Foster received the RIBA Gold Medal he asked Fuller to give the oration at the ceremony.[†]

A key reason why the technological strain of modernism took root in Britain was the presence of a strong engineering tradition. 'It wasn't just

---

[*] Speaking of the 1932 modern architecture exhibition at New York's Museum of Modern Art, Philip Johnson said, 'But we didn't think [Fuller] was an architect. So we didn't put him in the show.'
[†] Foster's introducer at the RIBA medal ceremony was Sir Robert Sainsbury.

the historical tradition of engineers such as Paxton and Brunel,' says Tony Hunt, 'it was the presence of a cadre of engineers who were interested in collaborating with architects.' Architects and engineers work together everywhere, of course, but in Britain it was the nature of the collaboration that mattered: intellectual, creative, and continuing from project to project. The British custom of close teamwork was influenced by the civil engineer Ove Arup. A pre-war Danish immigrant, Arup founded what has turned out to be one of the best-known – and most enduring – engineering firms in the world. His stated ideal was 'a relatively closely knit team, working in the same place and having a continuity of work on a few jobs at a time, so that the members could really learn to appreciate each other's qualities, or if necessary shed those members who didn't fit'.[17] Ove Arup & Partners was later to be the engineering consultant of choice for architects such as Foster and Rogers, and worked on the Hongkong Bank, Stansted Airport, the Pompidou Centre and Lloyd's of London.

Another immigrant engineer active in post-war Britain was Felix Samuely, a transplanted Viennese, trained in Berlin. Tony Hunt was an apprentice in Samuely's office under the celebrated Frank Newby. 'Samuely taught at the Architectural Association and always had several young architects in the office,' Hunt recalls, 'since British architects could do their apprenticeship with an engineering firm.' The tradition of collaboration was passed on to the younger generation – not only Hunt, but also the talented Irish engineer Peter Rice (who worked on the Pompidou Centre and briefly on Stansted), and Ted Happold, an Arup alumnus, who founded Buro Happold, which would collaborate with both Foster and Rogers. Newby could be critical of architects, and he once sarcastically defined high tech as 'the use of redundant structure for decorative purposes'.[18] Rice was more charitable. 'High-tech architects have concluded that the discipline provided by the engineer is the best framework in which to conduct architecture,' he said.[19] That sounds about right.

The second part of *Learning from Las Vegas* (1972), a seminal book for postmodern architects, was titled 'Ugly and Ordinary Architecture'.[20] The ordinariness that was referred to included using everyday materials and construction methods. Thus, the iconic buildings of postmodernism, such as Venturi's Vanna Venturi house, Charles Moore's Sea Ranch, Philip Johnson's AT&T Building, and Michael Graves's Portland Building, were structurally and technologically conventional. Architects such as Foster and Rogers, on the other hand, philosophically committed to advancing the state of the building art, were willing, even eager, to innovate and experiment. In that regard, they saw themselves as part of a tradition. 'I believe that architects have always used the very best technology and materials available at the time, and that's what Norman was doing,' says Roy Fleetwood. Referring to Graves, who had recently beaten Foster in the Humana headquarters competition, Foster associate Richard Horden told an interviewer, 'I think we [architects] are all like mountaineers. Michael Graves is the kind of eccentric chap who goes up all alone with a walking stick. We use crampons, pitons, and oxygen … and we go up higher.'[21]

Occasionally, they climbed too high. In the summer of 1985, during a regular washing of the Sainsbury Centre, workers who were hosing down the roof noticed cracks in the corners of some of the aluminium panels. There had been problems with some of the panels during construction, but now a detailed survey identified eighty-four defective roof panels; in addition, seven wall panels were found to have similar problems. The solution suggested by Foster Associates, then preoccupied with completing the Hongkong Bank, was simply to patch the cracks, assuming that the fault was a mechanical failure. But further investigation turned up a more troubling issue: water vapour was reacting chemically with the supposedly inert phenolic foam insulation, producing an acid that was corroding the panels from the inside.* Once research had shown conclusively that the

---

* The exterior of the laminated panels was protected by a rust-resistant layer of pure anodized aluminium, but the inner layer, which had the superplastic properties, consisted of a copper alloy that was susceptible to corrosion.

problem was endemic and threatened the integrity of the cladding, the hard fact had to be faced: all the panels would have to be replaced. Cupples Products, a leading American manufacturer and installer of curtain walls, estimated that the cost would be between £1.9 and £2.7 million.[22]

It was unclear exactly who was to blame for the failure – the manufacturer, the installer, the engineer, the contractor or the architect – and who would pay for the replacement. The university's legal position as building owner was complicated, since both the manufacturer and the installer were no longer in business; moreover, the seven-year statute of limitations for the builders' and architect's liability was about to expire. 'The university's solicitors advised us to immediately take out protective injunctions against all the parties involved,' says Peter Yorke, 'which we did.'

According to Steven Hooper, Sir Robert Sainsbury, who had no direct involvement in the affair, was slightly put out, for Foster had not informed him of the cladding problems and seemed to be avoiding him. But Hooper emphasizes that Bob felt a shared sense of responsibility, since he had encouraged Foster to innovate. 'For Bob, it was like having a favourite nephew encounter a problem – you helped him. Bob sensed it could have been a critical moment for Foster Associates, and the last thing he wanted was for the firm to struggle when it was on the verge of great things. It was similar to his attitude to Francis Bacon in the 1950s when he guaranteed his bank account.' David Sainsbury agreed with his father, and his charitable foundation covered the cost of the replacement. 'I swallowed hard and paid,' he says. The university's injunctions remained unserved.

Graham Phillips was in charge of the work. An architect who had graduated from the University of Liverpool, he had spent five years working for Arup before joining the Foster firm in 1975. 'I worked on IBM Technical Park before being assigned to the bank project, and I ended up spending seven years in Hong Kong,' he says. 'At the time I returned to London, a serious problem had developed with the cladding of the

Sainsbury Centre. This was very sensitive in terms of the clients, and since I was a new face, and also because I had worked with Cupples on the cladding of the Hongkong Bank, I was put on the Sainsbury project. "You've got to sort it out," Norman told me.'

The work was carried out during the spring of 1988. The removable panels proved their worth by making it possible to re-skin the building with minimal disruption to the fabric, although it was still necessary to close – and empty – the museum for six months. The new panels were not identical in appearance or structure with the old.[23] 'Cupples produced a more conventional aluminium panel with mineral insulation and a honeycomb backing for stiffness, so there was no need for ribs,' says Phillips. 'I assumed that the finish of the panels would remain silver. I remember a meeting with Phil Bonzon, the chief designer at Cupples, when Norman asked him, "If it was your building, what colour would you make the panels?" Phil observed that white was the best colour for reflecting the sun's heat. "OK," said Norman. "Let's make it white."'

Flat panels cost £500,000 less than ribbed, but the choice had less to do with economy than with the desire to present the repair to the world as an improvement. 'It has been decided to upgrade the panel system for a variety of reasons,' read a press release prepared by Sainsbury's communication office.[24] In a largely upbeat story titled 'Foster's Centre Sheds its Skin', the *Architects' Journal* reported that 'the plan is to upgrade the performance of the cladding in terms of insulation and to improve the ultraviolet filtering of the transparent glazing panels'.[25] The glass in the new panels, which had a low-E coating to reduce heat gain, was tinted rather than clear, and incorporated an ultra-violet filter, to protect the art works. According to George Sexton, this brought lighting levels down to a more manageable 150-lux range. So the story had a happy, if expensive, ending.

ARCHITECT REDUX

The Sainsbury Centre expands underground. Why it is rare for architects to add to their own work.

On Friday 24 October 1986, two dozen members of the Sainsbury family – children, grandchildren, cousins – gathered in the private dining room of a small manor house hotel near Oxford. The highlight of the weekend was a dinner to celebrate Sir Robert Sainsbury's eightieth birthday. David Sainsbury, who organized the event, had thought hard about a birthday present. 'What do you give someone like my father?' he says. 'It had to be something special, but trying to buy a work of art for him was hopeless. One of his favourite things was the Sainsbury Centre, so I thought it would be wonderful to give him a sketch done by Norman showing how the Centre might expand in the future.'

Foster drew his ideas on a poster-size birthday card that included an explanatory text in his characteristically spiky handwriting. In part it read:

> Last July David approached me with an idea for a present which he would give you on your Birthday. It started with the proposition that our thoughts on how the Centre could expand would provide a valuable record for the future. This touched a very sympathetic nerve, because for years I have been privately obsessed by the presence of a second design opportunity – albeit as a paper exercise. So David's proposal opened up a range of possibilities which have been bubbling around for years. This has led to a model which shows

a possible starting point for any such expansion and which David will be giving you on Friday.'[1]

Foster's drawing showed the building expanding eastwards in three stages. The first stage (illustrated by the model) lengthened the shed by about 10 metres, and added an outdoor sculpture court. This addressed a number of shortcomings. By extending the shed, and moving the café from the conservatory to the end of the building, Foster was able to enlarge the special exhibitions area and effectively place it deeper inside the building, further away from harmful natural light. He even proposed creating a small windowless gallery within one of the thick walls. He relocated the main entrance from the side to the end of the building, which made for a more impressive experience. The redesigned lobby accommodated a museum shop, and larger cloakrooms and toilets, which had always been inadequate for the public. The elevated bridge and spiral stair remained unchanged. The second stage added a basement below the sculpture court, and the third stage showed a free-standing pavilion, resembling a slice of the old building, on the far side of the court. 'Both the main building & pavilion could be linked internally from the basement below or accessed from the outside,' Foster explained on the drawing. 'Alternatively the entrance court could be roofed over as a conservatory.'[2] 'A BASIS FOR DISCUSSION!' he added at the bottom of the sheet.

The exquisitely detailed model shows part of the existing building, inside and out, and includes miniature people, cars, and even sculptures in the entrance court, as well as tiny electric lights that give it the appearance of a birthday cake. 'My father was immensely pleased with his present,' David Sainsbury recalls. 'He took it as a sign that I would look after the museum in the future.'

A week after the party, David Sainsbury and his father met for their regular lunch. Bob said how much he had enjoyed the weekend, and the thoughtful present. An extension to the Centre was a wonderful idea, he said. Then he made an unexpected proposal. 'Why don't we build it right away?' David Sainsbury was taken aback. He had meant the present to be, in Foster's words, a paper exercise. 'I intended that the drawing would simply be put in a safe, so that in fifty years time, if someone wanted to enlarge the Centre, they would know what the original architect had intended,' he says. But having raised the idea, he could hardly refuse his father, who even at eighty was eager for a new and exciting project. 'It turned out to be a very expensive birthday present,' David Sainsbury observes.

Foster and David Sainsbury had earlier discussed the potential expansion with Derek Gillman, the newly appointed keeper of the Sainsbury Centre.* Gillman, thirty-two, was not a conventional art historian. After graduating in Chinese studies from Oxford, he had spent a year in China learning Mandarin, before joining the British Museum as a curator in the Department of Oriental Antiquities. Once the decision to expand was made, David Sainsbury consulted Gillman again, as well as Steven Hooper, who would become an important link between the Sainsburys and the university.

Hooper had met Bob and Lisa in 1972, when he was twenty-two and working in the Department of Ethnography at the British Museum. His grandfather, James Hooper, had been a well-regarded collector of ethnographic art, who had founded his own museum, the Totems Museum, at Arundel in Sussex. Hooper revered 'Gramp', and inherited his enthusiasm for Polynesian art, which he shared with Bob. 'We liked to look at objects,' Hooper recalls. Bob was impressed by the detailed catalogue of his grandfather's collection that Hooper was compiling.[3] Nine years later, when the young man graduated from Cambridge with a PhD in social anthropology (he had spent three years in Fiji doing field research), Bob offered him a job: assisting him in editing a comprehensive catalogue of the Sainsbury collection. 'The Sainsburys also asked me to be a liaison between them and the university,' Hooper says, 'because relations at that

---

* Gillman's predecessor, Graham Beal, had come to the Sainsbury Centre from the Walker Art Center in Minneapolis. He stayed in Norwich only eighteen months, before returning to the United States, where he became chief curator at the San Francisco Museum of Modern Art.

point had become strained.' That was in 1982, when, with Thistlethwaite gone, the Sainsburys felt that the university was not paying sufficient attention to the Centre. Hooper's work, cataloguing and photographing the collection with James Austin, would last many years and overlap with another task. 'In 1984, after a visit to New York, Bob and Lisa got very excited about scholarly and exhibition activity in the tribal art world and they wanted to found – and fund – a specialist department linked to their collection,' says Hooper. 'They weren't sure how to go about it, and they asked me if I would think about how to organize such a department at the University of East Anglia.' Four years later the Sainsbury Research Unit for the Arts of Africa, Oceania and the Americas was born, with Hooper as its first director.

'When the idea of expansion was raised, Derek and I didn't think that simply making the building longer was a good idea,' says Hooper. 'That only added public spaces, while what we really needed were support functions.' The truth was that neither Sir Robert nor Foster had been experts in museum design when the original building was planned. The decision to reduce the area of the basement, for example, had proved shortsighted, and storage was now so inadequate that the Centre was obliged to lease space in a nearby industrial park. There was also a need for workshops and a proper conservation laboratory (curators currently used facilities in the chemistry department). Offices were required for the curatorial staff, which had grown in size, as well as for the newly founded Sainsbury Research Unit. As far as exhibition space was concerned, the Living Area functioned well, but special exhibitions remained a problem. 'Within the last decade, a set of international standards with respect to exhibitions and loans has been established and accepted by major institutions,' Gillman and Hooper wrote in a memorandum to David Sainsbury. The result was that 'the curatorial staff cannot in all conscience accept loans from other institutions which demand adherence to accepted standards.'[4] The best way to provide tight control over light, temperature and humidity, they advised, would be to build a new special exhibitions gallery, ideally underground. Hooper added to the list larger faculty offices with natural light for the School of Fine Arts.

'Bob and Lisa were very excited about the project,' says Hooper. 'There had been friction with the university for some years, and now with Gillman's arrival there was a sense of turning a page. The planned extension was a new adventure, an opportunity to have another go and to work with people they liked.' After weighing up several options, everyone agreed that the extension should include mainly back-of-the-house functions – there would be no new galleries – and since the Sainsburys were not keen on funding new offices for the School of Fine Arts, that idea was dropped, too. 'Bob was terribly practical,' Gillman recalls. 'He was also concerned about the size of the extension, since the cost would be borne by his son.'

Final decisions about the design of the original Sainsbury Centre had been made essentially by four persons: Robert and Lisa Sainsbury, Norman Foster and Frank Thistlethwaite. A decade later, Bob and Lisa remained very much the clients and Foster the architect, but there were also other people involved. As keeper, Derek Gillman had a keen interest in the building and, as he came to know Bob and Lisa, he was soon spending time at Smith Square. Steven Hooper also played a key role since he was close to Bob, and the Research Unit would occupy part of the new wing. Peter Yorke, who had been involved in the original building, represented the Estates Office (Gordon Marshall, who would retire in 1988, was not involved). David Sainsbury, whose charitable foundation was paying for the extension and who was particularly sensitive to cost issues after the recladding affair, was represented by his assistant Christopher Stone, who functioned as a sort of project manager. George Sexton was also part of the early discussions. Sexton had returned to the United States and opened his own consulting firm in Washington, DC, but over the years he had maintained his professional involvement with the Sainsbury Centre – and his personal friendship with Bob and Lisa.

The Foster team was new, since Roy Fleetwood, Birkin Haward, Richard Horden and Loren Butt had left the firm to strike out on their own. The design team was headed by Graham Phillips, who had established a good rapport with the Sainsburys during the recladding of the building, and included Richard Hawkins, Chris Connell and Heiko Lukas. 'It was a small team and an intensive project,' says Connell, today a partner in the firm. 'We all worked together on just about every aspect of it.' Tony Hunt was again responsible for the structure. George Sexton, who was familiar with the inner workings of art museums, oversaw the planning of the workshops and the conservation laboratory, as well as the design of the lighting. 'I had one of my people in Foster's office during the whole project,' he says.

Phillips remembers a meeting with Sir Robert early in the design process. 'If we do this project we must have no more problems,' Bob said forcefully, referring to the recent recladding. Foster's quiet response surprised Phillips. Another architect might have backed down, or sounded conciliatory. Not Foster. 'There will always be problems in building,' he said. 'Things will always cost more and take longer; that is the nature of the process.' It is a measure of the trust that had grown up over the last decade between patron and architect that he was able to speak so frankly.

It was twelve months before the design team was ready to present an architectural proposal. The problem was a lack of consensus about exactly where the new extension should go. 'The original building was a flexible tube,' says Phillips,' so the logical thing would have been to add more bays. But the Sainsburys wouldn't have it. They felt it was wrong to alter the building and they wanted something entirely separate.' Gillman and Hooper favoured an underground extension along the south side of the building at basement level, emerging from the slope; but burrowing beneath the existing building proved impractical. A smaller building was also considered, similar to the main one, sited parallel to and below it on the south side, and linked to it by transparent passageways. At one point, a separate utilitarian storage building was contemplated, and it was even suggested that it might be handled by a local architect, but Bob insisted that Foster remain involved.

'Our first solution was a free-standing building hidden among the trees and connected to the main building by a long tunnel,' says Phillips. This bare-bones option did not impinge on the original building, but nobody liked it: the university was not keen to build in the wooded area, and Gillman and Hooper felt that the remote location created functional problems in terms of access, convenience and security. The alternative was to extend the basement at the east end: with a grassed-over roof it would be invisible from the main building. 'The problem was that the curators wanted offices with natural light and a view,' says Phillips. 'The breakthrough occurred when we realized that, because of the topography, we could extend the basement until it emerged from the slope, so we could add windows.' Everyone agreed that extending the building in this direction made the most sense.

The new wing would house art stores, workshops, a conservation laboratory, a photographic studio, a seminar room and a students' workroom for the Research Unit, as well as offices for curators and unit staff. The brief was prepared by Gillman and Yorke. 'We kicked around the idea of a large multi-purpose space that could serve both as a 200-seat lecture room, which Peter wanted for conferences, and as an exhibition gallery,' says Gillman. This was a critical moment in the design of the wing since a lecture room-cum-gallery would require public access, which would greatly complicate the design. But Bob approved the proposal. He was sensitive to criticisms of the environmental conditions in the Sainsbury Centre, and liked the idea of a climate-controlled gallery for special exhibitions. The various uses added up to a significant area – 3,300 square metres – two-thirds the size of the original building's footprint.

The first version of the extension was a simple rectangle, the full width of the building, with a glazed wall at the east end. As the brief grew, the wing became longer and stuck out farther into the landscape. 'It meant that the glazing had to be longer and deeper,' says Connell, 'giving a more visible cut into the landscape and exposing the front of the building to a greater flood risk.' Moreover, since the number of offices had increased to a dozen, they could no longer be comfortably accommodated in the 35-metre width of the building. The solution was a splayed plan, which Foster sketched through several versions until it finally acquired a sweeping curve. 'Once we had the curve, it was natural to slope the glass to follow the grade,' says Phillips. The dramatic glass arc, which Lisa called 'a wonderful fish tail', gave the extension its name: the Crescent Wing.

The workshops, the conservation laboratory and the students' workroom had large (1.8-metre-diameter) circular skylights, with glass set flush into the grass. To amplify the light, Sexton designed parabolic reflectors, made from single sheets of spun aluminium. A long curving skylight, nicknamed the Slot, illuminated the corridor that led to the multi-purpose space. Hooper recalls visiting Foster's office and being shown a piece of masking tape stuck to a column to indicate the future ceiling height of 2.8 metres. 'It struck me as low because of my experience in horrible, long, low-ceilinged lecture rooms as an undergraduate.' In the final design, the architects recessed the floor of the multi-purpose gallery to create a generous 3.7-metre ceiling.

With the splayed plan and the arc, the extension achieved its final shape, and the Sainsburys and the university gave the go-ahead to prepare the final drawings, secure planning approval and get bids from builders. The last question that remained to be decided was how the public would enter the new wing. The ideal solution would have been to provide a connection through the existing building via a lift and stairs, but that modification would require closing the Centre. 'We had just reopened after six months' closure to reclad the building,' says Gillman, 'so closing again was out of the question. Digging a big hole outside and punching through to the basement was very attractive.' Since the extension would be connected to the main building only for servicing purposes, public access would have to be elsewhere. 'Bob and Lisa wanted a separate entrance to the new wing, which is how we came up with a ramp,' says Phillips. 'It was originally uncovered, but Lisa wanted a roof, so we added a glass cover.' Phillips describes Bob and Lisa as both extremely involved in the design process. 'We would have meetings not only in our office but also at Smith Square. Lisa tended to be more outspoken and forceful, but I sometimes thought that they played good cop/bad cop on purpose. There was nothing ostentatious in their manner, but they were a force to be reckoned with.'

In April 1989, just as construction was about to begin, the Sainsburys made an unexpected demand. They had just come back from their annual trip to New York, where they had visited the Metropolitan Museum's newly opened Henry R. Luce Center for the Study of American Art, designed by George Sexton. The study centre incorporated what curators call 'open storage' or 'open reserve', where artefacts are stored in such a way that they can still be viewed by the public as well as scholars. Sexton referred to the study centre as a 'library of objects', since the closely spaced, floor-to-ceiling glass display cabinets resembled book stacks.[5] Bob and Lisa wanted a similar facility in the Crescent Wing. The collection had doubled in size since the Sainsbury Centre had opened, and there was no longer enough room to display everything in the Living Area. Years earlier, they had admired the open storage of the National Gallery in Berlin, and Foster had included open storage in his early sketches for the Sainsbury Centre, but the idea had not gelled. 'On opening day, there was a small open storage area on the first mezzanine, with glass cases and sliding racks for drawings, but in time that space was overtaken by other uses,' says Sexton. 'The problem was that, in the 1970s, nobody, including the Sainsburys, understood exactly what open storage was.'

Study centres with open storage were rare in Britain, so the following month Sexton took Derek Gillman and Heiko Lukas from the Foster office on a tour of several North American museums. They visited the Luce Center at the Metropolitan Museum, as well as Silver Hill in Suitland, Maryland, the off-site storage facility of the Smithsonian Institution. 'This was not open storage,' says Sexton, 'but we wanted to look at the furniture, and at technical issues of storage.' They also visited the Victorian Doll Museum in Rochester, NY, whose large collection was openly displayed. The fourth museum was the brand new Menil Collection in Houston.

'Bob and Lisa really liked the collection,' recalls Sexton. 'The de Menils were the same generation, and they collected similar things: modern art, antiquities and tribal art.' In the early 1970s, about the same time that Bob and Lisa were beginning the Sainsbury Centre, John and Dominique de Menil had commissioned Louis Kahn to design a museum for their collection. Kahn had died before completing the design, and eventually Dominique de Menil, now a widow, picked Renzo Piano to be her architect. Open storage had been a central concern of the de Menils, and Piano located a study centre in a second-storey penthouse, which he named the Treasure House. 'We were very impressed by the Menil,' says Gillman. 'Its conservation lab became our model.'

Foster revised the plans. 'Good architects like Norman Foster have a great confidence in their ability to design,' says Gillman. 'What they demand is feedback: "Is this the building that you want?"' The Sainsbury study centre was located in an area previously intended for art storage, and Sexton began designing the glass cases and lighting. As in the multi-purpose space, he installed a recessed, flexible lighting system, 'This was the first time such lighting had been used in a museum to my knowledge,' he says.[6] On 5 June 1989, two and a half years after Sir Robert's birthday party, construction of the wing finally started. That year Foster suffered a heavy blow: Wendy Foster, who had contracted cancer, died. She left him with four sons, the youngest adopted only months before her death. Foster has described Bob and Lisa as 'second parents to me', which refers to the support that they gave him during this difficult period.

In 1990, the museum world was shaken by a spectacular art theft. Two men broke into the Isabella Gardner Museum in Boston, making off with twelve canvases, including a Vermeer and several Rembrandts. The Sainsbury Centre hired security consultants who reported that thieves in a helicopter could descend on the roof, cut through a panel, and slide down a rope into the museum. 'We installed alarms on the roof,' says Yorke. 'The art store and the open reserve in the Crescent Wing were protected by three layers of walls, so that was less of a problem.'

FOSTER MOVES FORWARD

Norman Foster in 1983 with drawings of the
Hongkong and Shanghai Bank, the project that
cemented his reputation as a major architectural
presence on the international scene. Although the
Hongkong Bank explored a high-tech approach,
the direct descendant of the Sainsbury Centre was
Foster's Stansted Airport (*below*), a vast top-lit shed
that integrated mechanical services, structure and
functional requirements.

New wing Crescent Nfoster

When it was decided to expand the Sainsbury Centre in 1986, Bob and
Lisa did not want to alter the appearance of the original building, and
Foster devised an underground solution, shown here in his freehand
sketch (*above*). The arc shape of the glazed office corridor gave the new
building its name: the Crescent Wing. The addition was designed to
cause minimum disruption to the original building during construction.
A cross-section (*opposite*) shows the relationship between the gallery, the
offices and the glazed corridor; part of the glazing swings up like a hatch
to provide emergency egress. As with the original building, the design
emerged from a close collaboration between the architect and his clients.

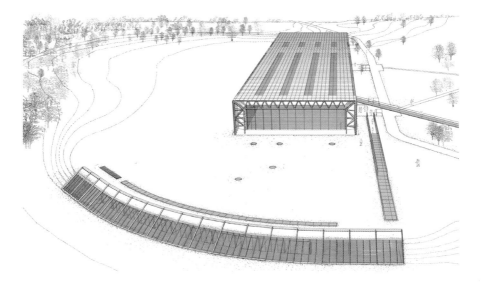

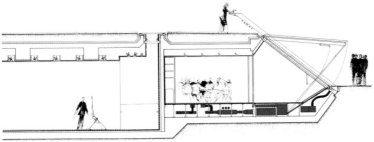

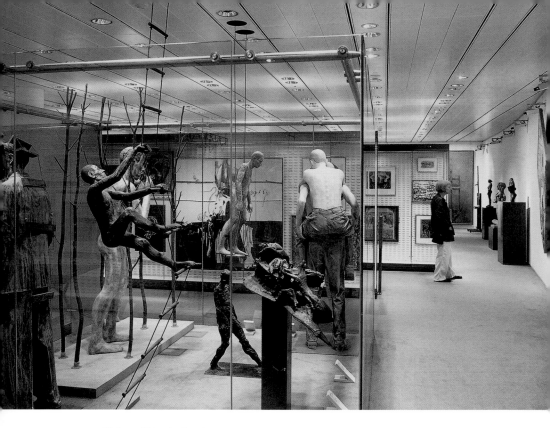

Bob and Lisa insisted on an open reserve – a storage area where works can be viewed – to house their growing collection (*above*). Their involvement with the arts also resulted in the founding of the Sainsbury Institute for the Study of Japanese Arts and Cultures in Norwich. This new initiative was a result of their growing interest in collecting Japanese art, such as this thirteenth-century figurine of a Shinto female deity.

The glazed office corridor in the Crescent Wing illustrates an
evolution in Norman Foster's style, to something sleeker and
simpler – almost Zen. He has characterized the architecture
of the original Sainsbury Centre as tent-like, in contrast to
the cave-like underground extension, which emerges from
the green slope in front of the Shed.

Norman Foster's 2002 sketch (*below*) of a weather-protected entrance to the Crescent Wing initiated a major refurbishment of the Sainsbury Centre. The underground Link houses the museum shop, galleries and classrooms. Also visible in the cutaway drawing are the open reserve, with its ranks of display shelves, and the wedge-shaped Lower Gallery. Large openings were cut into the floor of the existing building to provide views into the shop below.

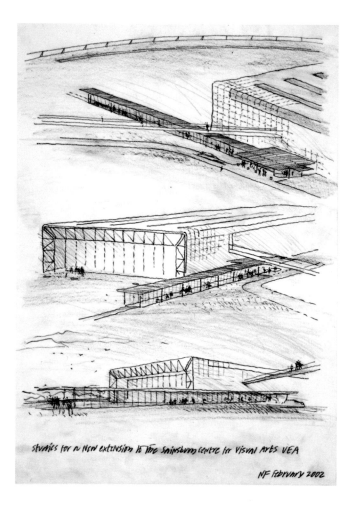

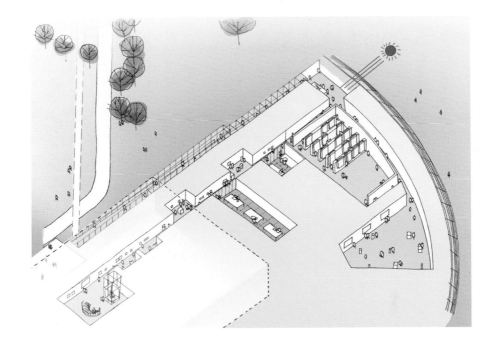

Never conventionally fashionable, the Sainsbury Centre
has successfully resisted becoming *un*fashionable.

Unlike the original building, the new wing was built entirely of reinforced concrete. The structural slab was hidden behind a suspended ceiling. The chief architectural feature, and the only feature visible from the exterior since the roof was entirely covered in grass, was the curved glass wall, sloped to match the angle of the hill. Early versions of the design had the offices on the exterior of the building, but in the final plan, the offices lined a brightly lit glazed corridor. In the architects' model, the curved bank of glass with the long building extending behind resembles the command cockpit of a great machine. The final building design enhanced this effect by providing a curved balustrade that resembles a futuristic ship's railing at the edge of the grassy roof. Standing there, looking down to The Broad, one has the feeling of being on board a large yacht.

The Crescent Wing opened in April 1991.* 'Foster is master of the grand approach,' wrote Hugh Pearman in the *Sunday Times*, 'be it a staircase, escalator or, as here, a ramp that gradually takes you underground, only to deliver you behind the great tilted glass wall. The architect, for all his minimalist tendencies, controls the event totally.'[7] Alastair Best, architecture critic of *The Independent*, was equally fulsome: 'The only big gesture, ironically, is something the public will not see: the corridor that sweeps round in a curve beneath the glass windscreen. Tiger-striped with shadows, this is a marvellous piece of pure abstraction.'[8] Gillman and Hooper had imagined the corridor as a social space, and had asked Foster Associates to design built-in benches outside the offices, where students and staff could sit and chat. The benches were designed, but were not installed at the time the building opened. Sexton remembers that Bob was rather cross about that. Foster argued that his clients should try it without the benches. 'We liked the simplicity,' Chris Connell recalls. 'Once the users had started living in the building and we realized how the corridor

---

* 1991 was a momentous year for Foster: the Crescent Wing opened, the Sackler Galleries at the Royal Academy were completed, the Willis Faber building received a Grade I listing from English Heritage (the youngest building to receive this distinction), and he remarried.

would be used, we put the benches in,' he says. 'I seem to recall Bob and Lisa particularly liked them and were keen to put them back.' However, in the official Foster monograph, the Crescent Wing corridor appears as it did on opening day, 'an ethereal space dominated by its silent sweeping view over the Norfolk countryside.'[9] No benches.

Museums regularly expand as holdings and programmes increase, but how common is it for an architect to be commissioned to design a major addition to one of his own buildings? Henry van de Velde was invited back to extend the Kröller-Müller Museum in 1943, five years after the museum opened. The architect designed several new galleries (the rooms in which the Sainsbury collection was exhibited) and a small auditorium, continuing his earlier low-key style and making the interior, if anything, even simpler, with rough brick floors and plastered white walls. Construction of the new wing was interrupted by the Second World War and, in 1953, more than thirty years after beginning the 'temporary' museum, van de Velde came out of his Swiss retirement to complete the work.

Another modern museum that has been extended several times by its original architect is the Amon Carter Museum in Fort Worth, Texas. Philip Johnson designed the original building in 1961. Although he had been a confirmed follower of Mies van der Rohe, this museum was the first of several buildings in which he explored a decorative style that one wag christened 'ballet classicism', a reference to the tapered columns that resembled a dancer's foot *en pointe*.[10] The Amon Carter Museum, which stands in a park, was conceived as a memorial to the successful newspaper publisher, who had established a collection of works by Frederic Remington. It consisted of a free-standing building with a portico and a single gallery.[11] The museum was hardly more than a garden pavilion, and two years later Johnson was called back to enlarge it. 'We are now engaged in more than doubling the cubage of that building,' he told an interviewer. 'We're making a museum out of it as well as a monument to

Amon Carter.'[12] In 1978, Johnson (working with John Burgee) returned to enlarge the museum still further. By then, he had moved away from the stylized classicism of the original pavilion to a more geometrical and abstract modernism. In 2009, the museum undertook a third expansion. This time the two earlier additions were demolished, and Johnson (working with Alan Ritchie) designed a large, two-storey, granite-faced block that left the original pavilion, a little gem that he described as one of his favourite buildings, intact.

The Amon Carter Museum remained loyal to Johnson for a remarkable forty years. Few client–architect relationships last this long. When the High Museum of Art in Atlanta decided to double its size after two decades in a building designed by Richard Meier, it commissioned Renzo Piano instead. When the Art Gallery of Ontario in Toronto extended its Beaux-Arts-style building in 1993, it chose Barton Myers as the architect; but eleven years later, it turned to Frank Gehry, now famous after the opening of the Guggenheim Museum in Bilbao, to overhaul and expand the museum.

Even if changing architectural fashions are not the issue, the passage of time often is. Van de Velde and Johnson were both in their nineties when they made the final additions to their earlier work, but few architects remain active for that long. Twenty or thirty years generally will have passed before a new museum undertakes a major expansion, by which time the original architect is usually either retired or deceased. When the Dulwich Picture Gallery was refurbished forty years after it opened, Soane was long dead, and his type of simplified classicism was out of fashion. The interior of the gallery was modernized – that is, Victorianized. Eventually, the almshouses, which were no longer in use, were converted into galleries, and in 1914 new galleries were added. By then, classicism was once more in vogue, and the architect, E. S. Hall, designed a sympathetic expansion, with a second range of top-lit galleries, which mirrored Soane's original plan. The exterior was in brick and Portland stone, more or less in the style of the original.

The Dulwich Picture Gallery is a combination of Soane and Hall, Soane setting the architectural theme with Hall in the role of accompanist.[13] One cannot tell where one stops and the other begins. Such blending is out of favour today, when most architects and critics believe that any architectural intervention must be recognizable and distinct. Consider the Kimbell Art Museum in Fort Worth, across the park from the Amon Carter Museum, and regarded as Louis Kahn's masterpiece. Kahn completed the building in 1972, and seventeen years later, the museum embarked on a major expansion. With Kahn dead, the commission went to Romaldo Giurgola, his friend and long-time colleague at the University of Pennsylvania. Giurgola's design duplicated Kahn's modular vaults and extended the building from 90 to 150 metres. (Part of the rationale for this solution was that Kahn had originally designed a longer building, which had been reduced for budgetary reasons.) Yet, just as the Sainsburys had not wanted their 'perfect' museum altered, many people considered Kahn's design inviolable. Paul Goldberger, the architectural critic of the *New York Times*, echoed a popular sentiment when he wrote: 'If the Giurgola addition is built, we will never again have the building Louis Kahn left us – but we will have a building that will look so much like Kahn's work that many people will mistakenly believe it is. Does this plan pay Kahn the greatest honor, or do him the subtlest form of dishonor?'[14] A few months later, the newspaper published a letter to the editor, whose signatories included such illustrious architects as Philip Johnson, Richard Meier, Frank Gehry and James Stirling. 'Why ruin the masterwork of Kahn's life with such an ill-considered extension?' they wrote. 'To put it bluntly, we find this addition to be a mimicry of the most simple-minded character.'[15] Giurgola's plan was shelved.

Compared to most architects, Foster had several advantages in working on the Crescent Wing: he was young when he designed the original building, the decision to expand was taken less than a decade later, and the Sainsburys were steadfast clients. Yet in many ways the Foster who designed the extension was not the same architect. In the intervening years, his practice had not only expanded but also evolved, taking on more complex problems that required more complex solutions. This was evident in an exhibition of Foster Associates' work that inaugurated the Crescent Wing. Among the twenty-eight projects on display were a law faculty for Cambridge, a town hall in Marseille, a commercial development in Barcelona, and underground railway stations in Bilbao, as well as master-planning studies for London, Berlin and Nîmes. Some of these projects, such as the Millennium Tower in Japan, which would have been the tallest building in the world, would not see the light of day, but the buildings completed or under way included an office tower in Tokyo, a telecommunications tower in Spain, and Riverside, Foster Associates' new studio on the south bank of the Thames, near Albert Bridge.

The early work of Foster Associates had been dominated by what Graham Phillips (who went on to become managing director and chief executive officer of the firm), calls a 'stretched skin' approach. The stretching was intellectual, as well as physical. 'A lot of our work was the result of a dialogue with industry,' he says. 'We would ask them "Why can't we do this or that?", they would explain the manufacturing issues, then we would push – stretch – the limits of the process.' Projects such as Renault and the Hongkong Bank represented a further development, more focused on how the buildings were constructed, and more articulated. Phillips sees the Crescent Wing as an important step in the evolution of the firm. 'The design of the Crescent Wing was a conscious shift. The interior of the Sainsbury Centre is all metal, but since the extension was below ground, we reasoned that it could be different, plainer and more sculptural, more minimalist, and more about space. This was the subject of much debate within the office, but with time this approach prevailed in the firm's work.'[16]

The Crescent Wing incorporates technical innovations, such as the upward-swinging panels of the tilted glazed walls that open to become

---

* Minimal did not mean cheaper. The cost of the extension is said to have exceeded £12 million, or £4.7 million at 1978 values – more than the original building. 'Foster's philosophy of design was to customize everything,' Derek Gillman recalls. 'He had just designed the Hongkong Bank, which was the most expensive office building in the world. We used to say that the new addition was the most expensive gallery in the world.'

escape hatches, and in the glazed corridor a graded frit that is intended to reduce heat gain (a very early use of this technology); but these devices do not call attention to themselves. Details fade into the background, and the chief interior wall material is painted plasterboard. The services are not integrated with the structure, which is entirely hidden, and instead of a subdivided universal space, there are individual rooms, tailored to meet different needs – display, teaching and conservation.

The Sainsbury Centre is a rare example of built biography. The original shed was the work of a young, ambitious architect testing the limits of technology, pushing a single idea as far as it would go. In the Crescent Wing, the architect has matured and significantly broadened his architectural palette. Eero Saarinen, an architect no less driven than Foster, underwent a similar evolution. He once told an interviewer:

> I think we have to design within our time, uncompromisingly, but we have to broaden the alphabet of modern architecture to face problems that it hasn't faced before … God knows I am very, very enthusiastic about Mies van der Rohe and the almost common vernacular style he has created and that we all accept as a very fine thing. However, I cannot help but think that it's only the ABC of the alphabet, that architecture, if we're to bloom into a full, really great style of architecture, which I think we will, we have to learn many more letters.[17]

In 1992, Bob and Lisa celebrated Lisa's eightieth birthday. Since her birthday, on 3 March, coincided with their wedding anniversary – this year their fifty-fifth – it was a grand affair, attended by many friends, and held at the Temperate House of the Royal Botanic Gardens, Kew, where Bob and Lisa supported an orchid conservation project. That same year they embarked on another scheme. Bob had had a stroke while visiting Paris, and in her practical way, while he was recuperating, Lisa decided that, having sold their country house at Bucklebury a decade earlier, they needed a second home, more suited to retirement than Smith Square. Moreover, she wanted a garden. 'Their garden was very important to them,' says George Sexton, whom she asked for advice about the move. 'The garden at Bucklebury had been not only a landscape – Lisa was an accomplished gardener – but also a place for displaying sculptures, two large figures by Henry Moore.'

Lisa decided on Dulwich for its proximity to London, and asked Foster to design a house. Graham Phillips oversaw the project. 'I always thought they should build themselves a modern house,' he says. In March, shortly after her birthday, Lisa took an American friend, Paula Deitz, to Dulwich to see the building site. They had met nine years earlier when Deitz had been writing an article for the *New York Times* about Lanning Roper. Deitz, the editor of *The Hudson Review*, was knowledgable about landscape architecture and gardens, and Lisa wanted her opinion. They looked at the architects' sketches, trying to imagine the house. The design was extremely simple, almost Miesian, with the main public rooms contained in a single, glass-fronted space, in the shape of an arc, like the Crescent Wing. 'The lot was on a hillside overlooking the town,' Deitz recalls. 'The steeply sloping site would have been hard to make into a garden.' After lunch, Lisa took Deitz to see an old house that was for sale nearby. The Grange stood at the eastern end of a long-neglected and heavily overgrown 1½-acre plot, next to a golf course. Two months later, Lisa changed her mind and bought the Grange. 'The lot was very suitable for a garden, and I think that finally swayed her,' says Deitz. 'She was also concerned that building a new house would take too long.' Lisa asked George Sexton to oversee the conversion of the Regency house. He gutted the interior, combined the dining and sitting rooms into a large living room, with a sitting room and library on the side, and, with Foster's help, added a modern-looking, stainless-steel-and-glass conservatory overlooking the garden. The interior of the house, with most of its decoration removed and walls painted white, resembled a spacious version of Smith

Square, though with less art. A new greenhouse was added at the foot of the garden, and Bob and Lisa commissioned the sculptor David Harvey to build a slate sculpture in the garden. Bob liked London, and wanted to keep their house in Westminster, so they only spent the summer at the Grange; but soon they were returning for extended weekends, and a year later they moved there permanently. Lisa called it their 'country place in the city'.

The Grange was less than a mile from Dulwich Picture Gallery, whose chairman of trustees was Bob's nephew John Sainsbury.* Bob and Lisa became involved with the gallery, and in 1994 funded a feasibility study for a refurbishment and expansion of Soane's museum. There were other projects. Bob and Lisa pondered adapting Smith Square into a venue for showing their Francis Bacon paintings and other modern art, but the practicalities and long-term management implications proved too complex. As a ninetieth birthday present to his father in 1996, David Sainsbury funded the new Sainsbury African Galleries at the British Museum, which allowed many of the museum's finest African pieces to be displayed for the first time. Bob and Lisa's relationship with the University of East Anglia was rekindled in 1995 with the arrival as vice-chancellor of Dame Elizabeth Estève-Coll, who had been director of the Victoria and Albert Museum.

Another new friend at the university was Nicole Coolidge Rousmaniere, a young lecturer in Japanese art. Bob and Lisa had acquired their first Japanese piece in 1963, and at the time the Sainsbury Centre opened the collection included about a dozen Japanese works. During the 1980s they acquired more paintings and sculptures, as well as Jōmon objects. Rousmaniere helped them to further enlarge the collection, which grew to include Buddhist and Shinto sculptures, Negoro and pre-Edo period lacquerware, as well as contemporary photographs by Hiroshi Sugimoto.[18] Bob and Lisa never visited Japan, but they developed close

---

* Lord Sainsbury of Preston Candover and his brothers were responsible for funding the Robert Venturi-designed Sainsbury Wing of the National Gallery in London.

relationships with leading Japanese dealers and acquired many notable works, including a large scroll by the eighteenth-century Kyoto master Maruyama Ōkyo.

In 1998 Rousmaniere and John Onians organized an international symposium at the university on British, European, North American and Japanese art. The participants were invited to the Grange to meet Bob and Lisa, and out of those discussions grew the idea that there was a need for more research on Japanese art. With characteristic enthusiasm, the Sainsburys proposed to found an independent research institute, which became the Sainsbury Institute for the Study of Japanese Arts and Cultures, which was affiliated not only with the University of East Anglia but also with the School of Oriental and African Studies of the University of London, and the British Museum. To fund this new project, Bob and Lisa sold their most valuable possession, Modigliani's *Portrait of Baranowski*, which they had bought as a mutual wedding present, and which had not been a part of the gift to East Anglia.*

One has the sense that Bob and Lisa were carefully tying up loose ends. Among the loosest was the catalogue of the collection, which was not published until 1997, when Bob was ninety. The work had taken so long in part because of Bob's enduring love of letterpress printing. The text was to be set in hot-metal type, by the Merrion Press in London, and then photographed for offset printing in Verona. The first two volumes were printed this way; the third volume was digitally typeset, since the typeface – Dante – had become available in digital form. Twenty-one art history specialists, including Peter Lasko and Graham Beal, contributed essays. 'I thought at one stage we'd never finish,' says Hooper, 'because of being so finicky – Bob was as bad as me, and of course the collection kept on growing. But we couldn't keep going back to contributors, so eventually we had to draw a line.' The catalogue, which comprised more

---

* The Modigliani was expected to fetch up to £10 million. However, while Sotheby's sold Monet's *Water Lily Pond and Path* for a record £19.8 million at the same London auction, the Sainsburys' painting sold for £4.3 million, much to Bob's disappointment.

than a thousand pages, included 866 individual entries. Bob and Lisa collaborated on the work, as they had on all their art projects. 'We hope that these volumes will provide intellectual stimulus for interested scholars and laymen alike,' Bob wrote in the Foreword, 'as well as visual pleasure for those of them and others who seek it.'[19]

In 1999, Bob and Lisa were awarded the Freedom of the City of Norwich (Foster gave the introductory speech). To mark the occasion, George Sexton and Steven Hooper produced for the Sainsbury Centre a commemorative booklet of selections from the collection. The works included the famous acquisitions of the 1930s such as Moore's *Mother and Child*, Degas's *Little Dancer aged Fourteen*, and Picasso's *Woman combing her Hair*. In addition to pieces by Bacon and Giacometti, there was the Gabon head that Bob had bought in Paris, the Khmer torso, a bird-shaped kava dish from Fiji, and contemporary ceramics by Hans Coper and Lucie Rie.[*] The most recent acquisition, a Japanese Kamakura wood figurine of the thirteenth century, had been purchased only two years earlier. Its acquisition number was 1146.[†] The twenty-seven objects represented a lifetime – two lifetimes – of appreciating and acquiring art.

The following year, at home and after a brief illness, Bob died. He was ninety-three. Six months later, a memorial concert took place in the old church of St John's, Smith Square, across the street from the Sainsburys' former home.[‡] Before the performance, there were several short testimonials: Steven Hooper talked about the collection; the naturalist Sir David Attenborough, a friend of Bob and Lisa's, described the research that they had supported at Kew; and Sir Guenter Treitel, an Oxford don who was one of the children from Germany that the Sainsbury brothers had provided for in 1938, expressed his gratitude for Bob's generosity. David

---

[*] Lisa's passion for contemporary ceramics led to the addition of more than four hundred pieces to the collection. Coper (1920–1981) and Rie (1902–1995) are considered by many to be among the twentieth-century's greatest potters.

[†] The Robert and Lisa Sainsbury Collection now numbers over 1,700 objects, including Lisa's twentieth-century ceramics and other personal items.

[‡] The concert took place on 3 October 2000. Fauré's *Requiem*, opus 48, was performed by the City of London Sinfonia with The Sixteen choir, conducted by Harry Christophers. The organist was Simon Preston.

Sainsbury spoke movingly about his father. 'He was a wonderful parent with clear and firm values, but he was also able to understand that these values could take his children and grandchildren in different directions from his own,' he said. 'He was also a man with a wonderful sense of irony and humour. I learned much from him, about people and about social justice and integrity, and I miss him a great deal.'[20]

The third speaker was Norman Foster. He recalled meeting Bob and Lisa at Smith Square, twenty-six years before. 'I have always maintained that in the best projects the true creators are the clients,' he said. 'I cannot think of a better example than the Sainsbury Centre, because it grew directly out of Bob and Lisa's vision, courage and generosity. They were far more than patrons, because patronage implies a certain detachment and aloofness, and nothing could be further from the truth.' Foster spoke from the heart, and his trenchant characterization of Sir Robert Sainsbury could serve as an epitaph: 'A common thread linked his art collecting and his approach to architecture, a combination of enthusiasm, intuitive gutsy judgement, and a taste for the radical and the experimental.'

NINE

A PLACE FOR ART

The third phase of construction. The Sainsbury Centre today.

AFTER BOB'S DEATH, LISA DEVOTED MOST OF HER ENERGY to the Sainsbury Institute for the Study of Japanese Arts and Cultures, but she continued to drop in at the Centre. Nichola Johnson, who was Derek Gillman's successor as keeper, remembers accompanying her on one visit. 'I think it must have been the first time that she experienced the building in the rain. By then, she was in a wheelchair, and she was wheeled down the long ramp of the Crescent Wing in a downpour. She complained a lot about that.' In February 2002, for his mother's ninetieth birthday, David Sainsbury asked Foster to devise a solution to the problem of accessing the Crescent Wing. The architect's sketch shows a glass canopy over the building's entrance, with a long extension enclosing the entire length of the ramp. Lisa's birthday was in March, and as they had done for Bob's eightieth birthday, Foster's office made a detailed model. It was a modest beginning for the third campaign of building at the Sainsbury Centre.

David Sainsbury felt a strong responsibility to safeguard his father's legacy; moreover, his long involvement with the project had given him a taste for modern architecture. 'The Centre is not really a building of my father's generation. I consider it a building of my generation,' he explains. 'It's actually a building I love, so that's a bit of luck.' As methodical as his father, he commissioned an independent assessment of the Centre's long-term maintenance needs. 'It became clear that the twenty-five-year-old building needed a total refit, which became the first phase of a ten-year maintenance programme,' says Stuart Johnson, who acted as David Sainsbury's representative and the project manager for the work. 'This required refurbishing the interior and furnishings, as well as replacing the electrical and mechanical systems that had reached the end of their useful lives.'

It is said that architecture is for the ages, but that is no longer literally true. For centuries, building technology was static: Renaissance builders used much the same materials and techniques as their ancient Roman counterparts (for that matter, so did Georgian builders). Upkeep meant simply maintenance: repointing brick, repainting woodwork, replacing roofing slates. Today, construction materials and techniques change with staggering rapidity. The useful lives of heating, cooling, ventilation, power and security systems, for example, are relatively short, and the performance of glazing, insulation and weatherproofing is likewise constantly improving. Standards also change; the current concern with buildings' carbon footprints, for example, has radically altered construction practices, and advances in communications technologies have produced new demands on infrastructure. This means that most modern buildings require a significant overhaul every three or four decades. The main advantage the Sainsbury Centre offered in that regard was that its mechanical and architectural parts were designed to facilitate replacement.

'I always thought that the weakness of the Crescent Wing was the lack of a direct connection,' says Foster. 'When it became clear that a major refurbishment was in the works, and that the building might have to be closed for some time, the possibility of an interior connection presented itself.' Under Foster's direction, Spencer de Grey and Chris Connell examined this option. Making a public connection at the lower level meant that additional space could be created in the basement. Initially planned as a gallery, this new space became an expanded museum shop, which was one of Nichola Johnson's particular demands. 'Our shop was much too small,' she recalls, 'the café needed upgrading and enlarging, and our educational programmes needed classroom space.' The new connecting corridor, which came to be known as the Link, was made sufficiently wide to include space for display. 'It became a third sort of exhibition space, smaller and more intimate,' says de Grey. The final major component of the work was the conversion of what had been a storeroom into a classroom. With the construction of the expanded underground connection, the different parts of the building became one continuous whole. 'This resolved all the problems and completed the building,' says Foster.

The refurbishment of the Sainsbury Centre began with emptying and stripping the main building. The two layers of ceiling louvres were removed and the trusses cleaned and painted; the louvred metal walls were taken down to reveal the mechanical equipment. The building now looked much as it had during construction in the summer of 1977. The next major task was cutting out a large section of the concrete floor slab in the lobby area and excavating below. Two sections of the glazed east wall were removed to allow earth-moving equipment to drive in and out of the building. Once the enlarged basement had been dug out, fresh concrete was poured in and a new floor installed. A matching section was added to the spiral stair to give access to the shop, and a new lift provided disabled access to the shop and the Crescent Wing.

Meanwhile, work went on in the rest of the building. The sealed glazing units of the skylights were developing condensation problems and an Austrian supplier replaced all 360 of them. New air-handling units were installed, the public toilets were entirely rebuilt, and the café was reorganized and equipped with a larger kitchen, located inside the thick wall. The exhibition lighting in the Living Area was upgraded with more efficient fixtures, display cases were repainted, and several new designs of case were added.

'At the time of the Link, I was in government and at arm's length from any activities of the trust,' says David Sainsbury. 'Since my father was dead and my mother was no longer intimately involved with the Centre, this was largely Norman on his own.' By then, Foster had become perhaps the best-known architect in the world, certainly the most visible. He had been knighted, appointed to the Order of Merit, and – in the same year (1999) – awarded the Pritzker Prize and created a life peer as Baron

Foster of Thames Bank. With the Swiss Re headquarters (the so-called Gherkin), the Millennium Bridge over the Thames, City Hall, and the roofed courtyard of the British Museum, he dominated London as no architect had since Christopher Wren. Foster + Partners, with more than a thousand employees, had grown far beyond its founder's earlier expectations, although its design philosophy remained unchanged, still guided by innovation, and impatient with conventional solutions. The Foster style had, if anything, grown simpler and more minimal, though paradoxically also more luxurious. This is visible in some of the new details of the refit of the Sainsbury Centre: the simple entrance doors have been replaced by automated, curved, sliding doors, the curved handrails of the circular stair, formerly plastic, are now tempered glass, and the toilets have been entirely rebuilt with opaque glass walls. On the whole, however, the building was restored, not redesigned. Most of the furniture is new, for example, but exactly the same as was installed in 1978 – Finnish easy chairs in the Living Area, Eames furniture elsewhere. 'Generally we continued the same aesthetic, maintaining the spirit of the original,' says de Grey. The free-standing screens in the Living Area were also redesigned by George Sexton to allow a slightly denser display, although it is hard to distinguish them from the earlier models.

The refit took twenty-one months and cost £12.5 million.[*] Lisa attended the opening ceremony on 20 May 2006. Thirty-eight years (almost to the day) had passed since she and Bob had informed Frank Thistlethwaite that they were leaving their art collection to the university. Their dream of a gallery where students would have 'the opportunity of looking at works of art in the natural context of their work and daily life' has been more than realized. Every year over 150,000 people – the public as well as students – use the facilities of the Centre, which has grown from 4,600 square metres to 9,000, and whose staff now numbers thirty, as well as sixty part-time volunteers. More than a hundred special exhibitions have

---

[*]   Adjusted to 1978 values, the 2006 refurbishment represented three-quarters of the cost of the original building.

been mounted since the building opened, and the Sainsbury Centre is a major presence among the hundred or so British university art museums. 'We always saw ourselves as an alternative to the Courtauld, although our collection was less mainstream,' says Derek Gillman. 'I believe that the Courtauld and the Sainsbury Centre are the two best museums of their type in Britain.'

The exhibition that inaugurated the newly refurbished Sainsbury Centre, curated by Steven Hooper, was titled 'Pacific Encounters'. More than 270 Polynesian objects were displayed all over the building – not only in the special exhibitions area, but also in the Link and in the multi-purpose space in the Crescent Wing. The exhibition design, by George Sexton's office working with Hooper, remained true to Bob's display ethos of presenting objects as fully and intimately as possible for the viewer. One Maori scholar called it the 'most comprehensive exhibition of Polynesian art and material culture ever assembled.'[1] Interestingly, the exhibits came mainly from museums in Britain, and included several items from the collections of James Hooper and the Sainsburys. Hooper dedicated the catalogue that accompanied the exhibition to the memory of his grandfather and Bob Sainsbury.[2]

The University of East Anglia today is a very different place from the one that Norman Foster and Kho Liang Ie visited in 1974. As Thistlethwaite predicted, the university grew westwards, and the Sainsbury Centre no longer stands in splendid isolation but is flanked by several new buildings. Lasdun's unified vision no longer dominates the campus, for later architects did not follow his lead – no more pedestrian decks, angular geometry or exposed concrete. In the early 1990s, the university undertook a major expansion, doubling its student population and adding several new residences. The end result is decidedly mixed. Neither a megastructure nor a traditional campus of quadrangles, East Anglia today is an unsettled combination of Lasdun's blunt modernism, Foster's precision, a smattering of watered-down 1980s postmodernism and, more recently, a modified white-box International Style.

In 2013, the University of East Anglia will celebrate its fiftieth anniversary. Fifty years is long enough for the pendulum of architectural fashion to swing from one pole to the other, yet compared to recent buildings at the university, Foster's shed holds its own. So, surprisingly, do Lasdun's ziggurats, which, at least from the front, still make a powerful impression, although the concrete has weathered poorly – Foster was right about that. The Sainsbury Centre, on the other hand, looks ageless, and not only because so much of it is literally sparkling new after the recent refurbishment. Never conventionally fashionable, Foster's architecture has successfully resisted becoming *un*fashionable. With its severe appearance, the metal hangar stands apart from its immediate neighbour, Constable Terrace, a curvy student residence that would be at home in Miami Beach.

The footbridge with its delicate glass railings still forms a slender connection between the Sainsbury Centre and Lasdun's concrete deck, although it now emerges from the treetops like an Amazonian sky walk. The trees that Lanning Roper planted more than thirty years ago have matured and make a leafy screen against the north façade of the building, which has changed little since the corrugated silver-grey panels were replaced by smooth, creamy white. The blank elevation, slightly mysterious since there is no identifying sign on the building, is relieved only by the irregular pattern of air-handling grilles. Foster was right not to move the front doors; their casual, unglamorous placement is an important part of the building's diffidence. The sole distinguishing features of the entrances are identical, thin, cantilevered canopies of milky glass – part of Lisa's birthday present.

Le Corbusier once defined architecture as 'the masterly, correct and magnificent play of volumes brought together in light.'[3] True, but architecture is also about enclosing space. Great architecture does more than simply enclose, of course: it creates an interior world. Passing through the glass drum with curved doors that slide open automatically with a barely audible whoosh, one enters Foster's world: a calm, rational place, coolly functional but not functionalistic, determinedly technical but not technocratic. And, almost in spite of itself, poetic. 'A lot of people think it's Foster's best building,' Graham Phillips told me, 'and I agree.' Roy Fleetwood voiced the same sentiment. George Sexton considers the Sainsbury Centre, with the Kröller-Müller and the Kimbell, as among the best modern museums in terms of providing a tangible sense of daylight. The apparently odd equivocation, 'a sense of daylight' is, in fact, exactly right, since one can't actually see light, only what it illuminates: the architectural experience of these buildings definitely depends precisely on the quality of the light. 'Clear as water,' Hugh Casson wrote of it in the Sainsbury Centre, a description that still stands.

Entering the building today, one has the impression of crossing a bridge, since large openings on either side provide views into the brightly lit museum shop below. On one side, Tony Hunt's spiral stair descends to the lower level; on the other side, a lift in the form of an open platform goes up and down in hydraulic silence. The Living Area remains the focus of the building. The turnstiles that some critics found objectionable are gone, and the entrance is now in the centre, not in the corner. After experimenting with different ticketing policies, the Centre has made admission to the Living Area free. Jacob Epstein's bronze busts of Lisa and Bob greet the visitor. 'It took me five years to get Bob and Lisa to agree to have a panel with text explaining their role in the Centre,' says Gillman. 'They didn't want any mention of themselves.'

The collection has changed over the years. As the number of objects has grown, some of the study tables have been removed and panels and cases added to make the display denser. The identifications are slightly more prominent (Bob had always insisted that labels be minute) but the essential concept remains: provide the viewer with unfettered access to the art. Moore's *Mother and Child* is out in the open so it can be touched, so is Giacometti's *Standing Woman* (1958–9). Further along is a case containing Degas's *Little Dancer aged Fourteen* and, near her, Epstein's head,

Baby Asleep (1902–4) – Bob's first sculpture. Like all personal collections, the wide variety guarantees its continuing relevance, since, as fashions change, now one piece comes to the fore, now another. Popular interest in Henry Moore's work, for example, which declined after his death in 1986, was renewed by the 2010 Tate exhibition, in which the wartime drawings that form such an important part of the Sainsbury collection attracted particular attention. Two new study tables incorporate long, low cases filled with tiny figurines, echoing Smith Square's Toy Department, a version of which is reproduced in a special eye-level case on the mezzanine. When the Centre opened, Bob was sceptical about having children under twelve admitted, but today groups of chattering schoolchildren traipse happily among the artworks and sit sketching on the floor. Their visits are arranged during the mornings, leaving the afternoons for quieter visiting.

Despite the easy chairs and the casual atmosphere, the Living Area lacks the intimacy of a genuine living room. In fact, the high ceiling, the absence of conventional walls, and the light filtering down from above give one the impression of being outside. Is that odd? Not necessarily. Many of the tribal artefacts on display were meant to be seen and used out of doors, and neither the Bacon paintings nor the Moore and Giacometti drawings demand a conventionally domestic setting. At the same time, the anonymous, undifferentiated surroundings allow the objects to assert their individuality. Just as at Smith Square, there is nothing decorative or pretty about the arrangement, nor is there anything pedagogical in the sometimes surprising juxtapositions. 'Like most collectors, Bob and Lisa wanted to remove the biography of the art,' says Gillman, 'and just have people look at the work.' Looking at the work is particularly comfortable since, in contrast to most museums, there are no uniformed guards looking over one's shoulder. Although there are no guards in the Living Area (there are cameras and a small, casually dressed security staff), Steven Hooper cannot recall any thefts, vandalism, or even instances of breakage. It may be that the open nature of the display makes surveillance particularly effective or, as Norman Foster speculates, it may be that the care and attention that have been paid to the design of the building affect the way people behave. Bob once told Hooper that during the student demonstrations at the time of the opening no one ever threw a pot of paint at the building, which he took as a sign of its transcendent qualities.

The special exhibitions area is still at the east end of the building, although The Broad is no longer visible since the blinds in front of the glass wall are permanently closed. The fig trees planted in the conservatory, where the café used to be, have been removed.* 'That caused a major furore,' says Nichola Johnson, 'since people really loved the trees, but we simply needed the space.' Descending to the museum shop, one reaches a passage that leads to the Crescent Wing. The Link is punctuated by recessed gallery spaces for works on paper (which require low lighting conditions), and a large vitrine that resembles a shop window. A glass wall looks into a spacious room with skylights, which accommodates art classes and children's programmes – The Studio. At the end of the corridor is the open reserve of the study centre, with rows of glass cases holding a dense collection of objects, large and small.

A long curving ramp descends to the multi-purpose room. Although what is now known as the Lower Gallery was designed to double as a lecture room, the space has been monopolized by special exhibitions, because of the time it takes to mount and dismantle shows, and because of the programming problems of dual-purpose spaces. During my last visit, the gallery was closed while an exhibition of prehistoric ceramic figurines from the Balkans and Japan was being installed. However, as Steven Hooper points out, if the government's budgetary cutbacks reduce the number of special exhibitions, the lecture room function could be reinstated. 'The Crescent Wing has gone through several functional changes since it opened,' he says. 'For example, after a year it was realized that the photographic studio was getting very little use, so the university collection

---

* The café was closed at the end of 2010. At the time of writing, the future use of that area was not yet determined.

was moved to that room, freeing up a meeting room for the new museology department. When our graduate students moved to new quarters on the first mezzanine, their room was converted into a classroom for the Culture of the Countryside programme, which is organized in conjunction with local schools and community organizations.'

The Link terminates in the Crescent Wing's reception area for the staff offices, which also functions as a small gallery for the collection of modern ceramics by Hans Coper and Lucie Rie. The long, curving glazed corridor that provides access to the offices is, in some ways, the most evocative space in the building. The view across a green meadow down to the sparkling waters of The Broad is particularly dramatic because the floor is about a metre lower than the ground, which creates the odd but not unpleasant sensation of being in a sort of glass bunker. A very luxurious bunker, for while the atmosphere in the Crescent Wing is just as modern and minimalist as in the rest of the building, it is considerably less spartan. Like the faculty offices in the School Court, the offices have glass walls, but here the similarity ends. The air-conditioned work spaces are square rather than long and narrow, the walls white rather than silver-grey, and the door-locks at the usual height.

'The offices have been rearranged several times, since partitions are moveable and allow us to make rooms of narrower widths to accommodate new staff and activities,' says Hooper. The flexibility that was designed into the building is most apparent in the changes that have taken place under the first mezzanine at the west end. The space that was originally administrative offices, and briefly also accommodated a lecture room, is today occupied by the Robert Sainsbury Library, which has grown four-fold and now includes over twenty thousand volumes. 'The modular form of the panels made it easy and effective to rejig walls and partitions,' says Hooper. 'From the library point of view, the architects' claims of the flexibility of modular elements have, indeed, been borne out in practice.' Half of the mezzanine above is occupied by gallery space, and half by new work spaces for students, fellows and staff of the Sainsbury Research Unit. The unit has flourished since it began in 1988. There are regular conferences and publications; faculty and staff have grown to a dozen; and alumni can be found in museums and universities in London, Edinburgh, Cambridge, Liverpool, Geneva, Leiden, New York and Washington, DC.

The second mezzanine, which once housed the Senior Common Room, today contains a gallery devoted to the university's art collection, as well as a meeting space for Sainsbury Centre volunteers. No one seems to remember exactly when the SCR was closed, but by the 1990s, interest in the facility had waned and, as the authorized history of the university drily notes, 'Senior Common Room gradually ceased to exist.'[4]

The School Court has changed little in appearance. The secretarial area has moved into one of the side offices, and there are more student study tables. With the SCR television gone – and no more typewriters – the area is peacefully quiet. The slide library has been transferred to a space in the skin and its original location has been redesigned, the light boxes and slide drawers being replaced by computer screens and key-boards for student access to digital archives. The faculty offices remain in place, although the sliding glass walls have adjustable blinds for privacy, and the hated floor-level locks are now operated by hand-held electronic remotes – no more stooping. A new elegant glazed screen with sliding side doors separates the school from the public entrance.

Foster has been accused of designing buildings that look innovative, but don't necessarily produce substantive changes in people's behaviour.[5] That is not the case with the Sainsbury Centre. 'The building works well in terms of engaging people,' says faculty member John Mitchell. 'It encour-ages interaction, since you can't shut yourself off. Of course, it's hard to do personal work,' he adds. 'Most people work at home.' According to Mitchell, who introduced a course in archaeology, 'the presence of the Sainsbury collection has had a major influence on our curriculum, which has changed radically. All our undergraduate students are now exposed to anthropology and archaeology.' Student enthusiasm, inspired by the collection, led to the teaching of non-Western art in the school, and the

Sainsburys sponsored a lectureship for three years in the mid-1980s, which was then taken over by the university. John Onians also championed a broader curriculum. 'Most art collections are organized into specialities; the collection in the Sainsbury Centre is like the world,' he says. In 1990, he suggested that the unique character of the collection would be better conveyed to outsiders if the Centre were to be renamed the Sainsbury Centre for World Art. 'Bob didn't like the idea at all,' Onians recalls. However, Bob had no objection to a change in the name of the school to accommodate a new world art perspective and a focus on museum studies. That is how East Anglia's School of Fine Arts became the School of World Art Studies and Museology.

'The new name allowed the school to acquire a new and stronger identity,' says Onians. In the government's national assessment exercise of 2008, the School of World Art Studies and Museology was recognized among the top three art history departments in the UK, and was ranked number one for world-leading research. In 2009 it was rated first among art history departments for student satisfaction. In 2010, the *Times Good University Guide* ranked the school number one in research, and called the Sainsbury Centre 'perhaps the greatest resource of its type on any British campus.'[6]

Bob and Lisa initially conceived of the Centre chiefly as a home for their collection, but the Sainsbury Centre has evolved since it was founded thirty-five years ago. 'When I got there, the Centre felt slightly disjointed, with the teaching and the collection separate,' says Gillman. 'Then Steven Hooper's research unit was formed, museology was introduced, and now teaching and the collection have moved closer together. With time, it's likely that the collection will recede and teaching and research will become more important, just as happened at the Courtauld.' This institutional evolution took an important step in 2010, when the university inaugurated the Sainsbury Institute for Art (SIfA), bringing together the work of the School of World Art Studies and Museology with the three Sainsbury endowments: the Centre, the Research Unit and the Institute for the Study of Japanese Arts and Cultures. This initiative formally recognizes that study and research in the arts, and by implication the Sainsbury Centre, are a leading strength of the university. And despite Bob's misgivings about art historians, the Centre has been a fertile training ground for museum directors: Alan Borg became director of the Victoria and Albert Museum, Graham Beal went on to lead the Los Angeles County Museum of Art and the Detroit Institute of Arts, and Gillman became director of the Barnes Foundation.*

Beyond the School Court is the so-called Garden Restaurant, a grand name for what is really a student canteen. But it *is* a grand space – tall, with one entire side composed of a magically seamless glass wall overlooking a green lawn. The white chairs around the tables are a Foster favourite, Eames fibreglass classics designed in the 1940s. The silver louvred walls are bare, almost monastic, with not a touch of anything that could be construed as décor. Yet it is a cheerful place, especially at lunchtime when it's full of chatting students, staff and faculty.

Foster has characterized the architecture of the giant shed as tent-like – in contrast to the cave-like Crescent Wing – and there is something delicate and almost provisional about the white struts that frame the view. The building perches daintily on the grass lawn. It reminds me of Palladian villas I have seen, with a similar sense of keeping nature at arm's length. The Sainsbury Centre also shares Palladio's humanist virtues. 'The humanist instinct looks in the world for physical conditions that are related to our own,' wrote Geoffrey Scott in his classic *The Architecture of Humanism*, 'for movements which are like those we enjoy, for resistances that resemble those that can support us, for a setting where we should be neither lost nor thwarted.'[7] Scott was writing about Baroque architecture, but his observation applies here. Nobody gets lost in the Sainsbury Centre, whose clarity communicates a palpable sense of order. Despite the building's embrace of technology and adaptability, this is not a machine but

---

* Nichola Johnson's successor, Paul Greenhalgh, was previously director of the highly regarded Corcoran Gallery of Art in Washington, DC.

a congenial setting for human activities: looking at art, studying, eating lunch, staring out of the window.

Outside the restaurant glass wall, a stand of trees forms a leafy backdrop to a large bronze sculpture, a giant reclining female form swathed in rumpled drapery – an almost magical presence when spotlit at night. Bob considered this one of Henry Moore's last great representational works. For twenty years, *Draped Reclining Woman* (1957–8) stood at the bottom of the Sainsbury garden at Bucklebury, until Bob, Foster and Roper together decided on the present location. Moore's sculptures have often been used as a foil to modern architecture, but never to greater effect. The massive figure looks back at the streamlined shed with what could be construed as a combination of wonder and contentment.

Notes

Abbreviations

BF   President's Files, Albert C. Barnes
        Correspondence. The Barnes
        Foundation Archives, Merion, PA.
        Reprinted with Permission
FP   Foster + Partners Archive
SRU Robert J. Sainsbury Archive, Sainsbury
        Research Unit for the Arts of Africa,
        Oceania and the Americas, University
        of East Anglia
SCVA Sainsbury Centre for Visual Arts
        Archive, University of East Anglia
UEA University of East Anglia Archive
UP   University of Pennsylvania Archive

PROLOGUE
(PP. 14–21)
1   Meryl Secrest, *Frank Lloyd Wright*
    (New York: Alfred A. Knopf, 1992), 169.

CHAPTER ONE - ONE HAS TO CHOOSE
(PP. 24–47)
1   *Sir Robert Sainsbury in Conversation*
    with Steven Hooper, September 1982 –
    November 1992 (privately published,
    2005), 14.
2   Bridget Williams, *The Best Butter in*
    the World: A History of Sainsbury's
    (London: Ebury Press, 1994), 89.
3   Jacob's father, Simon van den Bergh,
    founded the firm that became the world's
    largest producer of margarine, later
    merging with the British company Lever
    Brothers to form Unilever.
4   While Robert Sainsbury's mother was
    Jewish, the family was not observant.
5   *Sir Robert Sainsbury in conversation*, 7.
6   Ibid., 5–6.
7   Ibid., 34.
8   Ibid., 37.
9   Ibid., 25.
10 Ibid., 15.
11 Ibid., 43.
12 Lisa Sainsbury in conversation with
    Steven Hooper, 5 March 1996, unpublished
    typescript, 8.
13 'Arts Patron Sir Robert Sainsbury Dies,'
    BBC News Online, 3 April 2000.
14 Lisa Sainsbury in conversation, 6.
15 Ibid., 7.
16 Martin Vander Weyer, 'The New Statesman
    Profile – The Sainsbury Family,' *New*
    Statesman (12 June 2000). Posted
    at http://www.newstatesman.com/
    print/200006120013.

17 Lisa Sainsbury to David Sainsbury,
    18 March 1994. SRU.
18 Elizabeth Estève-Coll in conversation
    with the author.
19 *Sir Robert Sainsbury in Conversation*, 255.
20 Ibid., 99.
21 Ibid., 100.
22 Peter Yorke, in conversation with the author.
23 'La Collection de M. Robert Sainsbury,'
    Connaissance des Arts, 106 (December
    1960), 151 [translation by the author].
24 Lisa Sainsbury in conversation, 30–31.
25 *Sir Robert Sainsbury in Conversation*, 176.
    The guarantee was never lifted.
26 Nelson A. Rockefeller endowed the
    Museum of Primitive Art, which housed
    his personal collection, in 1957. In 1969, he
    closed the museum and offered the
    collection to the Metropolitan Museum
    of Art, where it now resides in the
    Michael C. Rockefeller Wing.
27 *Sir Robert Sainsbury in Conversation*, 197.
28 Robert J. Sainsbury, 'Introduction', *The*
    Robert and Lisa Sainsbury Collection,
    exhibition catalogue (New York: Museum
    of Primitive Art, 1963), unpaginated.
29 *Sir Robert Sainsbury in Conversation*, 102.
30 Ibid., 55.
31 Rudi Oxenaar to Mr and Mrs Robert J.
    Sainsbury, 8 December 1965. SRU.
32 In the mid-1980s, Peter Lasko, who was
    writing an essay for the comprehensive
    three-volume catalogue of the Sainsbury
    collection (published by Yale University
    Press in 1997), was worried about the
    authenticity of the *Virgin and Child*, and
    a subsequent X-ray revealed that the entire
    top, including the head, was a later addition.
    The figure was removed from display.
33 Robert J. Sainsbury to Rudi Oxenaar,
    25 August 1966. SRU.
34 Robert J. Sainsbury, 'Introduction',
    Collectie Robert & Lisa Sainsbury,
    6/8–2/10 1966, exhibition catalogue
    (Otterlo: Rijksmuseum Kröller-Müller,
    1966), unpaginated.
35 Ibid.
36 Robert J. Sainsbury, 'Holland/Speech'
    (July 20, 1966). SRU.
37 The museum's first choice to design the
    Sainsbury exhibit was Enrico Hartsuyker,
    a young Dutch architect. Hartsuyker was
    introduced to the Sainsburys, but for
    some reason was unable to accept the
    commission. Rudi Oxenaar to Robert J.
    Sainsbury, 17 January 1966. SRU.

38 Robert J. Sainsbury to Kho Liang Ie,
    26 August 1966. SRU.
39 Robert J. Sainsbury to Rudi Oxenaar,
    28 December 1967. SRU.
40 Sir Robert Sainsbury to Kho Liang Ie,
    21 March 1974. SRU.
41 José Manser, 'Private View,' *Design*, 278
    (February 1972), 50.

CHAPTER TWO - LIFE EVER AFTER
(PP. 48–83)

1   Bridget Williams, *The Best Butter in
    the World: A History of Sainsbury's*
    (London: Ebury Press, 1994), 152, 160.
2   *Sir Robert Sainsbury in Conversation
    with Steven Hooper*, September 1982 –
    November 1992 (privately published,
    2005), 100.
3   Ibid., 223.
4   Ibid., 242.
5   Robert J. Sainsbury, 'My Criterion for
    Acquiring – My Purpose in Disposing,'
    Robert and Lisa Sainsbury Collection,
    ed. Robert J. Sainsbury, exhibition
    catalogue (Norwich: University of
    East Anglia, 1978), 15.
6   *Sir Robert Sainsbury in Conversation*, 241.
7   Frank Thistlethwaite to Robert J.
    Sainsbury, 29 July 1964. SRU.
8   Michael Sanderson, *The History of the
    University of East Anglia, Norwich* (London:
    Hambledon and London, 2002), 249.
9   Ibid., 251.
10 Frank Thistlethwaite, *Origins: A Personal
    Reminiscence of UEA's Foundation*
    (Cambridge: privately published, 2000), 107.
11 Ibid., 108.
12 Since Alan Sainsbury divided his shares in
    the company among his three sons, David
    Sainsbury effectively controlled the firm.
13 Frank Thistlethwaite to Sir Robert
    Sainsbury, 27 November 1973. UEA.
14 Ian Ritchie, in conversation with
    the author.
15 Nikolaus Pevsner, *A History of Building
    Types* (Princeton: Princeton University
    Press, 1976), 111.
16 William Shakespeare, *1 Henry VI*, II, iii.
17 Terry Kirk, *The Architecture of Modern
    Italy*, vol. 1 (New York: Princeton
    Architectural Press, 2005), 67.
18 Dennis Farr, 'Desenfans, Noel Joseph
    (1744–1807)', in *Oxford Dictionary of
    National Biography* (Oxford: Oxford
    University Press, 2004), online edn,
    January 2008; Gillian Darley, *John Soane:*

An Accidental Romantic (New Haven: Yale
University Press, 1999), 181.
19 Giles Waterfield, 'A History of Dulwich
    Picture Gallery', in Ian A. C. Dejardin et al.,
    *Rembrandt to Gainsborough: Masterpieces
    from Dulwich Picture Gallery* (London:
    Merrell Holberton, 1999), 19.
20 Ibid., 56.
21 Farr, 'Desenfans, Noel Joseph'.
22 Darley, *Soane*, 206.
23 Waterfield, 'History', 29–30.
24 Pevsner, *History of Building Types*, 123.
25 John Soane, *Memoirs of the Professional
    Life of an Architect* (privately printed
    1835). Quoted in Darley, *Soane*, 273.
26 A Correspondent [John Summerson],
    'Architecture of the Mind', *The Times*
    (20 January 1937).
27 Waterfield, 'History', 37.
28 Darley, *Soane*, 271.
29 Albert C. Barnes, *The Art in Painting*
    (New York: Harcourt, Brace and Company,
    1925), 9.
30 A. H. Shaw, 'Profiles: De Medici in Merion',
    New Yorker (22 September 1928), 32.
31 Ibid., 29.
32 Howard Greenfield, *The Devil and Dr
    Barnes: Portrait of an American Art
    Collector* (New York: Penguin, 1987),
    34–35.
33 *New York Times* (14 January 1923), 17.
34 Greenfield, *Devil and Dr Barnes*, 76.
35 Ibid., 73–74.
36 Henry Hart, *Dr Barnes of Merion: An
    Appreciation* (New York: Farrar, Straus and
    Company, 1963), 23.
37 John Dewey, *Art as Experience* (New York:
    Minton, Balch & Company, 1934), ii.
38 John Lukacs, *Philadelphia: Patricians &
    Philistines, 1900–1950* (New York: Farrar
    Straus Giroux, 1980), 295.
39 Quoted in Elizabeth Greenwell Grossman,
    The Civic Architecture of Paul Cret
    (Cambridge: Cambridge University Press,
    1996), 114.
40 Paul P. Cret, 'A Recent Theory of the
    Natural Lighting of Art Galleries',
    Journal of the AIA, 11 (1923), 225.
41 'The Buildings of the Barnes Foundation
    at Merion, Pa.', *Architecture*, 53
    (January 1926), 1–6.
42 On 'French Renaissance' see: Lukacs,
    Philadelphia, 269; Hart, *Dr Barnes*, 81;
    and Greenfield, *Devil and Dr Barnes*, 72.
    On 'new classicism' see Grossman, *Civic
    Architecture*, 139.

43 Paul Cret, 'The Buildings for the Barnes Foundation', upublished typescript, prepared for Albert C. Barnes, 29 November 1922. BF.

44 Ibid.

45 Albert C. Barnes to Paul P. Cret, 23 October 1923. Paul Philippe Cret Papers, 1865–1976. UP.

46 Albert C. Barnes to Paul P. Cret, 5 September 1923. BF.

47 Albert C. Barnes to Paul P. Cret, 7 September 1923. BF.

48 Paul P. Cret to Albert C. Barnes, 26 February 1924. Paul Philippe Cret Papers, 1865–1976. UP.

49 Albert C. Barnes to Paul P. Cret, 25 October 1924. BF.

50 Theo B. White, ed., *Paul Philippe Cret: Architect and Teacher* (Philadelphia: Art Alliance Press, 1973). The nomination documents are in Paul Philippe Cret Papers, 1865–1976, UP.

51 Cret, 'Buildings'.

52 Hart, *Dr Barnes*, 80.

53 Ibid., 120.

54 Robert J. Sainsbury to Violette de Mazia, 27 February 1957. BF.

55 John Anderson, *Art Held Hostage: The Battle over the Barnes Collec*tion (New York: W. W. Norton & Company, 2003), 46–47.

56 One legal scholar has pointed out that trusts established by founders of personal museums are especially at risk of being altered since 'private donors, for better or worse, are focused on their own personal agenda. The donors do not have the humility … to realize that museums need flexibility for survival. Single donors are more likely to have stringent administrative terms. Single donors are likely to see a charity's endowment as their own money instead of being in the public trust and think they are only being prudent in leaving specific instructions.' Emmeline Babb, 'The Public Value and Legal Battles of a Single Donor Museum', Harvard Law School Student Scholarship Series, 4 May 2007, 16. Posted at http://lsr.nellco.org/harvard_law/.

57 Joshua Levine 'The Vision Quest of Helene Kröller-Müller', *Forbes Magazine* (8 June 2009).

58 Jan Van Adrichem, 'Collectors of Modern Art in Holland: Picasso as pars pro toto', *Simiolus: Netherlands Quarterly for the History of Art*, 22/3 (1993–4), 174.

59 Piet de Jonge, 'Helene Kröller-Müller', in Piet de Jonge and David A. Troy, *Van Gogh to Mondrian: Modern Art from the Kröller-Müller Museum* (Atlanta: High Museum of Art, 2004), 24.

60 Franz Schulze, *Mies van der Rohe: A Critical Biography* (Chicago: University of Chicago Press, 1985), 59.

61 De Jonge, 'Helene Kröller-Müller', 25.

62 Sergio Polano, *Hendrik Petrus Berlage: Complete Works* (New York: Rizzoli, 1988), 208.

63 Schulze, *Mies van der Rohe*, 63.

64 Richard Padovan, 'Kröller-Müller', *Architectural Review* (February 1978), 75.

65 Léon Ploegaerts and Pierre Puttemans, *L'Œuvre architecturale de Henry van de Velde* (Brussels: Atelier Vokaer, 1987), 342.

66 De Jonge, 'Helene Kröller-Müller', 30.

67 Patricia Cummings Loud, *The Art Museums of Louis I. Kahn* (Durham, NC: Duke University Press, 1989), 43.

68 Wim de Wit, 'Four Architects and a Museum', in de Jonge and Troy, *Van Gogh to Mondrian*, 118.

CHAPTER THREE - THE COLLECTORS AND THE ARCHITECT
(PP. 84–102)

1 'Proposed Gifts of Sir Robert and Lady Sainsbury and their Son David to the University of _____,' typed draft of the deed of gift, 26 March 1973. UEA.

2 Sir Robert Sainsbury to Kho Liang Ie, 14 November 1973. SRU

3 Frank Thistlethwaite to Sir Robert Sainsbury, 11 December 1973. UEA.

4 Ibid.

5 Frank Thistlethwaite, 'Denys Lasdun and the Development Plan', unpublished note, 3 July 1996. Muthesius Papers, UEA.

6 Memorandum, Patricia Whitt to Frank Thistlethwaite, 3 December 1973. UEA.

7 Frank Thistlethwaite to Sir Robert Sainsbury, 11 December 1973. UEA.

8 Frank Thistlethwaite, *Origins: A Personal Reminiscence of UEA's Foundation* (Cambridge: privately published, 2000), 110.

9 The list has many more errors: Ahrends Burton & Koralek are identified as 'Aarons, Behran & Comarze', Shepheard, Epstein & Hunter as 'Gabby Epstein & Peter Shepherd', and the winners of the Burrell Gallery competition are referred to as 'Messrs. B. Garsoon [Barry Gasson], J. Meunier and B. Anderson [Brit Andresen]',

the writer being, apparently, unaware that the last is a woman.

10 Kho Liang Ie, 'Open Space,' press release, Design Gallery VIVID, Rotterdam, 2000. Posted at www.vividvormgeving.nl/press-release/kho%20liang%20ie.htm.

11 Frank Thistlethwaite to Sir Robert Sainsbury, 11 December 1973. UEA. Kho, whose English was imperfect, gave Thistlethwaite the impression that he had previously collaborated with Foster on a project in the Netherlands. Foster confirms that there was no such project.

12 Bryan Robertson, John Russell and Lord Snowdon, *Private View: The Lively World of British Art* (London: Thomas Nelson & Sons, 1965), 158.

13 Tony Warner, 'Sir Robert Sainsbury,' *Artline* (summer 1989), 10. By 1973, Aalto was effectively retired; he died in 1976. The Sainsburys' interest in Aalto is mentioned in *Sir Robert Sainsbury in Conversation with Steven Hooper*, September 1982 – November 1992 (privately published, 2005), 246, and in Steven Hooper, 'Introduction', *Robert and Lisa Sainsbury Collection*, vol. 1: *European 19th and 20th Century Paintings, Drawings and Sculpture*, ed. Steven Hooper (New Haven: Yale University Press, 1997), lxxi.

14 'Sir Robert Sainsbury's Private Library (1996)', unpublished catalogue, compiled when the library was donated to the Sainsbury Research Unit. SRU.

15 *Architects' Journal* (12 April 1978), 676. Steven Hooper, in conversation with the author.

16 'Sainsbury Centre for the Visual Arts, Possible Architect', attached to letter sent by Frank Thistlethwaite to Sir Robert Sainsbury, 12 December 1973, annotated in Sir Robert Sainsbury's hand. SRU.

17 Sir Robert Sainsbury to the Rt Hon. Patrick Jenkin MP, 28 March 1984. SRU.

18 Hooper, 'Introduction', lxxi–lxxii.

19 Norman Foster, 'Meeting the Sainsburys', speech on the occasion of the presentation to Sir Robert and Lady Sainsbury of the Freedom of the City of Norwich, 23 June 1999, typescript. SRU.

20 Ibid.

21 Norman Foster, Arthur Batchelor Lecture, University of East Anglia, Norwich, 7 February 1978, typescript. SRU.

22 Frank Thistlethwaite to Bernard Feilden, 8 February 1974. UEA.

23 Sir Hugh Casson to Frank Thistlethwaite, 11 February 1974. UEA.

24 Acceptance speech at American Institute of Architects Gold Medal ceremony, 1994, Washington, DC. Quoted by Martin Pawley, *Norman Foster: A Global Architecture* (New York: Universe, 1999), 14.

25 'Fitzroy Street Project', *Architectural Design*, 42 (1972), 699.

26 David Jenkins, ed., *Norman Foster: Works*, vol. 1 (Munich: Prestel Verlag, 2002), 239.

27 Notes of a meeting, 4 April 1974. UEA.

28 Thistlethwaite, *Origins*, 109.

29 It is unclear exactly how the Centre was named, but it was probably decided by Bob and Lisa. Frank Thistlethwaite's letter of 11 December 1973 to Bob includes a reference to the 'Sainsbury Centre for the Visual Arts'. By the time of the April 1974 press release announcing the appointment of the architects, it was simply the 'Sainsbury Centre for Visual Arts'.

30 Notes of a meeting, 4 April 1974. UEA.

31 Ibid.

32 Press Release, B/15, University of East Anglia, 29 April 1974. SRU.

33 Kho's sketch has not come to light.

34 'Problems', Job 188, Sheet 26, drawn by Birkin Haward, Foster Associates, 28 September 1974. FP.

35 Michael Sanderson, *The History of the University of East Anglia, Norwich* (London: Hambledon and London, 2002), 141.

36 Peter Dormer and Stefan Muthesius, *Concrete and Open Skies: Architecture at the University of East Anglia, 1962–2000* (London: Unicorn Press, 2001), 64–65.

37 Sanderson, *History*, 143. Another linear campus of that period was Arthur Erickson and Geoffrey Massey's 1963 competition-winning design for Simon Fraser University in Vancouver.

38 'Itinerary', Foster Associates, 24 September 1974. SRU.

39 Foster, Batchelor Lecture.

40 Jenkins, ed., *Norman Foster: Works*, vol. 1, 386.

41 Ibid.

42 'Important New Structure in Houston', *Connoisseur*, 186 (May 1974), 59.

43 Jenkins, ed., *Norman Foster: Works*, vol. 1, 386.

44 Thistlethwaite, *Origins*, 109.

45 Andrew Peckham, 'A Critique of the Sainsbury Centre,' *AD Profiles 19* (August 1978), 6.

46 Norman Foster, 'Letters', *Architectural Design*, 49 (1979), 92.

47 Thistlethwaite, *Origins*, 109.

CHAPTER FOUR - THE SHED
(PP. 103–36)

1 Sir Robert Sainsbury to Frank Thistlethwaite, 5 January 1975. SRU

2 For the Willis Faber project, Foster had the American renderer Helmut Jacoby prepare two drawings to gain planning approval. After a four-storey solution was rejected, Foster presented a three-storey option (his preference), which was subsequently approved.

3 'Buildings and Shadows', Job 188, Sheet 15, drawn by Bodo Zapp, overdrawn by Birkin Haward, Foster Associates, 30 August 1974. FP.

4 Peter Dormer and Stefan Muthesius, *Concrete and Open Skies: Architecture at the University of East Anglia, 1962–2000* (London: Unicorn Press, 2001), 98.

5 See Michael Sanderson, *The History of the University of East Anglia, Norwich* (London: Hambledon and London, 2002), 171.

6 'Problems', Job 188, Sheet 26, drawn by Birkin Haward, Foster Associates, 28 September 1974. FP.

7 Sir Robert Sainsbury, lecture at the University of East Anglia, 20 November 1975, typescript. SRU.

8 David Jenkins, ed., *Norman Foster: Works*, vol. 1 (Munich: Prestel Verlag, 2002), 383.

9 Ibid., 354.

10 Martin Pawley, 'Sainsbury Centre, Building Revisits: Five', *Architects' Journal* (4 July 1984), 42.

11 Bernard Feilden to Frank Thistlethwaite, 19 May 1975. UAE.

12 Norman Foster, 'With Wendy', *Norman Foster: Works*, ed. Jenkins, vol. 1, 424.

13 Ibid., 425.

14 Norman Foster, 'Meeting the Sainsburys', *Norman Foster: Works*, ed. Jenkins, vol. 1, 366.

15 Kenneth Powell, 'Shed Aesthetics', *Architects' Journal* (14 August 2003), 35.

16 Norman Foster, 'Siting of the Sainsbury Centre for the Visual Arts', undated typescript. SRU.

17 Tony Hunt had been invited to join Foster Associates but he says that he preferred to remain an external consultant, which allowed him to work with other architects.

18 'It was also an early example of a low-energy "green" architecture.' Norman Foster, 'Meeting the Sainsburys', speech on the occasion of the presentation to Sir Robert and Lady Sainsbury of the Freedom of the City of Norwich, 23 June 1999, typescript. SRU.

19 Leonard R. Bachman, *Integrated Buildings: The Systems Basis of Architecture* (New York: John Wiley & Sons, 2003), 4.

20 Loren Butt, 'Environmental Engineering for the Sainsbury Center for Visual Arts, UEA', unpublished memorandum, January 2010. FP.

21 Loren Butt, lecture at the Construction Industry Conference, London, 15 May 1980, unpublished typescript. FP.

22 Jenkins, ed., *Norman Foster: Works*, vol. 1, 398.

23 Martin Pawley, 'Norman Foster 6.0, 6.0, 6.0', *Blueprint* (May 1984); reprinted in *The Strange Death of Architectural Criticism: Martin Pawley Collected Writings*, ed. David Jenkins (London: Black Dog Publishing, 2007), 93.

24 Roy Fleetwood, in conversation with the author.

25 Sanderson, *History*, 258.

26 See Paula Deitz, 'English Gardens with a U.S. Flavor', *New York Times* (13 May 1984), F79.

27 Paul Heyer, *Architects on Architecture: New Directions in American Architecture* (New York: Van Nostrand Reinhold, 1993), 303

28 John Walker, 'The Early Years', *Norman Foster: Works*, ed. Jenkins, vol. 1, 93.

29 'Foster Associates Recent Work', *Architectural Design*, 42 (1972), 686.

30 Jonathan Glancey, 'Engineering a Thing of Beauty', *The Independent* (23 January 1991).

31 Sir Robert Sainsbury to Birkin Haward, 23 November 1976. SRU.

32 Foster, Arthur Batchelor Lecture, University of Easy Anglia, Norwich, 7 February 1978, typescript. SRU.

33 Architect's brief for the School of Art and Music. The government allowance was, at that time, specified in square feet: it equated to 14.5 square metres. The fine arts school requested offices of 15.8 square metres, but were obliged to accept space of 14.9 square metres. The schools of Fine Arts and Music were administratively linked, even though by 1974, Music had its own building. The two schools separated in 1992.

34 'Fitzroy Street Project', *Architectural Design*, 42 (1972), 699–701.

35   John Mitchell in conversation with
     the author.
36   Alastair Best, 'In the Beginning', *Norman
     Foster: Works*, ed. Jenkins, vol. 1, 116.
37   Norman Foster to Sir Robert Sainsbury,
     7 September 1976. SRU.
38   Stephanie Williams, 'The Sainsbury
     Collection: Private Taste Made Public',
     Sunday Times Magazine (2 April 1978),
     79. Foster was referring to the famous
     scientist's quote about two cultures:
     science and the humanities.

CHAPTER FIVE - THE LIVING AREA
(PP. 137–49)

1   *Sir Robert Sainsbury in Conversation
     with Steven Hooper*, September 1982 –
     November 1992 (privately published,
     2005), 268.
2   Sir Robert Sainsbury to Andrew Ritchie,
     2 December 1975. SRU.
3   Ian Lambot, ed., *Norman Foster,
     Foster Associates: Buildings and Projects*,
     vol. 2: *1971–1978* (Hong Kong: Watermark,
     1989), 118.
4   Norman Foster, Arthur Batchelor Lecture,
     University of East Anglia, Norwich,
     7 February 1978, typescript. SRU.
5   Claude R. Engle to Norman Foster,
     6 June 1977. SRU.
6   According to Sexton, the lighting system
     of the Pompidou Centre was replaced two
     years after the building opened.
7   Sir Robert Sainsbury to Frank
     Thistlethwaite, 20 October 1976. SRU.
8   *Sir Robert Sainsbury in Conversation*, 286.
9   Sir Robert Sainsbury to Anthony Hunt,
     9 August 1978. SRU.
10   Norman Foster to Lanning Roper,
     17 August 1977. SRU.
11   Lanning Roper to Roy Fleetwood,
     15 July 1977. SRU.

CHAPTER SIX - LIFE AND LUX
(PP. 150–63)

1   The Robert and Lisa Sainsbury Charitable
     Fund contributed £25,000 towards the
     costs of the opening.
2   'The Sainsbury File', pamphlet of the
     Norwich and UEA Communist Party,
     1978. SRU.
3   Sir Robert Sainsbury to Frank
     Thistlethwaite, 10 April 1978. UEA.
4   Editorial, *Burlington Magazine*, 120
     (1978), 565.
5   The £4.2 million cost was covered by the
     original gift of £3 million; the interest on
     the gift, amounting to £1 million; David
     Sainsbury's gift of Sainsbury shares worth
     £1.5 million; the university's direct
     contribution of £632,000; a gift from
     Annabel Sainsbury of £120,000 to cover
     the cost of the footbridge; and an additional
     gift from the Robert and Lisa Sainsbury
     Charitable Fund of £50,000. When the
     costs had been met, £2.1 million was left
     in the endowment. Michael Sanderson,
     *The History of the University of East Anglia,
     Norwich* (London: Hambledon and
     London, 2002), 258.
6   Ibid. For the Pompidou Centre see Andrew
     Rabeneck, 'Beaubourg: Process & Purposes',
     Architectural Design, 47 (1977), 108.
7   Editorial, *Burlington Magazine*, 565.
8   Geoffrey Jellicoe to Sir Robert and Lady
     Sainsbury, 7 April 1978. SRU.
9   Edward Lucie-Smith to Lady Sainsbury,
     5 April 1978. SRU.
10   Malcolm Bradbury to Lady Sainsbury
     26 April 1978. SRU.
11   Charles McKean, 'When Architects Play to
     the Gallery', *The Times* (7 April 1978), 16.
12   Suzanne Stephens, 'Modernism
     Reconstituted', *Progressive Architecture*
     (February 1979), 50.
13   'Speaking of the Sainsbury Centre',
     AD Profiles 19 (August 1978), 28.
14   Ibid., 29.
15   Ibid., 30.
16   Ibid.
17   Ian Lambot, ed., *Norman Foster, Foster
     Associates: Buildings and Projects*, vol.
     2: *1971–1978* (Hong Kong: Watermark,
     1989), 114.
18   *AD Profiles*, 33.
19   Ibid., 28.
20   Ibid., 31.
21   Ibid., 27.
22   Hugh Casson, *Hugh Casson: Diary*
     (London: Macmillan, 1981), 33.
23   Norman Foster, Arthur Batchelor Lecture,
     University of East Anglia, Norwich,
     7 February 1978, typescript. SRU.
24   Stephanie Williams, 'The Sainsbury
     Collection: Private Taste Made Public',
     Sunday Times Magazine (2 April 1978), 79.
25   *AD Profiles*, 67.
26   Report to the Senate from the Board
     of the School of Fine Arts and Music,
     4 December 1978, Document K. UEA.
27   Andrew Martindale to Michael Paulson-
     Ellis, 1 February 1979. UEA.

28 Memorandum, M. D. Crowther to Estates Officer, 1 August 1979. SRU.

29 Martin Pawley, 'Sainsbury Centre, Building Revisits: Five', *AJ* (4 July 1984), 44.

30 Jos Boys, 'Too much daylight at Sainsbury Centre could damage exhibits', *Building Design* (8 September 1978).

31 Norman Foster to Sir Robert Sainsbury, 19 September 1978. SRU.

32 Memorandum, Loren Butt to Norman Foster, 10 October 1978. SRU.

33 Norman Foster to Alan Borg, 13 June 1978. SRU.

34 Casson, *Diary*, 33.

35 Frank Thistlethwaite to Sir Robert Sainsbury, 19 December 1979. SRU.

36 Sir Robert Sainsbury to Frank Thistlethwaite, 16 October 1979. SRU.

37 Borg stayed for four years at the Sainsbury Centre, before moving on to become director of the Imperial War Museum in London.

38 Sir Robert Sainsbury, private note to himself, 26 June 1978. SRU.

39 Sir Robert Sainsbury to John Fletcher, 6 December 1978. SRU.

CHAPTER SEVEN - FOSTER'S FORTUNE
(PP. 164–78)

1 Peter Cook, 'Criticism', *Architectural Review* (December 1978), 355–56.

2 *Times Higher Education Supplement* (18 August 1978).

3 Stephanie Williams, *Hongkong Bank: The Building of Norman Foster's Masterpiece* (Boston: Little Brown and Company, 1989), 49. In 1984, Graham joined Foster Associates as a director with responsibility for financial management, remaining in this role until his retirement in 1990.

4 'Hongkong Bank: Building of the Year?', *Progressive Architecture* (March 1985), 235.

5 Alastair Best, *Architects' Journal* (1 December 1982).

6 Jonathan Glancey, 'Hongkong Bank', *Architectural Review* (May 1981), 269.

7 Werner Blaser, ed., *Norman Foster Sketches* (Basel: Birkhäuser Verlag, 1992), 190.

8 The Sackler Galleries opened in 1991, seven years after Prince Charles's celebrated 'monstrous carbuncle' speech, attacking modern architecture.

9 Martin Pawley, *Norman Foster: A Global Architecture* (New York: Universe, 1999), 19.

10 Heinrich Klotz, *The History of Postmodern Architecture*, trans. Radka Donell (Cambridge, Mass.: MIT Press, 1988), 429.

11 Sir Robert Sainsbury to Derek C. Burke, 14 June 1990. SRU.

12 Reyner Banham, *Los Angeles: The Architecture of Four Ecologies* (Harmondsworth, Middlesex: Penguin Press, 1971), 233.

13 Ibid., 223.

14 Ibid., 230.

15 The architectural profession resisted standardized exteriors, so SCSD did not include exterior building skin components. More than 2,000 schools were built using the system. Chris Arnold, Andrew Rabeneck and David Brindle, 'BSD', *Architectural Design*, 61 (1971), 679.

16 Kazys Varnelis, ed., *The Philip Johnson Tapes: Interviews by Robert A. M. Stern* (New York: Monacelli Press, 2008), 43.

17 Quoted in Peter Jones, *Ove Arup: Masterbuilder of the Twentieth Century* (New Haven: Yale University Press, 2006), 274.

18 Martin Pawley, 'The Secret Life of Engineers', *The Strange Death of Architectural Criticism: Martin Pawley Collected Writings*, ed. David Jenkins (London: Black Dog Publishing, 2007), 175.

19 Ibid.

20 Robert Venturi, Denise Scott Brown and Steven Izenour, *Learning from Las Vegas: The Forgotten Symbolism of Architectural Form* (Cambridge, Mass.: MIT Press, 1977).

21 Martin Pawley, 'Norman Foster 6.0, 6.0, 6.0', *Blueprint* (May 1984); reprinted in *Strange Death of Architectural Criticism*, ed. Jenkins, 93.

22 A. G. McDowell to Foster Associates, 2 September 1987. SRU.

23 The new panels fitted more tightly together, which led to unpredicted problems with water run-off from the roof and smearing of the white wall panels with dirt. As a remedy, square-section downpipes made of grey rubber tubing were discreetly inserted into the vertical channels between the panels, which solved the problem, except in the heaviest downpours.

24 Christopher Leaver to David Sainsbury, 27 March 1987. SRU.

25 'Foster's Centre Sheds its Skin', *Architects' Journal* (7 October 1987), 9. The new panels substituted mineral or rock-wool insulation for the troublesome phenolic foam, although it is likely that this actually

reduced the insulation value, since rock wool has a lower U-value than phenolic foam. A. G. McDowell to Foster Associates, 2 September 1987. SRU.

CHAPTER EIGHT - ARCHITECT REDUX
(PP. 179–207)

1 Norman Foster, 'Happy Birthday!' October 1986. SCVA.

2 Ibid.

3 Steven Phelps [Hooper], *Art and Artefacts of the Pacific, Africa and the Americas: The James Hooper Collection* (London: Hutchinson, 1976).

4 Memorandum, Derek Gillman and Steven Hooper to David Sainsbury, 12 November 1986. Courtesy of Derek Gillman.

5 Paula Deitz, 'At the Met, 9,000 Objects in 40 Straight Lines', *New York Times* (11 December 1988).

6 The first use of a recessed, flexible lighting system was by Edison Price in the American pavilion at the 1967 world's fair in Montreal.

7 Hugh Pearman, 'Designed to Steal the Show', *Sunday Times* (12 May 1991).

8 Alastair Best, 'An extension with more to it than meets the eye', *The Independent* (8 May 1991), 19.

9 David Jenkins, ed., *Norman Foster: Works*, vol. 1 (Munich: Prestel Verlag, 2002), 446.

10 Franz Schulze, *Philip Johnson: Life and Work* (Chicago: University of Chicago Press, 1996), 255.

11 The museum originally had five offices, which were later converted into small galleries.

12 John Peter, *The Oral History of Modern Architecture: Interviews with the Greatest Architects of the Twentieth Century* (New York: Harry N. Abrams, Inc., 1994), 231.

13 In 1944, a German flying bomb severely damaged the museum. Most of the damage was to the mausoleum and the almshouses, which were rebuilt. Since Soane's genius was now recognized, the building was carefully restored to its pre-Victorian condition. The galleries built by Hall, were unharmed, and form a part of the museum today. See Francesco Nevola, *Soane's Favorite Subject: The Story of the Dulwich Picture Gallery* (Dulwich: Dulwich Picture Gallery, 2000), 146–63.

14 Paul Goldberger, 'Sincerest flattery or the subtlest form of dishonor?' *New York Times* (24 September 1989).

15 Letter to the editor, *New York Times* (24 December 1989).

16 Derek Gillman in conversation with the author.

17 Peter, *Oral History*, 211.

18 Nicole Coolidge Rousmaniere, 'Sainsbury Centre for Visual Arts: Sir Robert and Lady Sainsbury's Collection of Japanese Art', *Arts of Asia*, 39/4 (July–August 2009), 61.

19 Steven Hooper, ed., *Robert and Lisa Sainsbury Collection*, vol. 1: *European 19th and 20th Century Paintings, Drawings and Sculpture* (New Haven: Yale University Press, 1997), xiv.

20 The quotations from the testimonials were transcribed by the author from a privately produced compact disk, 'A concert in celebration of the life of Sir Robert Sainsbury, 1906–2000'. Recorded in St John's, Smith Square, 3 October 2000.

CHAPTER NINE - A PLACE FOR ART
(PP. 208–21)

1 Patricia Te Arapo Wallace, Review, *Contemporary Pacific*, 19 (2007), 661.

2 Steven Hooper, *Pacific Encounters: Art and Divinity in Polynesia, 1760–1860* (London: British Museum Press, 2006). In 2008, the exhibition was shown at the Musée du quai Branly in Paris.

3 Le Corbusier, *Towards a New Architecture*, trans. Frederick Etchells (Mineola, N.Y.: Dover, 1986), 29 [first published 1931].

4 Michael Sanderson, *The History of the University of East Anglia, Norwich* (London: Hambledon and London, 2002), 405–6.

5 'Foster is popular because he supplies the look of innovation without the pain of actually changing anything.' Rowan Moore, 'Norman's Conquest', *Prospect* (20 March 2002).

6 http://www.timesonline.co.uk/tol/life_ and_style/education/sunday_times_uni-versity_guide/

7 Geoffrey Scott, *The Architecture of Humanism: A Study in the History of Taste*, rev. 2nd edn (London: Constable, 1924; repr. Gloucester, Mass.: Peter Smith, 1965), 174 [first published 1914].

Acknowledgments

Many people contributed to this book in many different ways. First, I must thank David Sainsbury for open-handedly entrusting me with the story of his parents' magnificent project. Unfailingly generous and supportive – and never intrusive – he took time out of a busy schedule frequently to discuss his parents and answer my questions. His wife, Susie Sainsbury, likewise shared her memories of Bob and Lisa and made my many visits to London enjoyable and rewarding, as well as informative.

Norman Foster is, of course, a central figure in any biography of the Sainsbury Centre. It cannot be pleasant to have a stranger snooping into your professional past, and Lord Foster graciously endured my nosy questions and gave me several hours of his time during two extended conversations. I found his thoughtful insights into the design process richly rewarding. The observations of Lady Foster added to my understanding of Bob and Lisa Sainsbury.

One of the pleasures of researching this book was meeting the many friends of Bob and Lisa – and I was only scratching the surface. Steven Hooper, a skilled anthropologist, was the perfect witness – direct, thoughtful, and circumspect; he provided much useful information for my study, and took time out of his Christmas holidays to review the manuscript. Hooper's interviews with Robert and Lisa Sainsbury are an invaluable record, but in addition he gave me unrestricted access to the Robert J. Sainsbury Archive at the Sainsbury Research Unit. This proved a crucial source of information, for Sir Robert saved everything: correspondence, speeches, confidential memos, press cuttings, guest lists, itineraries, thank-you notes. The irrepressible Elizabeth Estève-Coll shared her many memories of Bob and Lisa, and having served as vice-chancellor of the University of East Anglia was able to provide interesting insights into the academic side of the story, and to suggest several valuable sources. My special thanks to George Sexton, who patiently explained the intricacies of exhibition lighting to a novice, and kindly shared many stories of his enduring relationship with Bob and Lisa and the Sainsbury Centre. This book also gave me the opportunity to renew my contact with landscape essayist Paula Deitz, a close friend of Lisa Sainsbury, who also provided useful information about Lanning Roper.

Norman Foster frequently stresses that architecture is the result of teamwork, and I spoke to many people – though hardly all – who worked on the design and construction of the Sainsbury Centre. My thanks to Ian Ritchie, who over the course of several pleasurable dinners, shared his memories of the early days at Foster Associates; Birkin Haward was helpful in explaining the genesis of the project; Loren Butt answered my technical questions and also explained the workings of the Foster office; during an interesting half-day, Roy Fleetwood recalled the evolution of the project, and described his memories of the Fitzroy Street studio; and Graham Phillips provided a thoughtful overview of the design of the Crescent Wing, as well as the opportunity to experience his beautiful Skywood House. The staff of Foster + Partners was invariably helpful. Senior partner Spencer de Grey was extremely accommodating throughout my research; long-time Foster collaborator David Nelson provided useful recollections of the Sainsbury project; Chris Connell explained the development of the Crescent Wing and the Link; David Jenkins facilitated my access to the Foster drawing archives, and the multi-volume *Norman Foster: Works* series, which he edits, was a consistently useful source. Katy Harris, Gayle Mault and Kathryn Tollervey were exceptionally helpful in identifying and assembling drawings and photographs of the building. Several consultants talked to me about the Sainsbury Centre project. The energetic Tony Hunt, now retired, explained the genesis of the structure of the building, and, having worked with Norman Foster on many projects, had invaluable insights about the early days of the firm; Claude R. Engle described the ideas behind the use of natural light in the Sainsbury Centre – one of its distinctive features; and Stuart A. Johnson elucidated the technical aspects of the most recent refurbishment.

A number of people helped me to understand the project through the eyes of the university. Frank Thistlethwaite, who unswervingly supported Bob and Lisa's vision, died in 2003, but his daughter Harriet Thistlethwaite was kind enough to provide a copy of the relevant chapter of his privately published memoir, *Origins: A Personal Reminiscence of UEA's Foundation*. Patricia Whitt, the vice-chancellor's long-time personal assistant, also shared her recollections. Gordon Marshall died in 1995, but his deputy, Peter Yorke, was a valuable source of first-hand information on both the original building and the Crescent Wing. The Frank Thistlethwaite Papers in the University of East Anglia Archive filled in some of the blanks, thanks to the help of librarian Bridget Gillies. I must also acknowledge Michael Sanderson's scholarly study, *The History of the University of East Anglia, Norwich*.

My thanks to my friend and colleague John Dixon Hunt, who once taught at the University of East Anglia, and who provided an introduction to Derek Gillman, keeper of the Sainsbury Centre from 1985 to 1995. Gilman generously shared his memories of the design and construction of the Crescent Wing. By coincidence, he is now director of the Barnes Foundation in my hometown, Philadelphia, and he also facilitated my access to the Barnes archives, where Katy Rawdon, Barbara Beaucar, and Deborah Lennert provided helpful assistance. Nichola Johnson, director of the Sainsbury Centre from 1996 to 2010, shared her vivid recollections of the design and development of the Link. Simon Kaner, assistant director of the Sainsbury Institute for the Study of Japanese Arts and Cultures (SISJAC) was kind enough to show me around that facility. Thanks also to Jon Cook, dean of the Faculty of Arts and Humanities at East Anglia, for explaining the newly founded Sainsbury Institute for Art (SIfA) programme.

I would like to express my appreciation to John Onians and John Mitchell, faculty members of the School of World Art Studies and Museology, for recounting their early experience of the Sainsbury Centre. Stefan Muthesius was likewise accommodating, and his penetrating study, *Concrete and Open Skies* (written with the late Peter Dormer) proved a useful guide to the architectural history of the university. Patricia Hewitt, librarian of the Sainsbury Research Unit, was extremely helpful in steering me through the archives, so was Matthew Sillence. Thanks to Nick Warr of the School of World Art Studies and Kay Poludniowski of the Sainsbury Centre for help in collecting and scanning archival images. Clare Wood of the Museum of London Docklands provided images from the Sainsbury company archive. Thanks also to Jonathan Makepeace, Assistant Curator of the Photographs Collection at the Royal Institute of British Architects. At the University of Pennsylvania, Heather Glaser of the Fisher Fine Arts Library Image Collection and Chris Lippa of the Van Pelt Rare Book and Manuscript Library were likewise helpful in scanning images.

Raymond Blanc provided information about Sir Robert Sainsbury's eightieth birthday party at the Manoir aux Quat' Saisons, a wonderful establishment as I learned from personal experience. Thanks to Penny Hughes-Stanton for sharing background about her half-brother Corin. My search for material on Kho Liang Ie's role in the Sainsbury Centre project was assisted by Kees Spanjers in Amsterdam, and also Ineke van Ginneke, the author of a Dutch monograph on Kho's work, part of which my friend and neighbour Lydia McAuliffe translated. Thanks to Robert A. M. Stern for reminding me of Philip Johnson's long association with the Amon Carter Museum.

In Lord Sainsbury's Westminster office, Chris Foy provided useful background information on current developments at the Sainsbury Centre, Jane de Brule and Joe Burns were helpful in matters great and small; Chris Neale and Tracy Mattinson helped to make my trips effortless and efficient. I enjoyed working with Rosemary Roberts, who did a sterling job of copy editing. Special thanks to my wife, Shirley Hallam, for putting up with my many absences, and for reading the manuscript aloud. Andrew Wylie, my agent, is always a valuable sounding board but in this case he played the role of literary midwife, and I want to thank him for his suggestion that I consider writing this book, and for his helpful support throughout the process. David Sainsbury read and commented on the manuscript, as did Steven Hooper and Norman Foster. Any errors of fact are my own.

W.R.
The Icehouse, Philadelphia
December 2006 – December 2010

List of Illustrations

Sketch of the site, showing six options for the location of the Sainsbury Centre, 1974. Foster + Partners.

Pages 112–13
An early plan drawing of the Sainsbury Centre. Foster + Partners.

Norman Foster's conceptual sketch of the building. Foster + Partners.

A cross-section detail, showing the roof and wall, and the basement. Foster + Partners.

The building under construction, showing the basement and partially completed trusses. School of World Art Studies and Museology, University of East Anglia.

Pages 114–15
The 'Living Area' from above. Nigel Young/ Foster + Partners.

The 'kit of parts', consisting of display cases, bases and plinths, and free-standing panels. Foster + Partners.

George Sexton adjusting the exhibition lighting. School of World Art Studies and Museology, University of East Anglia.

Norman Foster and Sir Robert Sainsbury at the opening of the building, 7 April 1978. © Ken Kirkwood.

Interior view of the Living Area. Nigel Young/ Foster + Partners.

Page 116
The Sainsbury Centre in winter. School of World Art Studies and Museology, University of East Anglia.

The Sainsbury Centre from the east. © Ken Kirkwood.

FOSTER MOVES FORWARD
Page 189
Norman Foster with drawings for the Hongkong and Shanghai Bank, 1983. © Ken Kirkwood.

Interior of Norman Foster's Stansted Airport building, 1991. © Dennis Gilbert/VIEW.

Pages 190–91
Norman Foster's sketch of the Crescent Wing. Foster + Partners.

Aerial view, showing the relationship of the new Crescent Wing to the shed. Foster + Partners.

Excavation work for the Crescent Wing. Foster + Partners.

Cross-section through the Lower Gallery and offices of the Crescent Wing. Foster + Partners.

The Sainsburys at work in Foster's studio. Foster + Partners.

Pages 192–93
The study centre in the Crescent Wing, housing the open reserve. Nigel Young/Foster + Partners.

Bob and Lisa Sainsbury, 1985. Courtesy of Steven Hooper.

Female Shinto deity, Japan, Kamakura period, 1185–1332. Robert and Lisa Sainsbury Collection, University of East Anglia (UEA 1146). Photo James Austin.

Interior view of the glazed office corridor in the Crescent Wing. Nigel Young/Foster + Partners.

Exterior view of the shed and the Crescent Wing. Nigel Young/Foster + Partners.

Pages 194–95
Norman Foster's sketches of an extension to the Sainsbury Centre, February 2002. Foster + Partners.

Cutaway drawing of the Crescent Wing, showing the Link, the open reserve and the new Lower Gallery. Narinder Sagoo/Foster + Partners.

Entrance to the Link and spiral staircase, giving access to the shop below. Nigel Young/Foster + Partners.

Page 196
The south side of the Sainsbury Centre. Nigel Young/Foster + Partners

The west end of the Sainsbury Centre, with Henry Moore's *Draped Reclining Woman*, 1957–8. School of World Art Studies and Museology, University of East Anglia.

Index